Praise for the book

I0220689

At a time when Islam is mostly analyzed through dry statistics, theories and principles, Tahir Abbas reconnects with the memoir genre to provide a unique insight into his journey as a Muslim and an academic in different cultures and political contexts. Highly recommended.

Jocelyne Cesari
*Professor of Religion and Politics at the University of Birmingham
and Senior Fellow at the Berkley Center for Religion, Peace and World Affairs
Georgetown University*

From being a Birmingham boy with Azad Kashmiri-Pakistani roots to becoming a Professor of Radicalisation in the Netherlands, Abbas sheds light on his journey of overcoming the obstacles on the road to his current destination of becoming a distinguished academic.

Alia Amir
*Associate Professor of English Linguistics,
Mid-Sweden University*

Tahir Abbas' story is partly a biography of growing up in a racialised, gang-ridden inner city where bullies mill across the schoolyard and narrow alleys, but it is also a reportage of a steadily changing Britain where race, the imperial past, so-called majoritarianism, and suspicions of the 'other' still anchor communal relationships.

Iftikhar H. Malik
Professor Emeritus at Bath Spa University

Tahir Abbas lets us peep into the family, social circles, mosque culture, and the hidden or not-so-hidden racism experienced by a British-Pakistani-Englishman with ancestral roots in Kashmir … For me, the book combines the wisdom of a teacher with the innocence of a student who is still 'reading' the world and does not shy away from sharing his ideas.

Samina Yasmeen
*Professor and Director, Centre for Muslim States and Societies,
University of Western Australia*

Thought-provoking contemplations.

Ziauddin Sardar
Editor-in-Chief of Critical Muslim

A charming and challenging 'coming of age' memoir of a young Muslim boy and his journey into political manhood in a strange and hostile land. A must-read that lifts the veil on Islamophobia!

Heidi Safia Mirza
Professor Emerita of Race, Faith and Culture at Goldsmiths and Professor Emerita in Equalities Studies at the UCL Institute of Education

As a post-Brexit UK struggles to accept that global dominance through an empire is no longer possible and that society is truly multiracial, multicultural, and multi-faith, this book captures the reality of growing up with immigrant parents and contributes to the creation of the newer society that is gradually emerging.

Sally Tomlinson
Emeritus Professor at Goldsmiths and an Honorary Fellow in the Department of Education, University of Oxford

The richness of the subject is matched by the excellence of the writing. Professor Abbas has reached a new level of literary attainment.

Akbar Ahmed
Ibn Khaldun Chair of Islamic Studies, American University

Ruminations is a poignant reflection on Tahir's formative years and distinguished career. It is an incisive analysis punctuated with tender moments of introspection at the juncture of what makes us all human—individuality, community, and metaphysical longing.

Uzmah Ali
Poet and Public Servant

RUMINATIONS

Books by the Author

The Education of British South Asians (2004)

Islamic Radicalisation and Multicultural Politics (2011)

Contemporary Turkey in Conflict (2017)

Islamophobia and Radicalisation (2019)

Countering Violent Extremism (2021)

Islamophobia and Securitisation (2022, with L Welten)

RUMINATIONS

Framing a sense of self and
coming to terms with the other

✧

TAHIR ABBAS

Published in the UK by Beacon Books and Media Ltd
Earl Business Centre, Dowry Street, Oldham, OL8 2PF, UK.

Copyright © Tahir Abbas 2022

The right of Tahir Abbas to be identified as the author of this work has been asserted in accordance with the Copyright, Designs and Patents Act 1988. All rights reserved. This book may not be reproduced, scanned, transmitted or distributed in any printed or electronic form or by any means without the prior written permission from the copyright owners, except in the case of brief quotations embedded in critical reviews and other non-commercial uses permitted by copyright law.

www.beaconbooks.net

ISBN: 978-1-915025-12-8 Paperback
ISBN: 978-1-915025-13-5 Hardback
ISBN: 978-1-915025-14-2 eBook

Cataloging-in-Publication record for this book is available from the British Library

Cover design by Raees Mahmood Khan

◈

This book is part memoir, part social commentary. Various names have been changed to protect privacy.

tahir-abbas.com

What you seek is seeking you

Rumi

Contents

Dedication

To all those who believed, here I am, and to all those who did not, here you are.

Acknowledgements

I am a reader as well as a writer; a settler and a sojourner; an insider and an outsider. This book takes the reader on a journey that begins with awareness of the self and progresses to knowing the other. It is an attempt to understand the cycle of being and existence through a social lens, in which self and other are always interacting, conversing, struggling, and exchanging. I am grateful to all those who have helped shape my life, good or bad, right or wrong. It is through these interactions that I come to know myself and to know you. I would also like to thank the team at Beacon Books for taking up this project and for supporting its production, in particular Siema Rafiq for her meticulous reading of an earlier version of the manuscript.

Part I
Framing a sense of self

1

A Land Forgotten

*What matters in life is not what happens to you but what you
remember and how you remember it,*
Gabriel García Márquez

Travelling-it leaves you speechless, then turns you into a storyteller,
Ibn Battuta

*I only read biographies, metaphysics and psychology. I can dream up
my own fiction,*
Mae West

It all started over two centuries ago, when Allah Ditta and his two broth-
ers banded together to build Ankar-Bachlakra, a settlement in Kashmir.
Ankara is a group of ten villages that make up "the larger Ankara," with
Bachlakra (the "one in the middle") at its centre. Altogether, there are another seventy villages distributed across a plain in the rocky, mountainous *tehsil*
(sub-district) of Dadyal in the district of Mirpur in what is now Azad Kashmir.
These young men were descended from Bhatti Rajputs. During the reign of the
Mughals, their ancestors converted to Islam. Since the village's founding, these
Bachlakrans have progressively expanded to form thirty households. Some Bachlakran women married out, while most married into the clan. However, the
settlement is nearly deserted now. It has become a ghost town, with only traces

of the once-thriving community of interconnected family members who had long-standing relationships with other nearby communities remaining. The Bachlakrans who emigrated became transnational and developed diasporic communities, particularly in England and the United States.

Life in this area of the world is often harsh, with hot summers, heavy monsoon rains, and cold winters followed by a chilly spring. In the past, Kashmiris survived on subsistence-level economics, but if the crop failed, they suffered greatly. But when the crops became insufficient to fulfil the nutritional demands of the local people, and with no alternative economic opportunity, the early generations were driven to seek a better living elsewhere and to travel throughout the world. The British were still in India in the 1930s. The word got out that the Bombay-based British Merchant Navy was looking for people to help fuel its fleet's fires. A few men from the village made the long journey in search of work and the prospect of a better future. Because of the high demand, recruiters urged the frequent dispatch of more individuals to join the current band of devoted labourers. However, the English were also racially biased in believing that Indian men, as they were at the time, would find employment less pleasant in the face of the hot coal-furnaces that powered the steamships and transported products to service the British Empire. The work was rough and arduous, but it was significantly safer than life as a poor farmer.

My paternal grandfather, Zaman Ali, along with his brother Abbas Ali, joined these men on their journey to Bombay. They came home to their families on occasion, but they were usually gone for months at a time, sailing the high seas, and visiting all the world's main ports. The Second World War began in 1939, and the Merchant Navy eventually played an active role in transporting critical products and equipment to the war effort in impacted areas. These two gallant men, along with many others from the same village, were unavoidably caught up in the action. The Germans sank their steamer, which also carried other Bachlakrans, in 1944, during the Battle of Singapore. It went down into the water. Some of the survivors were shot at as they tried to jump into the ocean. Surviving the unrelenting onslaught, these two brothers, along with others, were rescued from the water by the allies. Others were less fortunate, and they were later imprisoned in Japan's notorious prisons in Burma.

◎

Their release and return to work came soon after the war's end, but partition in 1947 marked the beginning of a new era. Many communities in and around Ankara were Muslim, but some were also Hindu. It was Hari Singh's and the Dogra *zamana* (era). Hari Singh, as ruler of Kashmir, debated whether to merge the state into Pakistan or India. Eighty percent of Jammu and Kashmir's area was Muslim, as it is today, but Hari Singh, influenced by Nehru, of

Pandit Kashmiri ancestry, and Sheikh Abdullah, a Kashmiri Muslim dubbed the "Lion of Kashmir" by some, and a strong secularist, did not want Kashmir to join Pakistan. Abdullah believed that feudalism would prevail, and that Mohammed Ali Jinnah exaggerated his own importance. As Kashmir became a part of India under the leadership of Hari Singh, it sparked a wave of communal bloodshed. Naturally, Pakistan was disturbed since the letter "K" in Pakistan stands for Kashmir. Elders in the village seldom discussed the indescribable incidents of women and young girls being kidnapped and raped on both sides. Other official and personal reports reinforce the assumption that this is what happened between the time partition was proclaimed and Hari Singh's decision less than two months later.

Because the Hindus around Bachlakra were outnumbered, they fled to the Indian side. Other Muslims later arrived in the surrounding communities and claimed the area as their own. However, the notion that there was an indivisible, unified Kashmir in the first place is incorrect. It is still split today, as it was then, even though both India and Pakistan claim part of the region and have battled each other twice over it. In 1947, Pakistan seized a chunk of the territory to the east of Jammu, which became known as Azad Kashmir. Azad Kashmir, which is neither Kashmiri nor wholly Pakistani in actuality, has its own distinct identity but no international legal standing. Before partition, Azadis from Jammu started the campaign that led to the battle for unification with Pakistan. This region may have had a higher level of violence and war (as a proportion of the population). There is still a forgotten history of the people of Azad Kashmir, as historians and political scientists focus on the more numerically significant displacement of the people of Punjab. That area of what was India was brutally divided down the middle, leading ten million people to flee and one million people to die because of communal violence on both sides. It is still the twentieth century's greatest forced exodus.

Domestic demand in the United Kingdom began to rise following World War II, but indigenous British workers were unprepared to work in less desirable occupations. They want a higher standard of living. Zaman Ali refused to dwell in England. He obviously could not stand the weather. Abbas Ali did, and he came to live in Birmingham. His decision, along with many who followed him into manufacturing positions in the late 1940s and early 1950s, triggered a wave that lasted two decades, peaking in the early 1960s. My father, having successfully completed his high school matriculation tests—a rare occurrence in those days—arrived in Birmingham in 1957, at the age of sixteen. These men came to live and work in some of the poorest areas of towns and cities, sometimes in multi-occupancy houses with up to ten people per room. Many would work "night shifts," sleeping during the day while day employees were at work, and vice versa. The main goal was to save as much money as possible to send back to their home countries as remittances, but they also saw their stay as transitory. The bulk of society has shared this viewpoint. Men from Azad Kashmiri villages settled in Birmingham and Bradford, where they worked in the manufacturing and engineering industries. Caribbean workers moved to poorer areas of west and south London to work, mostly in the transportation and health industries.

◈

Back in the Mirpur district of Azad Kashmir, it was decided that Pakistan would build the biggest dam in South Asia in that region. Construction started in the late 1950s, but it needed the submergence of almost two hundred settlements. These villagers were compensated for the loss of their land, and some of the younger and fitter men began to migrate to England with other men as part of a chain migration process. This alarmed British officials in general, and the white-English working classes. The latter was beginning to show more active racism, which had been passed down through British colonialism, scientific racism, and the civilising missionary zeal of old. By 1962, law had prohibited primary economic migration, replacing it with a voucher system under which new employees may enter the nation only if sponsored by current workers. This hastened the chain migration process. My father made the choice to return to Azad Kashmir and marry my mother, who hails from Jhelum, a city close to the west of Azadi territory. It is near to the spot where, over two thousand years ago, Alexander the Great, who had conquered extensive territories east of Macedonia up to that time, eventually met his equal at the River Jhelum at the hands of Porus, a fierce Indian ruler.

Abbas Ali was gravely injured in a horrific car accident in 1961. A leg had to be amputated, but he died a few days later in the hospital. He was the first to be returned to the village to be buried, and this practise continued until the late 1990s, when later British-born generations desired to bury their loved ones closer to them. From the 1940s through the 1960s, young men departed Bachlakra in droves, with spouses following the men who had gone earlier; children were married to other children in the UK. The graveyard in one area of the village still includes unmarked graves and those of the elders, although the dates of those who died cease around the early 2000s, with few exceptions. In 1964, Peter Griffiths, a Conservative Party candidate, won the Birmingham seat of Smethwick with the iconic slogan, "If you want a nigger for a neighbour, vote Labour." Such statements would be unthinkable to use today, but every general election since then has included some mention of the "immigrant problem."

When British MPs changed the law again in 1968, terminating the voucher system, the Azad Kashmiris were forced to choose between staying in Britain alone or taking their dependents with them. Many chose the latter, but this resulted in the inevitable concentration of the population in the same impoverished parts of towns and cities, as well as an increased demand for housing, education, and health care in already under-resourced regions. Many of these problems are still present today. Though the strategy was intended to reduce immigration, it had the opposite effect. It did not help to alleviate existing racial tensions between impoverished whites and visible minorities, which endure today in the context of the country's deindustrialisation processes, which have touched all working-class groups. Now, Birmingham-based grandparents are dwindling, yet some Bachlakran grandchildren continue to marry across the generations. Traditions and conventions of cultural life remain with little or no change, often to the chagrin of newer generations.

❖

In visiting the ancestral village in mid-2014, I found myself back to where it all started. It was the birthplace of my father and his father before him. This land is in my blood as it is its heritage. But I was saddened to discover an empty village with next to no-one left. There were only a few of the original Bhattis, as most call themselves, still left in the village. Their presence dates to my earliest memories as a child and of all the times I visited the place over the years. Many of the elderly in the village are quite old and often quite ill. From time to time, their middle-aged children are routinely invited back from England or New York to take care of them.

With only a few days in the village, I spent much of my time with three people. Uncle (all males of my father's generation who have either near or distant relatives to him are referred to as uncle) Quyum, then in his early sixties and now unfortunately departed, did not leave the village because he needed to care for his late mother. Then there was Khanam Jee, my *dadi* (considered as my paternal grandma), who was in her late eighties (she passed on the same day as HM The Queen in late 2022). She was the last of those still alive from my trips beginning in the early 1970s. She was quick-witted, engaging, and has great recall. Another notable figure during that time was Uncle Liakat. He arrived in Birmingham as an 11-year-old youngster in the late 1950s and is now in his late-80s. He and his wife had returned to the hamlet for three months to care for his mother, Khanam Jee, who had lately lost her husband of more than seventy years. In the 1950s, her late husband, Fazal Hussain, worked aboard commercial ships. In the 1960s and 1970s, he did light assembly work in England, and then, in the 1980s, in New York City, he worked in a pen factory before retiring to Bachlakra to tend to his land and livestock.

A day into my journey, Uncle Liakat returned to Birmingham. Three days before my arrival, Uncle Quyum had returned to Bachlakra. It was following his first visit to the United Kingdom. He had been in Birmingham for 11 weeks with his three sons and two daughters, as well as their many offspring. He was not in a good mood and had few positive things to say. He began by saying, "people are abandoning Islam. When greeting one another, they do not utter salaam. They instead say *ka hal he"* (how are you?). He went on to say that the "elderly live on their own and that people just do not see or meet with one another as they do in the village." And this is not a matter of proximity. There is just no regard for the elderly. "Unless there is a death or a wedding, people don't see each other," he continued. He emphasised that older people living alone is not a good thing since boredom and idleness would lead to terrible ailments with no cure. He had a valid argument. He also mentioned another subject. He began by saying, "women." After which he said, "in the old days, we used to get a stick and strike them over their heads if they showed any insubordination. You can't even touch your child these days because social services will take them away." Uncle Quyum was characteristic of many men of his generation who still have similar attitudes about women, albeit for those who have migrated to the west, much has been mitigated by adaption to society and seeing their own children grow up and become parents themselves.

On the other hand, Uncle Quyum raised some intriguing points about family groupings. English society is increasingly made up of atomised individuals, rather than families in the traditional sense. People work long hours, and some parents are unable to spend enough time with their own children, let alone see or interact with other families and their children in houses dispersed throughout huge metropolitan conurbations. Despite efforts to keep familial interconnectivities, they exist at a much greater micro-dynamic level. Uncle Quyum's greatest worry was assimilation; "marrying out, living like *dengar* (animals)," he remarked. He believed the long-term outlook was bleak, as more of the younger generations began to marry outside of the *biraderi* (patrilineal clan-kinship-network system). He was happy in the village where he had lived his whole life. It was the one location he knew best and had the greatest faith in. The subject of the British Azad Kashmir integration-assimilation process has been debated for some time, but the question now is how to prepare for its unavoidable repercussions. One way ahead is to have a greater understanding of and appreciation for the legacy. Understanding who we are allows us to better understand where we are. Much of this is lost to future generations born in other countries. My own children's feelings of connectedness are even more distant than mine, even though they are wonderful, well-rounded young people on all other levels. People undergo an unavoidable process of change, although certain other elements never profoundly change.

For several political reasons, including infighting among the more landed farmers who also happen to be political leaders, and the requirement or impact of kowtowing to the authority of Islamabad, the territory of Azad Kashmir has seen almost no economic progress. The economy is back to where it was over a century ago. Craftwork, artisans, low-level farming, small-scale trade, and minimal state investment in education and health have resulted in the majority of Azad Kashmiris looking to flee to either larger cities in Pakistan or, better still, overseas. Today, if the houses in the villages are not vacant, they are filled with "asylum-seekers," as Uncle Liakat characterised them. "Come on, they are non-related family groups hired to care for a house they live in for free, while they have all the ability to toil the land at their whim without contributing a single rupee to the proprietor in return," he replied when asked if this was a derogatory comment. Various such statements were often made by some of Birmingham's elders throughout the years, who would say things like, to para-phrase somewhat, "look at these Somalis coming to our neighbourhoods. They are stealing our jobs (as taxi drivers), starting small companies, moving into our houses (sometimes as tenants of Pakistani property owners), and living ful-ly off the welfare state (often as do many Pakistanis)." Hearing these statements many years ago, it occurred to me how some of the more established ethnic minority populations began to internalise the deep-seated traditions of English racism, such is its continuing legacy.

Even though change is afoot in Birmingham, the village's long-term sta-tus is still uncertain. The neighbouring dam had recently completed its first significant enlargement in thirty years. Its high-water levels have now risen to the point that they have submerged crops on three of the four sides of the set-tlement. It will have ramifications for social connectedness, considering how long it has taken to set up basic services like electricity and the battery-powered feeds that kick in when the main power supply is cut for up to eight hours a day. The winding route down to the bottom of the now-electrically-powered well that serves the whole community would become impassable.

◈

It had been a long time since I had visited the village. But it was clear to me now that my main connection to the place was nostalgia. As I sat under the mango tree in the courtyard of the recently-reconstructed family "summer villa," as my father likes to call it, many vivid ideas raced through my head. Certain Azad Kashmiri communities in the UK continue to invest in luxurious housing complexes emphasising status and position in the UK and Azad Kash-mir, although these structures serve little use other than to satisfy an ego-driv-en urge to be represented by authoritarian imagery. It is not unusual to find them empty, lifeless, or an eyesore in the middle of a beautiful vista. Memories of my trips throughout the years came flooding back, as did memories of all those loved ones who were no longer with me, prompting me to dwell even more on those exceptional personalities with their steely spirits and determina-tion in the face of adversity. They were the ones who opened the doors that my generation and our children are now passing through. We owe them a debt of appreciation. Integrity, honesty, forthrightness, commitment, and respect for others were qualities they had that are often absent in others today. In more developed cultures, we are increasingly connected to one another, yet these links are shaky, occasionally merely virtual, and sometimes overtly instrumentalised in practise.

I peered into the brilliant night sky with the stars shining brightly as I lay in my *kat* (traditional bed) late at night, having pulled it towards the centre of the family house's forecourt. A particular type of timeless charm could be sensed when the calm air swept over the mango tree's limbs. The Bachlakran diaspora is now in its fourth generation, and about 3,500 of the 4,500 or so descendants of the three brothers who started this process over two hundred years ago are in Birmingham, the city where I was born and where my children live. A few hundred are dispersed around the Midlands and North, with one hundred in Bradford, thirty in New York City, and me in Istanbul at the time. We only have memories of the past, but the future lives on.

2

First Lights

I must confess, I was born at a very early age,
Groucho Marx

There is nothing like returning to a place that remains unchanged
to find the ways in which you yourself have altered,
Nelson Mandela

To truly laugh, you must be able to take your pain, and play with it!
Charlie Chaplin

I was born in 1970 in Small Heath, Birmingham, to Pakistani and Azad Kashmiri parents. As a small child in Azad Kashmir, I have a few of my earliest recollections. My sister was around two years old, and I was about three. We were spending a year away from our birthplace, going with our mother as she oversaw the construction of a brand new home in our ancestral village of Bachlakra. When my father moved to Birmingham as a young man in 1957, he worked tirelessly to accumulate money for this housing project. The building of the village house was in full swing in the summer of 1974, with my mother directing the activities. Running around the various huts that most people still lived in, roaming freely and effortlessly between the houses of my extensive extended relatives, in the dusty forecourts that each home had, and through the rich, lush fields that surrounded us all, was an everyday occurrence that blended into one enchanted experience as an inquisitive child.

After seeing the birth of a calf one day, I ran to my mother, who was busy cooking a *paratha* that had been asked of her, and said, "look, the baby is not standing up, and its mother is dying". "'Don't be afraid, *beta* (son)," my mother said calmly. "The baby is okay, and she will soon be able to stand on her own," she claimed.

When I returned to see the miracle in action, I noticed the young calf labouring and battling to control the movements of its legs until it eventually stood up. The small brave animal fought valiantly, but not in vain. Later that afternoon, as I calmly chewed my ghee-laden flatbread, my thoughts raced with the notion of nature at work. The miracle of birth is a remarkable sight, and seeing life appear in such a spectacular way moved me closer to nature. It also prompted me to consider Allah or God for the first time.

In another event, when I was looking at the ground one day and saw what looked to be a mile-long stretch of ants all travelling in a tidy straight line, I asked my friendly but simple uncle Quyum, "Where are they going?'"

"They're obeying Allah," he explained.

"But why?" I inquired.

"Because this is what Allah demands," Uncle Quyum explained.

This concept of Allah causes some disquiet. Allah, who or what is this? Is it a human? Is it a man or a woman? How can we be sure it is there if we cannot see it? What does it expect from us? What brings us here? The answers that came back to me were that Allah created the universe and all its subjects, and that they are all subordinate to Him alone. He is the all-powerful master-planner, whose presence can be seen someplace in the sky. Standing in the centre of the villa courtyard, gazing up at the sky and the airy vapours enclosed there, I thrust my hands out as far as they could go while standing on my toes, elongating. Those massive fluffy white clouds did not appear to be all that far away. A taller person could one day touch them. I am getting closer, reaching up so high that I could run into my maker. I can then ask him or her all of my never-ending inquiries. What if I was born a second before or after I was really born? How different would I be from the person I had already become? Individualities and personalities are given to us by Allah at any point in time, or they are determined through social interactions between individuals in various locations and periods. What distinguishes humans as individuals? If we obey Allah like the ants, do they have distinctions like humans? How do ants connect to humans if we are all Muslims?

It has since come to my attention that the physical world, with its blue skies, oceans of water, and volcanoes alive and ready to erupt, is a delicate ecological balance of air, fire, earth, and water, whether it is animals, such as our closest genetic relative, the chimp, or meagre ants and their colonies. All biological things are composed of at least one element: carbon. Our relationship with our environment has developed over millennia as we have built sophisticated towns, cities, and civilisations, from tiny groups to tribes to finally countries, but we are all the same as human beings. But humans are sensitive beings, and this is especially true today, when walls, whether manufactured or natural, divide, separate, and finally govern us.

Even though I was not aware of it at the time, those early days in Azad Kashmir shaped my perspective. Reflecting on them throughout my life has shown the depth of their significance to me, both then and today.

◈

When I returned to England, my birthplace, it was a world far away from the heat and dust of Azad Kashmir. I do not remember much following my return until I entered a nearby primary school. It was the summer of 1976, and it was scorching. The sun had been shining for six months, and I had devoured far too many soft whipped ice creams for my own good. The heat sizzled the skin as I ran around in my sleeveless vest, appearing like a young kid in many a scene from any number of Amitabh Bachan films released and viewed during this period. The only choice would be to jump into the lido in the neighbourhood park and return home to a frustrated father who feared for my safety as well as my personal hygiene.

Small Heath is where we live, and after returning from Azad Kashmir with the house in the village fully built, we moved back to Britain to live in a home close to the one where my parents were renting a room and where both my sister and I were born. My father and his one and only elder brother, Fazal Rehman, bought our new house together, and it was the six of us, including my elder cousin, who were now living in this inner-city terraced late-Victorian, dilapidated, obsolescent abode, which, instead of being torn down and replaced by new homes, was owner-occupied, like many thousands of Pakistanis and Azad Kashmiris in the area. Where else could we live? In the early 1970s, wider society was hostile to Pakistanis, and a limited salary meant a restricted ability to move away, so we needed each other because no one else wanted us there. Our desire to live in close-knit communities arose from a lack of options, not from a longing to do so. When others in the area, such as Ugandans or Kenyan Asians, could afford to leave, they did so quickly, leaving only the poor and unfit to live in the deteriorating environment of the inner cities.

One of my distinguishing recollections from this period is Eid in 1976. On Eid, all the men in the household awoke early, showered, and prepared to walk to prayers at a nearby mosque. Although there was no actual religious basis for it, every male and female dressed in traditional Pakistani and Azad Kashmiri attire on the day. This was the only day I felt comfortable wearing

13

these traditional garments outside of my house. Although some of the other people in the vicinity mocked our "parachute pants," there was confidence in numbers. We were not the only ones. They were free to say anything they pleased as we passed by their houses. It was our day, and we were confident in our appearance. Aside from the two major Eid days of the year, we were rarely seen outside the house dressed in such garb. The threat of unwanted attention was uncomfortable merely because of the hazard posed by those who regarded the outfit with scorn at best and hatred at worst. Later that year, in downtown Birmingham, a completely new mosque, The Central Mosque, was erected, which is still in use today. It meant that we could meet in our hundreds for an act of worship to commemorate an important occasion without having to pray outside on the road or in an unpaved parking lot, since space had become an issue due to the rising population. Passers-by mocking during Eid, on the other hand, stayed a common occurrence for some time.

◇

To our left was the home of an old English lady. We never got the opportunity to speak with her in depth. This was terrible, given that she was extremely lovely when seen outside of her house. Her house always looked beautiful from the outside, with vibrant flowers and dazzling plants adorning her external landscape. Living alone and tired of strangers, she had nowhere else to go, and the growing number of non-white individuals in the area who no one wanted to know or care about certainly made her feel even more isolated. The houses on our block were tiny, poorly lit, and reeked of strange semi-gaseous odours. The floorboards squeaked, the windows let in frigid air, and the bathrooms were either outdoors or at the back of the home. And most importantly, it was constantly gloomy and wet outside, day or night, summer, or winter. There were Muslim Pakistani, Azad Kashmiri, and Indian households to my left and right, as well as everywhere else on Byron Road. There were one or two non-South Asian homes in between the houses, but we did not see or hear anything from them. Most of the residents on the block were Pakistanis, and I made friends with other boys and girls from the neighbourhood, with whom I played various board and role-playing games. We went to the nearby park, where we played cricket, cycled, and sometimes brought a choice of little sandwiches for a "picnic." We were always left alone. I am certain that it had a huge influence on my developing a sense of independence.

At home, we really enjoyed playing games. One was a sort of world power game in which I sat behind a huge table pretending to be the president and my companions pretended to be prime ministers or secretaries. I was always the president because I talked the most and forced my long-suffering friends into minor roles. My behaviour was certainly more autocratic than democratic, but

I was never dictatorial, disciplinarian, or brutal. For me, being president meant doing the right thing for the people, even though we had no idea how to do it in practice, aside from making speeches to cameras at the time. One thing was certain, however, and that was that I needed a large desk, which we duly created out of whatever furniture we could muster.

My friends' houses were comparable to mine, either precisely the same or a mirror image, albeit the gardens were occasionally different. There were times when there were no gardens at all. There was nothing but ruins surrounded by a six-foot-high fence and a pair of railroad lines to look at. All the rear gardens on one side of the street shared a walkway. Some of us went through it several times, chasing each other for distinct reasons. It was possible to do so without being apprehended or having to struggle through deep vegetation, fences, or tiny barrages. It was just something to do, and it was slightly hazardous and hence adventurous. What I was doing with the local head petty crook was more by chance than intent. Asif was the son of one of my mother's many local female associates. Because my father worked most days and nights, I often had to join my mother on her rounds to visit some of her local acquaintances. I was told they were all my aunties, so I addressed them all as "auntie." They were my parents' acquaintances, formed because of religio-cultural clan-network ties. They were not blood relatives, but part of a loose network of associates.

I thought we had many relatives at the time. Many were true matrilineal and patrilineal cousins and second cousins, but many were not. I treated them all equally, albeit I did prefer some over others. Asif had taken a fancy to me since I was always cheerful. He also appreciated the calculator that my grandpa had gotten for me, as well as the Elvis recordings that my father had gotten from Reader's Digest. One of the four Elvis cassettes, as well as an authentic 1970s LED calculator, vanished. Soon, Asif vanished as well. I yearned for the return of the missing objects, but Asif would never return. It was eventually revealed to me that Asif had spent some time in a correctional facility, however short, sharp, and shocking it may have been for him.

❖

I never worried about spending so much time with so many aunties since I did not know or care about what they were talking. I sat in front of the television when there were no other kids around to play with. I must have come off as decidedly uninterested or entirely uninteresting because someone was usually giving me something to eat or letting me play with toys. This is the one thing I truly cherish about growing up as an Azad Kashmiri in Birmingham. It is the way we go about things to help or be mindful of others. It is both cultural and religious in nature. Being friendly, open, and attentive to welcome visitors is a global tradition that spans all civilised worlds. My aunts appeared civilised to me, even though they spoke languages that only my parents understood and took part in fully. I was constantly preoccupied with larger issues, such as the possibility of nuclear war or how to survive the end of the world, which my friends, their parents, and my own parents were persuaded was imminent.

While we lived on Byron Road, the other streets and roads and roads around were named after famous English poets: Wordsworth, Tennyson, Malmesbury, Cooksey, Bolton, Oldknow, and Lloyd. It was special to think that we lived in a place where road names might be recognised in this manner. A few minutes away, on Waverley Road, was an older cousin of mine who was a bit of a geek with his brown suits and technologically constructed brain. He once started teaching me chess, since I had picked it up at school and found it intriguing, but I quickly lost interest because he was usually distracted by his many interactions with other people in the room. I was able to establish the fundamentals but not go beyond them. Later, I persuaded my father to get me a chess set, but he lacked the patience and time to work with me on it. Noreen, my younger sister, pretended to be uninterested.

Techie Zulf, this nice nerd cousin, has a massive poster of Kashmir, or rather Azad Jammu Kashmir, on his front room wall. The names of towns and cities were printed in Urdu, and I interrogated him about the whereabouts of our respective "back home" residences. He pointed to them, but they made no sense to me, nor did the concept of a dividing line in Kashmir. "Who placed that there?" I timidly inquired one day.

"The Indians and Pakistanis went to war over this region of the world twice recently, and because there was no resolution, a line split the territory into two," he responded.

"What was the cause of the conflict between Indians and Pakistanis over Kashmir? Surely the Kashmiris would want to be left alone to deal with their own issues?" I returned.

"The Kashmiris are a part of Pakistan ... and they should have joined when Pakistan was created by Mohammed Ali Jinnah, who eventually received a distinct position for Muslims in 1947, but the British were involved in a rapid and divided withdrawal, and it had a disastrous consequence," he continued. As a seven-year-old, it felt strange, insignificant, and so far in the past that it did not need to bother me. I could not see why he was concerned by a setting where he only had childhood recollections himself. He was plainly political in his views on ethnic, cultural, and economic concerns in Pakistan and Azad Jammu and Kashmir (AJK), and why not? I was more intrigued by the prospect of having another location to call home, somewhere other than Birmingham's chilly, damp, and dreary weather. Away from those who despised us and called us names. People with short hair and enormous, tall Doctor Martin's boots would yell at us, "Go home, Paki," or Caribbean youths who would threaten Asian youngsters in the local park, shouting forcefully, "Give me 10p or I'll take your bike." Every time, the ten pence set up for ice cream was sacrificed. However, this was not the case for everyone.

Most people were polite and easy to converse with. I had no fear of anyone except those who were blatantly hazardous to me, which were skinheads and yobbos. And it was nice to know that I, like many of my friends on my street and in my neighbourhood, had access to other locations that we could call home. I was fond of Techie Zulf. He was unique, and I could spend hours poring over his encyclopaedias and maps. I enjoyed flipping over the pages of Jacob Bronowski's *The Ascent of Man* in particular. The stunning sights and images of other countries and people fascinated me. Other volumes in his collection were Muammar al-Gaddafi's *Green Book*, which looked like a comic when I initially picked it up, but I had no clue what it contained when I finally started reading it. I became fascinated by the world and its people, past and present, science and technology, and I could not get enough of books with photos and representations of everything.

Techie Zulf's wedding was the first of several South Asian Muslim marriages in Britain that I recall. It is the start of a yearly wedding season that continues to this day. For the marriage to be conducted, tradition with folklore and Islamic rites of passage have to be engaged. Although their practical utility is limited, their symbolism is significant. It was warm and lovely to be among other young people and among the seniors. They were all kind folks but communicating with the golden agers was usually a challenge. It was a vital opportunity for us, as Azad Kashmiri and Pakistani communities living away from "home," to appreciate what we had. It resulted in sentiments of being able to prove a sense of self while still celebrating our cultural, religious, and ethnic history. We would return to our usual daily routines once these mega-events were done, but they were ours for a few days out of the year.

❖

I learned how to use a photocopier while spending an entire day in the town library with the elder brother of one of my friends from across the street, Azar, who is now a biotechnology engineer working in California. I vividly recall making an A3 photocopy of a bright photograph of the full moon. The original photograph was vivid, but the photocopy was inverted. In a white sky, it appeared dark. When I brought it home to show my parents, they were happy that I had spent my ten-pence pocket money on something other than ice cream. The photocopy conveyed a metaphor—reversing light and dark—that I would remember for the rest of my life. My parents told me that this is how the moon will appear at the end of time, which was a terrifying concept.

During these early years, I would often push myself upon my parents' efforts to have a night out by themselves to see the latest Pakistani movie from

Lahore. The location was the Walford Road Cinema in Sparkhill. However, after a while, I discovered that I no longer enjoyed going to these movies. The films were at times loud, brightly coloured, and completely illogical. Ladies with large boobies and men with massive moustaches, *bundook*s, and long skirts with turned-up slippers were running about in what appeared to be fields near what I recognised as rural areas, which perplexed me. The 70mm film was projected onto massive screens, accompanied by a thunderous sound and what I can only describe as a musical accompaniment for the deaf. In the end, it was too much for me. I could not hear what the characters were saying because they were yelling at each other while glaring directly at the audience. Others did not leave when I did. The South Asian film industry has grown to become a popular form of entertainment in the United Kingdom, although my film watching habits had nothing to do with it.

I would rather sail across space. It was 1977, and the world was captivated by a single film, *Star Wars*. It was going to be my first trip to the movies to watch an English film, and I was not going to miss it. Techie Zulf wanted to join us, so my father took us both. We knew it was a major picture, and Techie Zulf used his frontal lobes to ensure we arrived with plenty of time to get our tickets at the theatre. However, it was much too late. People were lined up three-deep around the building, trying to buy tickets. In the end, we were only able to secure three separate tickets for a later showing. We had some spare time. It now meant two things: ice cream and a trip to the railway museum, which was only a short distance away from *The Gaumont*, a massively grandiose independent cinema in central Birmingham.

As we entered the auditorium, we were divided. It was like a large amphitheatre, with people seated up and down and to the sides. A mysterious man in a black velvet dinner suit spiralled up from the stage as he tinkered on the ivories of a grand piano prior to the screening. After a few rounds of bite-sized classical music, he vanished through the same hole. Some of the tunes were familiar to me since my father had bought a collection of classical music audio cassettes from The Reader's Digest. Chopin, Debussy, and Rachmaninov excerpts came and went in a flash.

The movie started, and the screen erupted with the words, "*A long time ago, in a galaxy far, far away...*" From that point on, I was enthralled. In a parallel reality, I was fighting evil to rescue the rest of humanity. I fantasised about holding my own light sabre and flying into the stars. It was an awe-inspiring, young-person-friendly action-adventure fairytale that changed the imaginations of a generation. It would permanently reinforce my love of science fiction, technology, and big-budget action sequences. I had discovered proper movies, and I'd be eternally grateful for it.

When the Princess Leia character returned to the big screen six years later in *The Return of the Jedi*, I found myself looking away from the screen as she appeared to me as Venus coming to the seas in the manner of Botticelli's masterpiece. This portrayal of Leia triggered feelings that I recognised as entirely sexual. Leia was dressed like an angel in 1977, but she wore almost nothing in 1983.

3

Life in a Box

I think God, in creating man, somewhat overestimated his ability,
Oscar Wilde

I believe in God, but not as one thing, not as an old man in the sky. I believe that what people call God is something in all of us. I believe that what Jesus and Mohammed and Buddha and all the rest said was right. It's just that the translations have gone wrong,
John Lennon

I find your lack of faith disturbing,
Darth Vader

Apart from the odd trip to the movies to see the latest blockbusters, there wasn't much else to do in town. Nothing was bought from the stores in the city centre on a regular basis. My father knew and trusted the local shops that supplied our family's meals and goods. Shopping at upscale department stores was reserved for the privileged. They were a million miles apart from anything we knew or cared about. But something happened in the late 1970s that transformed our lives forever. With colour television already in use, we received our first black-and-white goggle-box in 1977. It was a little dinky, finicky gadget that was often defective and seldom turned on, sitting in the corner of the room staring back at us. However, when a refurbished colour television came to our home in early 1978, it completely changed our viewing habits. More details could be seen on a larger screen, but because it was the only colour TV in our Bhatti family, we would have to sacrifice my cartoons or cowboy westerns for the news or live debates between Sadat and Begum at the UN, for example, with elderly male relatives eagerly focused on the major debates of the day. My uncle Fazal Rehman used to keep us all quiet and say, "Shhh ... the news is on ... listen quietly." Then he would turn to my father or Techie Zulf and ask, "What did they say?"

Television and film introduced me to a whole new universe. It provided me with invaluable insights into the workings and brains of many individuals and communities. Of course, a lot of it is made up, but not all of it. During the late 1970s, there were a range of incredible television events. The death of Elvis Presley in 1977, as well as footage of a motorcade that extended far into the horizon, remain vivid in the mind. The Iranian Revolution of 1979 is shown through images of hundreds of thousands of protesters dressed in black and a frightening-looking bearded old man kissing the tarmac at Tehran Airport. Shortly after, the Russians invaded Afghanistan, and ITN's Sandy Gall covered it every day. The Afghans were our Muslim neighbours since our origins were near Pakistan. The Russians had helicopters and tanks, while the Afghans had none, yet they battled valiantly. It was freezing outside, and they were dying in droves, but these Afghans were the west's allies, helping in the fight against the terrifying "Ruskies." Television also introduced me to popular culture. I was intrigued by the dark-haired vocalist when I watched ABBA on TV, but I wished she had blonde hair like her bandmate. A common ideal of beauty, Kate Bush, was also on TV, and we thought she was stunning yet terrifying. When watching the battle between Muhammad Ali and Leon Spinks in 1978, with Ali losing terribly, the entire Bhattis gathering was pretty upset to see how an incredible human being was being pounded to a pulp. For many years, I was shaken by images of Ali being pounded repeatedly as he gazed back, slumped, and unable to respond, almost smiling numb with pain.

In terms of Pakistani news, a significant occasion occurred in 1979, when the world awaited word on the fate of Zulfiqar Ali Bhutto and whether General Zia ul-Haq would hang him. Clemency was a possibility until the very last moment, but it was not granted. The Bhatti elders gathered around the radio to hear the official announcement that Bhutto had died. The assassination of John Lennon in 1980 shocked not just music enthusiasts, but also anti-Vietnam War protesters.

With television came the mini-screen, as well as VHS and "pirate films." When the fever first struck the Bhattis, we would gather every weekend at Techie Zulf's house. We sat on the floor on cushions, competing for the most comfortable spot, and watching Bollywood film after Bollywood film on the little screen. They would last all weekend since whenever somebody rented a VHS player it came with a giant basket of badly-copied flicks. It took some time to get the player to function every time, but we got there in the end. The tweens would appear from a weekend-long orgy of music, dance, thrills, and romance, anxiously expecting the reassuring return of Esther Rantzon and her BBC *That's Life* (1973–1994) crew late on Sunday night.

Bruce Lee in *Enter the Dragon* (1973) was one of my favourite non-Asian pirate flicks (although these, too, made me dizzy in the end and I began to avoid them). It is a great film, full of amazing action sequences, although it's an orientalised Hollywood rendition of an eastern narrative. I memorised key lines and practised them in school. I used to tell my friends at school, "Bullshit, Mr. Han-man, you come right out of a comic book." When I was happy with anything, the words "you have our ga-rata-tude" would come next, in a semi-comical, semi-racist Chinese accent. Among the teenage Bhattis, the main discussion was whether Bruce Lee was as excellent as Jackie Chan. *Drunken Master* (1978) and *Snake in the Eagle's Shadow* (1978), both starring Chan, are among the best vintage Hong Kong Kung Fu films ever made.

When the electricity was turned on during the chilly winter months, my father could see I was watching a lot of television, but he also wanted to control what we watched or did not watch. He insisted on making me watch *Weekend World* with Brian Walden on a regular basis. It was terrifying. Every weekend, probes into nuclear bombs and the cold war made me feel as if the world was about to end. The officials on the TV seemed and sounded deadly serious, and they undoubtedly believed in the prospect of nuclear devastation. The Russians, Brits, and Americans were always asked how many Polaris, Cruise, Tomcats, or MiGs they had. And how many nuclear bombs were to be produced for deterrence purposes rather than actual combat? What a strange thing to construct bombs for the sole purpose of scaring governments rather than using them on the people for whom they were intended. The fact was that they could never be used against others since, even if only a part of them were fired, the entire planet would be wiped out.

In a dream about the end of the world and how I would survive it, I worked out that if there was a nuclear holocaust, I could walk over the burning rubble, hot ash, and solidifying lava that engulfed humanity as I escaped Armageddon by wearing Doctor Martin's high-laced boots with their extra-protective rubber soles. It would mean an added opportunity to compete in the fight for survival, all because of the boots, which were more likely to be worn by skinheads and National Front members at the time than as proper footwear in the case of the world's end.

❖

Throughout this period, my Islamic and cultural education had been entrusted to a small mosque a short walk from my house. Ashfaq, a friend from across the street, and I were told to enrol in an after-school programme for Islamic studies, Arabic, and Urdu. We were around nine or ten years old, and our parents thought it was their responsibility to teach us in the Islamic manner. We went reluctantly because any number of dangers could cross our path, from enraged Irish kids riding their bikes to National Front yobbos eager to "bash a Paki" or two, to Caribbean guys fleeing (or running towards) other lads of various kinds or from the police. We had heard about the local gangs' impact, with names like Panthers, Lynx, and Redheads being thrown around. The Redheads were primarily Pakistanis and Azad Kashmiris, many of whom were locals, and the mosque we visited housed several members of this gang.

The mosque was a lot of fun because of the characters we met, but Ashfaq and I did not learn much other than how to survive the hostilities of frustrated young British Muslims and how to take advantage of the often absent Pakistani-trained Molvis with their deep-set eyes, big bellies, and overall look of frustration. We learned more about Bruce Lee's life and times because of his enormous popularity among young people in the late 1970s. Lee was a legend whose existence was made even more heart-breaking by his premature death at the pinnacle of his talents. When the Molvis went missing, we spent more time debating how Lee died. Had competing gangs poisoned him? Had demons possessed him? Did he die because of too much sex, or was he only acting and would reappear one day?

When we chewed gum, the Molvi was completely disgusted. Wasim, a young man, chewed ceaselessly while our Molvi dealt with one of the other fifty pupils in the class. When Wasim was caught chewing, he managed to hide the gum in his mouth, but the Molvi never found it. He informed us that he had figured out how to make it appear like a tooth, and even when we tried, we could not see it. "Sit like a chicken" was the penalty for chewing gum or general disobedience. Any young boy who was to be punished was compelled to crouch on the floor, putting his arms around the inners of his thighs. He would have to put his head between his knees and clutch his ears until he was commanded to let go. It was excruciatingly unpleasant, and the chubbier youngsters had no chance. The Molvis took tremendous joy in this, and it was amusing to see. It served as a good deterrent to those who were considering pulling any fast ones over the Molvis.

At the mosque, we were given many scriptures to memorise as well as instruction in ceremonial activities such as bathing, washing, fasting, and praying, but it was never said why or for what vital reason, other than that it was our responsibility to Allah. In terms of design and substance, this curriculum was *Jamaat-e-Islami*. Not as literalist as others, but with stronger *Sufi Barewli* leanings than other Sunni Islam varieties. At this point in our lives, our parents did not pray daily, but they wanted us to study and fulfil all the laws. We were not interested in the messages or the acts, but in the antics of the other lads.

Ashfaq's father died the previous year. He had always worked in industry and had been a chain smoker. Ashfaq did not have anybody else. His brothers were significantly older than him. Most of the time in the mosque, Ashfaq and I avoided the rabble and sat with the quieter youngsters in the rear, rocking along in front of the large, elevated boards that served as desks, trying to articulate the difficult Arabic.

Mohsin, a young mosque goer, had the nicest eyes and the friendliest grin. His facial lines suggested someone a little older and wiser than others, calm, at ease, and completely comfortable around him. Every time I went to the mosque, whether with or without Ashfaq, we would hunt for him and sit next to him. It was wonderful to discuss the topics that young guys wanted to talk about. Mohsin looked uncomfortable as he sat slumped against the side wall one day, wearing his normal hip and stylish black *Happy Days* mock-Fonzie faux-leather jacket. He appeared broken when I looked into his eyes. He was trying to take his gaze away from the situation. He had a swollen and crimson corner of his mouth. I kept asking, 'What happened?' "I fell," he said with a wry grin. He was not being completely honest with me. How could this kind, gentle, and clever young man be so broken? "You're lying, so tell me the truth." He said that he had been beaten up by the other lads. Instead of being a sinner, Mohsin was a saint. As much as possible, he stayed away from shady company. Mohsin, on the other hand, would never be the same. Anyone or anything may have caused him to appear messed up. Mohsin, like many other youths, vanished from the mosque shortly afterward. Mohsin had left town with his family.

The Molvis were absent from class for an extended period. For some reason, we preferred it that way since they were completely worthless. The elder boys would hold court and try to educate us on culture and the South Asian way of life. We knew nothing except this life, so learning anything new about other people, no matter how bizarre, was a revelation. We were informed about the "blacks," "Irish," and "white" people, and how they were leaving the neighbourhood in droves. This was perfect since it would allow us to move around without worry. Later, it became clear that they were all fleeing the "Pakis": us.

The older lads dropped a tremendous bombshell on us one day in the mosque. "You don't realise it, but your marriages are already fixed," they remarked. We were aware that marriages required some planning; there was the car, the wedding hall, the dress, and the cake to consider. We were also aware of the concept of arranged marriages because my mother and aunties would routinely discuss this or that wedding or arrangement, and sometimes even this or that young girl running away from home and how shameful it was. These females were always portrayed as "loose women" who didn't care for the South Asian way of life and were more intent on getting their "white-English thrills," which were seen as unclean, decadent, or plain illegitimate in Islam.

It finally dawned on me after some time. Arranged marriages have the same effect on young Muslim males. The older guys informed us that our mums and dads would sit down with other mothers and fathers and decide who would marry whom, and that this is often done when youngsters are just three or four years old. Surely, we are born free to choose what we can and cannot do in relation to issues like marriage. What advantage might parents see in this situation? How can they predict how children will develop into adults? What about language, education, and cultural disparities, especially when one spouse is British, and the other is from Pakistan or Azad Kashmir? Although I tried to convince myself of its merit—namely, the vast support mechanism it provides for young couples—it seemed confining to me, and this sounded crucial given the environment of dread and animosity that characterised our existence. I then realised that these traditions are more cultural than religious, and I decided not to entertain the concept anymore.

The mosque was uninspiring, and when it came to memorising the many different verses of the Qur'an, which still tends to be the dominant approach taken in most Islamic centres and mosques in the UK, many of us gave up after a while. We could not memorise it, and the Molvis's dejected expression was too much for us to bear. I could not always remember sophisticated pieces of Arabic-sounding language, and Molvis' replies panicked me. I informed my father that the Molvis were assaulting the boys by striking them with sticks, which was correct even though I had never experienced it. My father instantly escorted me out, but he then brought me to another mosque. I quickly quit that as well. The loss of my brand-new trainers influenced my father's decision. I took them off before Friday prayers, never to be seen again, and returned home in the rain wearing a pair of damp, faded size fourteen plastic *Bata* slippers.

⟡

Unfortunately, there were a plethora of similar mosques in the surrounding region. The next mosque was only a short distance away, so it was quick to get there. It was a terraced home that had been turned into a mosque. It was either this or another decommissioned plant. By this point, Asfhaq had given up on his Arabic studies since he could not be bothered, and he stayed at home with his mother, sister, and older brothers. I was back where I had left off, in the middle of a long, narrow, poorly lighted room, rocking to Arabic sounds, reading, and revising the same material as before. The only difference this time was that at the end of the two hours, a pupil was requested to stand up, and if they successfully memorised a brief verse upon request, they were each tossed a green apple from the enormous crate situated before an amazing and amusing Molvi. He would throw this orb to those who recited it correctly, and it was always an enjoyable moment at the end of our sessions. Some displayed amazing composure when reading aloud, yet no ball control whatsoever when clambering over each other to grasp this flying green thing. When this happened, no one laughed louder than the Molvi. This Molvi had a good sense of comedy. He was able to excite, inspire, and reward the youngsters who found the events quite hilarious, and we were at ease, letting go of ourselves whenever it happened.

A few Molvis, recognising how learning and pre-pubescent children's brains come together, were admirable in using different methods for embracing the sacred books, even though we still had no understanding of what it all meant. My favourite Molvi, on the other hand, had moved on. Instead of starting over with another Molvi, the next choice was to try reading at home. My mother, who could read Arabic, began to catch up on our Qur'anic teaching. She even invited Ashfaq and his sister Azra to join us in learning to read and recite together. When my mother had to deal with an issue or leave the room, I couldn't help but sing the Arabic to the tune of Boney M.'s *The Rivers of Babylon*. My behaviour was naturally unsettling to the others in the reading group. When I realised it was making everyone laugh, I thought it would be a clever idea to sneak it in now and then when reading with my mother. Uncontrollable laughter from my sister, and then from the others, meant we could not go on blaspheming. Finally, we simply quit reading. I used to think that listening to Qur'anic Arabic was preferable to reading it.

We would often discuss religion at home as my parents tried to get me to study, pray, and visit the mosque, but the discourse usually drifted to "the end of times," which was a scary subject. I had the notion that Islam was a religion that punished severely and rewarded sparingly. That Islam was more about what not to do than what to do, and that any minor error would result in endless hell-fire and damnation.

"But why?" I countered.

"Because this is how it's supposed to be... Because Islam needs complete obedience, and avoiding prayer, cleanliness, or fortitude leads to harsh punishment," was the typical reaction I received.

I would argue that I am learning to read and recite, but I am not sure why or for what purpose.

My father would always say, "Be good, my son, and you will be rewarded."

I tried to adhere to this rule. When my mother was helping me dress for school one morning, she remarked to me, "You know, your father will do everything for you as long as you listen to him." That would be easy to follow because I wanted a Scalextric racing set for Christmas. Furthermore, if I behaved well at school and at the mosque, I would be able to watch films that my father had originally banned on television. This setup seemed to work well for me. My father struck me as a sensible man. He always spoke to me in English since he was one of the few in his generation to have passed the difficult matriculation examinations at the age of sixteen, which was unheard of in the

1950s. My mother never learned more than a few words of English, owing to her lack of formal education. However, she did get substantial Qur'anic and Islamic studies at home from her maternal grandmother, Aisha. Most importantly, my father wanted me to succeed, to get ahead, and to be a good Muslim. That is something I could get behind. With the world set to end in a nuclear holocaust and the end of times approaching as prophesied in the holy writings, I figured we had about twenty years before it all went up in flames. If my Maker were waiting for me, he'd want to hear only positive things. I had best not let Him down, with the curious inkling that my father rather enjoyed his role as our immediate patriarch-God.

4

Schools Apart

Education is what remains after one has forgotten everything he
learned in school,
Albert Einstein

The whole educational and professional training system is a
very elaborate filter, which just weeds out people who are too
independent, and who think for themselves, and who don't know
how to be submissive, and so on—because they're dysfunctional to
the institutions,
Noam Chomsky

I had a terrible education. I attended a school for emotionally
disturbed teachers,
Woody Allen

Argentina hosted the 1978 World Cup, which sparked worldwide football mania. It was my first memory of a major tournament, and it is still the most thrilling. The Argentineans were dressed in blue and white striped shirts; their hair was long and curly, and they wore short beards as they rushed about the grounds. The ticker tape and the noise generated by the people were the most memorable aspects of this World Cup. The stadiums resembled massive coliseums.

Argentina was clearly the favourite, since they were winning games easily and scoring beautiful goals that enthralled both analysts and spectators. The brilliant Socrates from the second-outstanding squad in that World Cup, Brazil, was the one man who scored all their goals. His talent shone brightly throughout the games. During the phases of the competition, with some world-class players undoubtedly at the pinnacle of their physical and mental capabilities, it was always remarkable how they managed to avoid hitting globules of unpleasant spit on their companions. By adopting the technique, I thought I would convey an air of hardness and coolness that will deter some of the ruffians from picking a fight with me. However, it was just the nonconformists' domain to do so at school. When I got off the school bus one day, I spat on the ground, exactly like my football idols. My father happened to see this act of spitting on the ground because the bus stop was directly across the street from our house. I could see he did not think it was cool, and he waited patiently at the front door as I approached. For that moment, time stood still.

When I was dragged inside the home by my collar, I was told not to spit again, and that if I did, I would face severe punishment. I was instructed that spitting was reserved for rebellious undesirables and football players. I soon abandoned it since it had not yet become a habit. But the story did not end there. My father was certain that my peculiar behaviour was the result of negative socialisation, and he explicitly blamed my primary school. I was attending an inner-city Church of England school with a sizeable proportion of Irish, black, Indian, Pakistani, and Kashmiri students, more than the total number of white students. Being surrounded by too many "others" was viewed as the defining element in my seeming demise. The primary frame of thought was that I could only have learned it from my fellow comrades. I did in the end, but I am not sure that is where it started. My father was likewise furious when he caught me swearing in Mirpuri. It is a lot of fun to use Mirpuri curses as adjectives. Whole dialogues might be built around swear words or make-believe swear words. Mirpuri is a dialect with a limited vocabulary, not an official language. With only land and cattle to worry about in Azad Kashmir, elaborate vocabulary to depict a more evolved way of being was simply unnecessary. Mirpuri was extremely difficult to learn through parents, and I discovered that people either took it up or did not. Speaking English with my father and sister allowed me to avoid having to speak Mirpuri with anybody else, even my Mirpuri schoolmates. Because English was the *lingua franca*, I simply required Mirpuri to amuse myself and the people around me. I dreamt in English, watched English television, and read English books. I was only South Asian because of the colour of my skin, what I ate at home, who my friends were on the local streets, and because I went to an Asian-dominated school. Still, my father blamed the school and nothing else, so the decision was taken to move me. I was transferred to a Roman Catholic school directly across the street from my existing school, which had three non-white students, two of whom being my sister and myself.

I missed my old school, my friends, and my teachers. I was head over heels in love with one of my former teachers. It was the first of many love-at-first-sight experiences. She was a stunning blue-eyed, blonde-haired woman with the hair and chin of Farah Fawcett and the figure of Lynda Carter. I did all I could to not offend her, including helping her in selecting veggies from a nearby greengrocer when I happened to notice her shopping there once. I was with my mother at the time, but I ran to my teacher and practically begged to aid her. She complied, hoping not to disenchant me. I used to adore sprinting around the playground with my friends, connecting our hands with each other to form what looked like two car drivers. We were *Starsky and Hutch*, but never *The Professionals*' Bodie and Doyle. Leroy and Karl, two Caribbean students in my class, were both intelligent and amusing. Others were simply cool cats, both guys and girls. I wanted to be with them all as much as I yearned for the freedom to be myself. All my familiarity, comfort, and consolation were snatched away from me in an instant.

My new school was hideously white. It was dominated by Irish Catholics, with a small visible minority of 'other whites'. I instantly realised that I was an outsider who needed to accept and adapt swiftly to survive. I developed a Mirpuri-free sense of humour and tried hard to satisfy my teachers, who were all pleasant and accessible to me. My father insisted that my sister and I attend this school since it was vital for our religious and cultural education. In Islam, Jesus is eulogised, and I was taught that Islam and Christianity were the same religion, with minor distinctions. I was advised to "leave out the miracle birth, son of God, walking on water, and you'll still be a good Muslim." It was all right to me. Others thought I was all right. Soon, a warmth come over me, which was encouraging, and I began to miss my old pals less and less.

❖

One day, my teachers and parents were debating whether I should go to confession. I said that I would be delighted to do so. I recall being escorted into the confessional chamber and then going down on my knees and looking up to talk to the priest who was seated. I had watched *Jesus of Nazareth* (1977) with my family and understood precisely what I had to say. "Please forgive me, father, for I have sinned. I am nasty to my sister and I defy my parents," I blurted out. I believe I could have said these words to any senior religious authority, but the padre looked at me bewildered, not knowing what to say or do because here was a Muslim youngster begging for forgiveness from a Catholic priest. In a calm and peaceful voice, he said, "Arise, my son, your sins are no more." This is amazing, I thought. I can go now and commit some more sins before returning next week to be cleaned again. This was a laid-back religion, not much different from Islam. The extravagant costumes of prayer leaders, the concepts of Lent and Ramadan, paradise, and hell, and how the Lord's Prayer sounds eerily like *Surat al-Fatiha*, the first verse of the Qur'an, all seemed quite rational to me. Every Monday morning, we would discuss the Sunday Mass lesson, which I never attended.

David and Goliath, The Good Samaritan, and The Prodigal Son were three of my favourites. Singing beautiful hymns, psalms, sonnets, and Cat Stevens songs each morning seemed necessary and enjoyable as well. I succeeded academically, and now that I had a new set of NHS spectacles, I found pleasure in playing the affable and funny nerd who was becoming popular with everyone.

During this period, I grew increasingly conscious of disparities in myself related to my beliefs and the colour of my skin as viewed by others. Because I was at a white school, I and a few others stood out like sore thumbs. Our differences were clear in how other people saw the few "darkies" who came to school. Apart from a general feeling among some parents that I was undesirable, I was also getting it from the teachers. Mr. Devoti, the music instructor, was an old, overweight Italian man who was the school's sole music teacher. We had two hours with him every week, but they were not ones I looked forward to. Mr. Devoti would choose students from the class to play specific instruments as part of an impromptu group. I vividly recall never having the opportunity to play the guitar, viola, bass, or keyboards. I was almost never asked to play anything. It would be to play the drums if I were. Every time, I agreed grudgingly, not because I despised drumming, but because I wanted to play one of the other instruments. I occasionally dwell on my first true understanding of music making and ponder long and hard about how I may have been exposed to it more favourably.

My interaction with Mr. Devoti was insufficient to make an impression. However, one teacher's remark left me cold, shivering, and helpless. Mrs. Clarke was well known as a tough teacher. She was grey in her clothes, grey in her demeanour, and grey in her hair. As was customary, I approached her in class one scorching day to ask her a question. I had seriously hurt my nose a few months before following a tumble at the local park, as due to its size, it typically fell first when striking the ground. As a result, my snout was not completely healed, and I was prone to sniffling. I was also suffering from hay fever. I felt the need to sniffle as I approached Mrs. Clarke, who was sitting behind her desk in front of the class. At that moment, she abruptly halted me in my tracks and told me directly, "don't you ever come near me sniffling like that again, young boy." To prove my point, I was ordered to return to my desk, clean my nose, and then return to her to ask the question I had requested. She responded appropriately, but ever since that day, I have kept a handkerchief in my pocket for such moments when any unnecessary sniffling is out of the question for a conk the size as the nose on this Concorde, which was one of many nicknames at the time.

As part of a class assignment on policing in the United Kingdom, a police officer paid a visit to the school. During the demonstration of how finger printing is done, which was a long, drawn-out, dirty, and tedious procedure involving asking for volunteers from the class to take part in the inking process, I was unsurprised when the officer pointed his own finger at me and said, "you'll do". I was getting acclimated to it by this point, and I could see the patterns reappearing repeatedly. I could also hear comments like "he's a mugger" or "no point in finger-printing him, his hands are too dark" from some of my more agitated classmates. I ignored these statements from my peers since I had become accustomed to their jabs and insults. Later, sensitive to these themes of racialisation and criminalisation, the police officer allowed me to freely examine the motorbike he brought to the school, and I asked all the questions I could. Later, when we went to the police station as part of a school field trip for the second stage of the class project, the same officer recognised me and let me touch the police horse and ask more questions. These encounters left me with the idea that race matters in how people interact with one another, but there are many more white English people who are polite, courteous, compassionate, and helpful than not. However, it is usually the few who inflict the grief, anger, and outrage that loom large in the mind and, at times, define the lasting viewpoint.

Mrs. Jones was the English teacher who oversaw my primary school. I recall one incident that was unpleasant to me for a long time. I wasn't eating the meat dishes that were generally offered during the lunch hour since I was attending the mosque and growing up with Islamic values on *halal* meals. This was brought to Mrs. Jones' attention, and she took action to correct the situation. One lunchtime, while it was scorching outside, I was sitting alone eating my food when Mrs. Jones peered over my shoulder and said, "the dinner women are telling me that you are not eating the meat."

I said something to the effect of "I can't eat that," without fully clarifying that it was because my faith required me to eat only *halal* food.

"Of course you can, there's nothing wrong with it," she said, bringing over a platter of what I now believe was beef and saying, "you're not a Hindu, so eat. It's beneficial to your health."

She cut the meat herself and shoved it into my mouth. I did not take it easily since I thought I was committing a deadly sin, and I began to cry. I kept weeping but was instructed to chew and swallow. The tears cascaded onto the dish in a slow but steady stream. Strips of meat were swimming about on my plate and floating in a pool of brown water in no time. I was ashamed and completely perplexed because I thought I had transgressed. My friends thought it was hilarious, and I felt completely alone.

This event was reported to my father. He walked into Mrs. Jones' office and challenged her. I am not sure what he said to her, but she had a rudimentary understanding of Islam by the end of her chat with him. However, the result was less than ideal. I had to wait a little longer for my lunch so that one or two of the nicer dinner ladies would scramble an egg for me or let me take something off the staff menu. My helpful dinner ladies were not always available, and for many days I had to make do with a cold lunch that was sometimes nutritionally deficient, just enough for a growing kid. I have avoided beef with a fury since then, even if it is *halal*.

There were several incidents at school that affected my confidence and self-esteem at the time, and there were plenty of fellow students cracking racist and sexist jokes. I often laughed aloud with them, not realising how horribly hurtful they were at the time. I will not repeat them here, but they had everything: racism, homophobia, misogyny, sexism, and a Benny Hill-esque smutty ending.

Mr. O'Brien was the physical education instructor. He understood that, as someone with a South Asian sub-cultural heritage, cricket was in my blood. True, I played as much as I could at the neighbourhood park, and I could pick up a bat and bowl a solid ball. He instantly assigned me to the cricket team. But one day in class, Mr. O'Brien gave me the most perplexed expression. When he took over as art instructor one day, he asked us all to design a depiction of ourselves as other people would perceive us. When we were asked to draw ourselves without thinking, I sketched an image of someone who looked particularly black African, that is, dark skinned with huge eyes, curly hair, a large nose, and thick lips, while everyone else drew portraits of white Europeans.

"Who is the image meant to be of?" Mr. O'Brien inquired.

"Me. Isn't this how everyone sees me?" I responded in kind.

He seemed really bewildered by me. It was my impression of myself through the eyes of others. At that school, I was the sole boy of colour amid the whitest of environments. In the late 1970s, black males were often portrayed on television news as muggers, rapists, or unwelcome antisocial pariahs. Black people were reduced to basic notions based on beliefs of difference that were the most unlike white European self-conceptions and that all non-white Europeans are the same mass of undifferentiated individuals. In the lack of any distinction, I was just the opposite of everyone else. I could have passed for a black person while having a brown complexion.

❖

Sport has a significant role in bringing people together. Cricket taught me the most about this. For many people in South Asia, Australia, and the Caribbean, cricket is more than simply a sport; it is a way to "kick the buttocks" of the colonial overlords who once dominated the planet. Cricket was introduced to the colonies to keep the ex-pats entertained, but once the indigenous started playing it, it felt wonderful to defeat the colonials, who felt supreme in all other ways and methods. Pakistan reached the semi-finals of the second newly constructed World Cup competition in 1979, hosted by England. The television was once again the centre of attention in our home, as the older males watched anxiously in the hope that their "home" team would win. A decade later, the dilemma of who to support, England or Pakistan, would resurface with the not-so-wise comments of Conservative Norman Tebbit MP, who questioned British-born Muslims from Pakistan like myself, "Which side are you on?" There was obviously a sense of glee in smacking the flailing English in the late 1970s, and many first-generation men got a lot of enjoyment out of it. For me, it was more perplexing back then, and a decade later, when I believed I could not lose when England and Pakistan faced off. Additionally, if the games were good, a third winner would appear. Cricket.

The English side, on the other hand, rarely stood for the breadth and depth of skill of the many English-born minorities. If selectors could understand that cricket is in the blood of British-born ethnic minorities with heritage from the former English colonies, the English game might become the most thrilling in the world, but this does not happen. The game in 1979 was tight, and England won in the end, but the 1980s were a dreadful period for the English and a brilliant time for India, with players like Sunil Gavaskar and Kapil Dev, and the West Indies, with Viv Richards and Clive Lloyd. In 1983, I attended my first cricket match, an England vs. India test match at Edgbaston. Imran Khan was rising through the ranks, and he was undoubtedly Pakistan's most renowned export throughout the 1980s. He was a fantastic all-rounder and an Adonis to see on the field, guiding his team to a World Cup triumph against England in 1992. When Ron Atkinson brought three Caribbean players to West Bromwich Albion in 1978-1979, fans and sports writers called them "the three degrees." There were no black players in cricket, and this stayed the case for many years. Being denied the opportunity to play for your country, let alone fully take part in the society that welcomed you in the 1950s, were factors that contributed to many second-generation British-born Caribbeans rioting on the streets in 1981, and the same would happen two decades later to British-born Pakistanis and Bengalis.

◈

People who did not engage with me had no idea I existed in the late 1970s, even though I was a cheerful young man who had a good relationship with teachers and classmates equally. On one occasion, while hurrying across the city on a school excursion, one of the parents who went with us stared at me as I walked to cross the pelican lights with others and asked, "Are you with us?" I stood in the centre of the road, unsure which direction to go in. One of the teachers promptly intervened and informed them that I was legitimate. This was a strange incident for me because I knew the parent had seen me previously. Was this question meant to humiliate me or my friends? Was it a deliberate attempt to make me feel unwelcome as an outsider, or an outlier? Was it a deliberate attempt to halt me in the middle of the road so that I would be run over? I never gave it much attention at the time since I assumed this individual had just forgotten. But it is obviously an experience that is still in my memory, as does the very confrontational behaviour of a difficult English student who insisted on calling me "Oi Paki" rather than my name. He was a self-avowed and proud member of the APL (Anti Paki League). To the chagrin of the teachers, he had just recently started at the school and made an immediate impression on the rest of the class with his raucous overtures about Pakis. I would avoid this young man on the playground since any tiny touch would turn him aggressive. I raced as fast as I could, but his Doctor Martin's boots were enormous and strong, and they were not being used in the way I imagined: devastation rather than survival. I still have a scar on the right side of my skull from where I felt his boot and the fury that came with it.

I was having trouble getting chosen for football and cricket team matches, even though I could wow my friends by showing ball handling or telling hilarious anecdotes. I mostly made friends with loners and the underprivileged. They hung around on the outside of the school playground, and I could see they were not comfortable with me, but they were content enough to know that as the official school Paki, I was not a particularly awful person. Yvonne Parker was one such girl. She was a modest young woman whose mother knew my father from her frequent use of his bus. Yvonne lived close to the school, and we occasionally walked home together. Her warmth and friendliness drew me in, and she smiled at my jokes, which I could not stop telling her. I believe my interactions with her began to take on romantic connotations. I was ten years old, just like she was, except she was Catholic, and I was Muslim. In the 1970s, such a relationship would have been looked down upon by society. Nonetheless, I recall her scent, which had the consistency of milk, and the dress she wore on one non-uniform day. It was as brilliant and golden as the sun. My father picked me up from school one day in his enormous double-decker bus, which he had to himself for an hour. Several schoolchildren hopped onto the bus to obtain a free ride to the top of the road, and this earned me a lot of friends for a few days following the event.

Later that year, the actions of "Maggie Thatcher the Milk Snatcher" finally led to the discontinuation of our daily dosage of pasteurised milk in the mornings, and we were also informed that it was she who had raised the prices of our mid-morning crisp snacks. The Iron Lady came to power in 1979, ushering in a new era of thinking and doing that favoured the individual and entrepreneurship. It would put an end to the lights shutting off often or the occasional lack of hot water. With a political agenda that allowed us to strive to potentially live comfortably, I asked my father one day, "Are we poor or middle class?" He did not respond directly, claiming that "we are not so poor that we go hungry or cannot afford special items when we need them, but we are not so affluent that we drive huge cars or live in enormous houses." The majority of the young Muslims I met and knew at the time did not have working mothers or fathers.

I had also learned in school that they were impoverished Africans who did not eat every day. My Catholic school saw it as a job to not only provide them with food but also with faith. I felt sorry for them since, in Islamic history, the first person to cry out the *azan*, or call to prayer, was called Bilal. Bilal was an African slave who was emancipated by Islam. Even if they are portrayed as inferior or backward in books and on television, black people are no different than white, South Asian, or Chinese people. That had been taught to me by seeing *Roots* (1977) with my family, but how I was to learn it all intellectually occurred many years later.

I wanted to be with the "in group," but I had also painfully realised that the people in the "out group" were not there by chance, but on purpose. I was occasionally made a member of this "out group" by the behaviour of others toward me, and I knew it was not because of anything I had said to them, but of what they had perceived or imagined. Such is the function of authority in the face of a lack of creativity.

5

Surviving the Unfit

It is not the strongest or the most intelligent who will survive but those who can best manage change,
Charles Darwin

Civilization is a race between disaster and education,
H.G. Wells

Fear is the path to the dark side. Fear leads to anger, anger leads to hate, hate leads to suffering,
Yoda

The year was 1980, and I was reaching the conclusion of my time in primary school. We were preparing for secondary school. As one of the more intelligent students in the class, it was assumed that I would take the 11+ with my trusted classmates Aidan, Adrian, Gerald, John, and Kieran. But there was a snag. As it turned out, it was a giant "brick in the wall."

Mrs. Jones, the principal of my primary school, felt obligated to limit my attempts to attend grammar school. She persuaded my father that I was not yet ready and that failing the exam would leave me damaged for life. She had assumed that I would fail. We did not have a choice on the issue. Schools may only recommend students take the examinations back then. We were in a bit of a bind. My father sent me to Holy Family in the first place because he believed

I needed a solid educational foundation on which to grow. Now I was being denied the chance to take a test that might or could not lead to an educated future full of hope and anticipation, or not, as nothing in school is guaranteed.

Looking for a local secondary school meant eventually enrolling in a contemporary comprehensive on the other side of my world, where I would never see most of my Irish Catholic and English friends again. Waverley School had been a thriving state-funded grammar school until 1973, when educational comprehensivisation turned many of these formerly strong intellectual gymnasiums into semi-functional entities. One immediate effect was that elderly white teachers were leaving year after year. When I arrived in 1981, South Asians and African-Caribbeans were the minority groups. By the time I left the school five years later, most of the students were non-white and South Asian. This once-great learning institution instructed a different group of students with teachers from a bygone period. These teachers wore tweed and corduroy coats to school and were humorous and unconventional. We were exposed to many of these excellent teachers since we were placed in the top set because someone believed I was clever enough, along with the knowledge that I could tie my tie and my parents had bought me a fitted school blazer. These teachers were incisive, amusing, open, and alive. Other year groups did not have access to these outstanding educators. They had to deal with newer instructors who had just graduated from teacher training college and were eager to assert their newfound positions, often harshly. The older teachers were unflappable and unquestionably more interested in us as individuals.

Mr. Hassle was the name of one of the teachers. He would often refer to himself as "mad as a Hatter." He had a beautiful way of creeping up on people and checking to see what they were doing as he walked up and down the gaps between the perfectly set desks. When he was in full flow, he would go up and down the front of the classroom at breakneck speed, sliding around on the dusty, gleaming oak floors while wearing his brogues. He would tell all sorts of amusing tales about the French language, which he taught with great zeal. But he was quite quirky. That is why we all admired but also dreaded him. Mr. Jones was our math instructor. He had a kind demeanour, but he was also extremely brilliant and witty. He had produced all kinds of amusing mnemonics to help us recall certain sections of trigonometry. Various triangular signs were characterised as "SOHCAHTOA," which translates as "some old horses can't always hear their owners approach." Mr. Jones was always considerate and explained everything thoroughly. He fell ill for a time, and when he returned, the entire class applauded as he moved towards the door. It was clear that he was moved by it all, but he did not want to show it. Mr. Ellis smoked a pipe and was a strict geography teacher. He usually spoke quickly, yet his knowledge was astounding. He and many others left as the boys became increasingly rebellious because of changing circumstances at school. Sometimes it was due to sickness, but often, it was because they were tired of always trying to control youngsters who did not want to be there.

Although it was never directly said, we were compelled to look down on the lower groups with scorn, viewing them as less capable, even if we were instructed not to. It was not always easy to avoid them entirely, especially because some of the classes had diverse abilities. It was not an option not to mix. Accents, smartness of dress and appearance, demeanour, and elegance were all characteristics I became acutely aware of. In other situations, I thought the people in the other classes seemed average in contrast. I was functioning through the prism of class consciousness, which served to promote the idea that my position was as it should be, and that those who were not part of the selected few were simply less capable. It was a social-Darwinian worldview that was instilled through the procedures of a typical comprehensive system in which students were put into sets based on perceived aptitude. It is a microcosm of life in general. All these ideas were shaped by dominating social systems and were based on socialisation and the perceptions of others. The way we had to act was a method to legitimise the current system.

Later, I saw that children from impoverished households not only found life more difficult overall, but it also had an influence on their ability to rise above their poverty and isolation. Because they lacked the opportunity frameworks of other working-class and lower-middle-class families, they would be labelled in such a way that they would be perpetually diminished, while those doing the labelling legitimised their positions and those like them. In this way, elitism and the status quo are reinforced. Meanwhile, the many continue to compete on the razor's edge of life, uninformed of or unaffected by their more powerful counterparts' means, attitudes, and behaviours. An acute schism that centred on a chosen few while excluding a so-called unworthy majority was completely discriminating. It became clear to me that many of the children in the lower groups were kinder and friendlier than some of the children in my own group, though it was obvious that I should avoid making too many friends with these so-called undesirables for fear of being excluded from dominant groups. Staying at the top of the food chain was going to be critical for survival in life. Or was it?

Aksar's teeth protruded from his mouth like Freddie Mercury. Despite his obvious physical flaws, he had an outlandish sense of humour. He dressed formally but brought little else to school. He did not have a satchel, a coat, or any accessories. He was a gentle and compassionate young man, but due to his pressures, he was known to go missing every now and then. It came out that he was bearing most of the duties put on the shoulders of four young brothers in a Pakistani shopkeeper family. His father would gradually entice him into the business, while his other brothers pretended to be academically inclined. I remember him and I playing Starsky and Hutch at my first primary school.

We were proficient at knocking over some of the other guys in the playground at the time, I recall. Aksar found me hilarious as well. We shared comparable interests and found comfort in one another's presence, including films, television, and a weirdly developed sympathy for people who were less fortunate than ourselves. When things began to go terribly wrong at the school, this proved useful and vital.

Aside from Aksar, all my friends were in the same ability group as I was. Besides, I did not have a choice. I had gained a fancy English accent after leaving a good Catholic school. This contrasted with the other South Asian youngsters who had mostly left primary schools, where most of the pupils were from similar backgrounds. To avoid being picked on since I was now too sophisticated a South Asian for most, I stayed close to a small group of individuals, not venturing out at all. Even then, I was too pretentious for some of the South Asian youngsters in the higher class, and I was routinely mocked as a result. Bullying and harassment are common occurrences for children in schools as well as later in life when they become adults and enter the world of work in huge hierarchical organisations. To overcome the immediate problems that confronted me, I had to adopt the image of a brilliant clog to gain the necessary attention from teachers, but I also had to be street smart enough to avoid being perceived as an outsider-within. Aksar was my best friend outside of the top sets, where most individuals were, to put it mildly, mediocre. He and I had a wonderful time together. It was secure, safe, and unobtrusive.

⟡

The Rubik's Cube was introduced in the early 1980s and quickly became affordable to the public. This problem was always supposed to be difficult to solve, but some people were able to complete it in less than thirty seconds. There appeared to be a limited supply of the formula on two sides of a folded A4 printed sheet in tiny type. Manz and Sham, two of my Bhatti cousins, had a paper copy of the answer. Sham meticulously copied down by hand the directions to solve this perplexing brainteaser since she did not have access to a photocopier or could buy a solution anywhere. But, for some reason, she had not copied down the last page's part. I memorised the answer, which allowed me to solve 95% of the cube but not the remaining four corner pieces. In the schoolyard, I took joy in impressing many youngsters who were astounded to see me so eager to spend so much energy work solving most of the cube. The novelty faded off quickly.

I did well in school, succeeding in math, English, science, arts, and languages with little or no effort. I was never overwhelmed, and I had mastered the art of memorising facts for examinations. That was all there was to it. Looking back, it was clear that I was never pushed. In truth, many people, including myself, were not encouraged to work harder. The better ex-grammar teachers were leaving in droves, while the newly-qualified younger teachers were still learning a lot. When people are not pushed to excel and there is ability in a person based on aptitude as well as desire, the hazards are that these young people grow complacent. When this happens, all kinds of distractions appear, some of which are not necessarily beneficial. I began to develop an interest in table tennis and soon became known as the best in the school. The PE instructor saw some ball control, and before I knew it, following a very lengthy set of technique and control tests, I was named captain of the cricket team and the opening bowler. It was a privilege, but it did not endure. At some level, believing you are good enough is crucial, but the mirror cracks when you face a stronger opponent.

Our first game took place away from home. We won the toss, and I chose to bat first. Things were not looking good because we were up against the league's toughest club. Most of Small Heath Cricket Club's players were Caribbean. They were large, towering boys who were up for the challenge. My team was made up of skinny, gangly Imran Khan wannabes and English boys who were skilled at football and very fit. The top order was knocked out by the opening pair. I chose to bat fourth because I wanted to get a feel for the opponent and didn't think I had the temperament or patience to bat first in my first game. It was two-for-two. My teammates had a habit of stepping back from the crease to create more room to hit the ball onto the mounds that surrounded the school-pupil-sized cricket ground. What they did not remember is that it is critical to examine the trajectory of the approaching sphere before trying to launch it into the outer stratosphere. They all fell one by one. I was able to put on a run before arriving at a 4-for-9 final wicket stand. My last companion soon followed suit, and we were all out for four runs. What a colossal blunder and a total embarrassment. My sole redeeming quality was that I was not out.

I began the opening spell with jokes from the field that I would not be able to bowl my first over before the game was ended. I gave up two runs, but by the next over, it was all over as the second bowler threw a wide and was hammered for a four on his next ball. I was happy since I was not out and did not give up the winning runs. However, our post-match team meeting was cancelled. Apart from expressing my dissatisfaction to my teammates, I had nothing to say. Mr. Warrior-Law, the enraged PE instructor, stormed into the changing room and told us that if this happened again, he would be too uncomfortable to continue.

We then played at home. Mr. W-L shuffled the order himself. He believed I had not proven myself sufficiently among the lads. He may have been correct, but such traits are learned, and I did not have much time to make an impact. A single game could never be sufficient. We headed into the field, chasing a low total. The batters were all instructed to keep their stance and not be intimidated by the bowling. The goal is to hold your ground and put pressure on the bowler to deliver the ball offline and off length, allowing offensive shots to be struck. Stepping out of the crease and trying to thump the ball for a six is typical of Sunday cricket in the park. Unfortunately, the pressure to make an impression on Mr. W-L, the desire not to be intimidated by the process, and a lack of self-belief meant that after we lost three wickets, and with me being caught at mid-on by a slower ball after only two runs, the rest of the order collapsed for only three more runs. After that, it was all over. For the next few years, the school did not set up teams or take part in competitive school league cricket.

Table tennis, on the other hand, was different. I used to play against my kitchen wall, striking the ball repeatedly while pretending to have someone else to play with. My sister did not want to know, and my father pretended to be elderly. But I played and met other people who shared my enthusiasm for the sport. Mr. Rabbani, one of the senior Bhattis, played for his firm, British Telecom, and he saw my keen interest in the game. He would take me to competitive games that were held after work hours. I began to play with his son, Shahzad, fondly known as *Slimfast* at the time (he grew into a very tall chap who could not sit still for more than a few seconds). When we visited each other, we sometimes used the tiny table in our separate living rooms. We spent the day and night tip-taping away by building a net out of cassettes placed on their sides across the centre of little tables. It irritated the seniors in the other rooms, who were absorbed in Bhatti banter.

I was the usual captain of the school team, and we competed against other school teams from across the city. This taught me a lot about how various schools were: clean, unclean, drab, colourful, bright, or depressing, and it was reflected in how the students appeared as well. Although I was the best in my school, there were students on other school teams who were brilliant. Some of the selected school students appeared emaciated and geeky. Others were chubby and oily, but most table tennis players fit into a variety of categories. I did not have the matching Lacoste headband, sweatband, sweat-socks, trainers, T-shirts, small towel, large towel, or equipment bag. I was okay in my urban eco-wear and did not mind the hubbub. Some of my teammates took immense joy in temporarily dominating their middle-class grammar school rivals.

I realised I was decent at sports but never great at them, which was an unpleasant revelation. Was it also connected to my intellectual ability? Is it possible to overcome it? I began to consider my place in life's pecking order and the ever-present significance of that food chain. Surely, if I had greater resources to use, such as trainers, sports camps, or inspiration from home, this would be a more crucial element. Was it nature or nurture? Aside from that, there is also athletic psychology to consider. Aside from the significance of skill, technique, and enthusiasm in cricket and table tennis, the game is often won or lost moments before it is played. Each player believes that they will win or lose. I intended to apply this philosophy to everyday life. I got started right away.

◈

In 1982, we learned that our house would be razed to make room for a motorway that would pass directly to the town centre. This is a common trick used by many post-industrial town planners throughout the western world. When obsolescence becomes a feature of the local area, with long-term decline setting in, middle-class employees living on the outskirts are placated rather than investment programmes to revitalise the local area. These declining areas are often flattened, and a motorway built over them to a) ensure that middle-class workers can arrive at their destination quickly and b) avoid having to look at the rabble as they drive by because they were considered more important to the local economy. As it became clear to local inhabitants, some of whom were fleeing quicker than ever before, including Pakistanis and Azad Kashmiris, that nobody cared about the local neighbourhood any longer. We had to wait until the local authorities could re-house us, but until then, we were in a state of suspense. But, amid all of this, our own home had become unfit for human occupancy. The houses at the back had been unoccupied for a few months, and various people had been throwing their rubbish into the now-abandoned gardens. This pile developed into a jumble of broken home furniture, bust-up prams, kitchen sinks, bathroom fixtures, ancient settees, and boilers emitting foul odours. Nobody came to clear it up, and the mound grew and expanded until we could not see out of the living room window anymore.

Things did not get any better when a snake was discovered in our neighbour's garden a few weeks later. Mrs. Kaneez was cleaning her outdoor toilet when the dreaded blighter appeared from behind a metal container. Mrs. K quickly summoned my father, the closest senior South Asian male patriarch to be located. By hacking the head off this snake, it is as though Indiana Jones came to the rescue. My father informed my sister and me that special personnel had arrived and that a poisonous snake had escaped from the zoo. He was playing us all for fools. For several miles, there was no zoo. The second notion was that it had evolved genetically from the rubble and rubbish that had erupted at the rear of our house. For some reason, which was too terrifying to contemplate, I did consider the possibility of life being produced in this manner for a moment. It was a black adder, an innocuous English grass snake that had escaped from the nearby park.

We left the house where we had lived for the previous six years as a family in the winter of 1982. The local authorities gave us a home that was a short walk from my school at the time. This new house was on the opposite side of Small Heath from where all the Bhattis lived. A year earlier, Uncle Fazal

Rehman purchased a beautiful Victorian house with two stories, an attic, and a basement. We used to go there a lot because it was on the opposite side of the park. His Eid celebrations were legendary. Our former house and much of our old road vanished, along with all our tangible memories. Ashfaq, Azra, Azar, and a bunch of other friends from my neighbourhood vanished across Birmingham, and I tried to remain in touch with them as best I could.

Our new home was freezing, but it had plenty of natural light and huge front and back gardens. The local council had rearranged the upstairs to fit three bedrooms and a little bathroom, and we had a huge living area downstairs. The house was a significant upgrade on the one we previously lived in. The notable difference I saw was that all the people on the street were white, with many of them appearing to have been unemployed for years. Some would describe it as a council estate. The neighbourhood's white youngsters appeared uninterested in their South Asian neighbours and were dismayed to find that their favourite impromptu BMX freestyle dirt-track outside our house would have to be abandoned. Two elderly couples lived on each side of our house. If we spotted each other in the gardens, we would welcome each other warmly. I continued kicking various balls into each of the gardens, which frustrated both couples because it required bending over to slowly hunt for various coloured and sized items amid the dense rose bushes and forget-me-nots. So, I stopped playing in the garden so as not to bother them too much.

❁

One night shortly after we moved here, a neighbour going home from the local pub, after one too many jars of ale, chose to hurl a brick through our window while Techie Zulf and some of the Bhattis were visiting to talk about something or other. For a few seconds, we were afraid, but because we were all together, we felt strong in numbers. My father stepped outside and conducted a citizen's arrest. My sister and I found this amusing, partly because we wanted him to go inside so no one on the street could see him in his shalwar-kameez. The offender was quite intoxicated at the time, and he did not get past the words "ffffuck off back home Paki," to which my father replied, "Come on now ... that type of language is unnecessary, young man." Pat, as his name was revealed to be, eventually managed to flee just as the police officers arrived. They hauled the brick away for inspection, even though everyone knew it was Pat from number seven. Nothing came of the inquiry, but Pat began walking home on the opposite side of the street when he returned home late from the pub until he vanished entirely.

The spectre of hate was often real, and I dared not go out on the streets alone, or at all, at times. While my parents discussed turkey in the living room and my sister did her own thing, I spent most of my evenings in the now-larger kitchen, slamming table tennis balls against the wall.

6

Cruel Discoveries

My style? You can call it the art of fighting without fighting,
Bruce Lee

An eye for an eye will only make the whole world blind,
Gandhi

A leader leads by example, not by force,
Sun Tzu

In 1984, Big Brother was not watching. My father felt compelled to push my sister and me to value our ancestors, fearful that we might lose part of ourselves if we continued to Anglicise culturally and socially the way we were. His choice, and his alone, was to transfer my mother and sister to Azad Kashmir for a year. The main goal was to rebuild an abandoned and rotting home that he had sponsored to completion a decade earlier. There was also the worry that my sister might do something that would bring shame and dishonour to him or the clan. Not because he felt compelled to do so based on first-hand facts, but out of fear that something bad might happen. It was a result of power, patriarchy, and sheer terror at the prospect of being despised by his community. She was also being tentatively signed up to marry her cousin, and with an increasing number of stories of problems with 'wayward' young women who refused their first-cousin suitors, the dread would only grow in a climate of isolation and among a community that amplified entrenched lives.

I imagined it was a form of conditioning. But I do not believe my sister was thrilled because it meant leaving her school friends behind, and she went to a wonderful school. But she went nevertheless, determined not to offend our father. She enrolled at a school a mile away from the village after moving to Bachlakra for a year. Even by the mid-1980s, there was not much in the village "back home," except for a few old people. The majority of the Bhattis and their descendants were now scattered over Small Heath. What was significant for me was that I was separated from my mother and sister during a critical moment in my mental and physical development, and I felt it. I was fourteen years old. My thoughts were always racing. I had so many questions, but no answers, just more questions. Furthermore, my father and I did not always agree. I wanted to be modern and relevant in today's environment, and I saw the globe as one big, wide field. His point was that Islam is the only religion that satisfies all human issues and concerns. I did not completely disagree with him, but his point of view was shaped more by a cultural viewpoint than a religious one, and the cultural diktat felt more restrictive and self-serving than my preferred way of looking at life. It was a terrible period for me since I felt really alienated and cut off. Because there was not much else to do or take part in, I began to focus increasingly on television.

◈

Popularity and success do not always bring many friends at school, especially if some of the other guys are becoming bigger and angrier as part of their own journeys of self-discovery and intergenerational alienation. In 1984, several local schools in high-density ethnic minority areas were closed, and the schoolchildren were transferred among existing schools around the borough. The argument advanced was that cuts were being made across the board and that there was no other choice. We would be growing, with several students from other schools being added over the school years and courses. The schools from which we recruited our new students were in an area of town where there were a lot of Pathans. My classes now included several intelligent but bulky Afghans, and across the school, many new Pakistani, Kashmiri, and Afghan students were trying to adapt to the new system.

Some of the young males were physically intimidating. Their overall calm was marred by a strong tinge of hostility. Individuals and groups striving for pride, prestige, and recognition increased the number of clashes in schools. These brawls quickly devolved into melees, with rival gangs from neighbouring schools often joining in on the action in after-school violent clashes. The new teachers appeared worried; all the older ex-grammar schoolteachers had either left or retired. Omar, a Kattak clan Pathan who wore a combat jacket, was huge and physically formidable. He was dressed in high-laced Doctor Martin's combat boots. He was the leader of the new school pack. He plainly eulogised the Afghans in Afghanistan as they continued to fight the Russians. As history has often proven, the Afghans were proving to be tenacious. Omar's famous party trick was to wander about with his bunch of harebrained brutes, and when he came across a lone Azad Kashmiri or Pakistani, he would grab them by the arm as if to hit them and ask, "are you a capitalist or a communist?" Even when they argued that both communism and capitalism had risks and benefits, that the evidence that one was superior to the other was not always clear-cut, and that there was certainly some kind of half-way house between the two that could be classified as socialism combined with competition, as I myself stated, his arm was pommelled until his mind was changed. That was the more balanced answer, leaving room for ambiguity and the need for further information, but the uncompromising were not going to accept it.

His approach was physical rather than psychological. He would tap softly at first, then go on to more ferocious assaults, depending on how long it took him to persuade his unyielding compatriots to accept his ideas. Some of the more independent-minded males took their time surrendering, and I, too, suffered a beating before admitting that I would prefer communism over capitalism only to satisfy him. I was fourteen at the time, and I thought capitalism stood for freedom, competitiveness, profit-seeking, and a market economy, while communism stood for little or no freedom and no competition. In a communist society, everyone was paid the same, and the state governed a centralised economy. We had spoken about it in social studies, and I was not certain that maximising individual happiness was always preferable to meeting the needs and desires of the many, or that it was preferable to let individuals do whatever they wanted rather than doing what everyone should. As a result, a balanced capitalist economy had an advantage against the brand of communism promoted by the Afghans. Furthermore, while Islam was totalitarian

to me, people appeared to be free enough. There were restrictions in place to prevent individuals from doing anything they wanted, which is a good thing given the potential for excess in a free society. I might have rejected capitalism, as my friends in arms were commanding, but I was hesitant to adopt communism because I wanted to be free to think, to be human, even though I understood I did not want to satisfy every material or bodily urge. When a maniacal bruiser was battering my arm, I had to think hard about the matter, but I pushed these public vs. private, the good of the many against the good of the few, debates to the outskirts of my consciousness.

✧

At school, violence was becoming the norm. Someone who was physically tough was higher up the food chain. They were crushed if they were feeble. Alternatively, they learnt to tell jokes and run quickly. Despite gaining a reputation as the school boffin, owing partly to NHS spectacles and a physically-smart demeanour, I was not immune to the testosterone-fuelled hijinks that affected every other young male in the school. Because of demographic changes in the surrounding neighbourhood and inside the school, there were now more South Asians than whites in the school. The whites were now a minority, and they were forming identities along separate ethnic and racial lines in the face of a dominating other—the South Asian other. It also encouraged a substantial number of Pakistanis, Indians, and Bangladeshis to develop a collective identity; the concept of an "Asian invasion" was widely circulated. It also increased rivalry at the very top of the hierarchy. With the whites retreating into the distance, the South Asians sprang to the fore, seeking respect and position. It meant that none of us could escape the ever-increasing efforts of some to impose an order of physical toughness on the school. I had managed to keep myself out of it up to that point. I did not like the concept of a violent fight in figuring out a position, and I did not want to remember what it was like to be the target of indiscriminate physical attacks, as I was at primary school.

All my attempts to be a good boy, however, were futile. I was being bullied by my peers into picking a fight with AN Other, as I had yet to prove my worth in the field of war. I had to prove that I was not a "chicken." Kamran, who was thankfully smaller than the average person, was making some snide remarks with the intent of unsettling me, and members of my social groups were encouraging me to "give him a lesson." He was also being pressured to assert his place in the school's power, prestige, and status structure. I let it linger for months before succumbing. I was under constant duress. I felt compelled to show my hand. I challenged Kamran to a fight after school, but on the condition that only two people would be present. The entire year group was aware that this fight was about to take place, but they were also conscious that it was a private affair with only two witnesses. Many of the tougher boys were eager to give me pointers on how to get through it fast. I had seen some of the fights after school, and they were tremendously fierce, but also incredibly swift. It will end sooner rather than later in my situation. We could then all go home and prepare for the myriad further challenges that were ahead of us. Throughout the day, I prepared for this moment.

The drama began at 4 p.m. in the afternoon after all the schoolchildren had gone home. Some people told me during the day that if I wanted to finish the fight fast, I should squat on top of my opponent and box his face in. The impression was that it would be quick and effective, and that it would be over in minutes. My strategy was to wrestle him to the ground and then lay into him. Or, at the very least, this is what I was instructed to do. We eventually started scrapping after the cliché remarks that often occur, "you start ... no, you start." The two onlookers watched as the rough and tumble unfolded in front of their staring eyes. We rolled about on the floor, pushing, pulling, biting, and scratching each other until I was on top of him. He lay there ready for a hammering to the face, but I could not bring myself to do it. I went completely still. At that very moment, I realised I did not have it in me to injure this person or anybody else. I pulled away from him and stopped fighting. Kamran was still game. He was also jeered on by witnesses who said they would testify that it was a non-contest if there was no more activity. He kicked, shoved, and punched me, and I did nothing in response. I was face-down on the ground; my ribs being pounded by kicks to the side. "Get up. Get up," he said, and I refused. The war had ended. Kamran had proven himself to be the victor, and therefore his task was complete. By then, I had already admitted defeat. At this time, amid the silence, an Englishman cycling by came to a rapid halt. He got off his bike and came up to me. He shooed the others away, and after a short glance at me, he decided I was okay to go home. The rider felt I was being picked on, but he had no idea it was a pre-planned school brawl. Kamran and I had both agreed to go on with the fight. There was some blood dripping from the side of my lips, and I was wobbly but all right. I looked like I had gone into a wind tunnel, but I continued walking home, which was just ten minutes away.

When I came home, an elder relative who was visiting at the time unlocked the front door for me. I even gave him and my folks a friendly salaam before I excused myself and dashed upstairs. I washed my face and examined myself in the mirror. I at once burst into tears. I had held all the anguish I was experiencing throughout my body, but in an instant, I could not hold it in anymore. I wept and wept till it was all out of my system. My folks did not suspect a thing when I arrived downstairs. At the very least, they did not have to know, which was a positive thing. I do not need to irritate them with my careless behaviour. I am not sure if my classmates who finally learned what occurred respected me more or less than before, but I did not care. Accepting the challenge but then giving up when success was within reach was not a sign of moral triumph for individuals whose currency of trade was no longer intelligence or moral fortitude but how to live in an era where violence was the prevalent paradigm. I never mentioned the incident again, and I have avoided any violent confrontations since. I realised that violence produces no results. Kamran, I believe, was also being gentle with me. He could easily have punctured a kidney or broken my nose if he had wanted to.

Over the next several weeks, I saw some after-school brawls that were built up to be massive fistfights with an audience of fifty or sixty gathered around, but they tended to be over in seconds, with one or many young boys hobbling away semi-naked, with teeth missing, bleeding, and permanently injured. I know I got off lightly, and I am relieved that it did not have a negative impact on me in the long term. Bullying others never appealed to me but being bullied by others stayed a feature—an issue that took me a long time to fully understand. My skill at dealing with them, on the other hand, did not grow. It is never a clever idea to give in to bullies. Later in life, I learned not to do this. Kick me to the ground and I will eventually get up but stopping people from kicking me again in the future needed more than apathy or a moral compass on my side.

I did not want to be the monster who lived by violence and whose acts legitimised the concept that violence had become the norm by which people interacted with one another. At the school, there was no simple answer to this situation. It had collapsed quickly, and there was no one to pick up the fragments. It was every worst fear imaginable. There was no leadership in the school; fighting was the norm, and few people knew what to do. What could not be predicted was that things would deteriorate further.

◈

According to George Orwell, Big Brother was meant to be in authority in 1984. Waverley School, on the other hand, was run by no one. The national teaching unions had resolved to go on strike over salary and conditions. Teaching across the country was disrupted, and our school was especially hard hit given the already poor teacher morale, never-ending disputes, deteriorating values, and ever-shrinking resources. Maths, Science, French, and Computer Studies were all severely affected. It did not help that we only had one Sinclair ZX81 and one dot matrix printer for the entire school, even though we were informed that personal computers would revolutionise how we learned and did business in the next ten years. Teachers just stopped showing up to teach. It also had an impact on the attitudes and behaviours of the schoolchildren.

Aksar and I were now taking more classes together since he had advanced a band and the Afghans and new Azad Kashmiris were filling the ranks of the so-called lower ability classes. Because resources were so limited, classes were no longer streamed. Every morning, Aksar would knock on my door to walk to school with me. I lived 10 minutes away, and because he was a punctual businessperson, he would come at 08:40 every day. Teachers' strikes had now become a regular event, lasting for the better part of two school years. We would come to school each morning and discover some minimal information that showed to us that we had one or two lessons that day, but nothing else. The decision was straightforward. Hang around at school and the famed library with no books, trying to gain access to the one computer while evading the formidable Afghans on their warpath or vanishing for the day. We chose the latter.

We were not returning home any later than usual, at least not at first. Then we started to leave for school at 08:00. We had, in fact, discovered UK 8-ball pool. Den's Den, a local working man's café, had one excellent pool table, and with Aksar having access to the many ten-pence pieces we would need every day, we hogged it morning, noon, and day, and we played and played. We left my house early to ensure that we got to the table before other truants came, as they, too, were facing similar issues due to a lack of teachers at their schools. Den was friendly, and he understood we needed to go to school, but he also recognised that school was not working for us. We did not bother him, and he did not bother us. Only the taller Caribbean youngsters did, as did those who needed ten-pence pieces for the gambling machines more than we did for the pool table.

We had to leave Den's Den soon since it was becoming overcrowded with kids who were no longer attending their own schools, so Aksar and I went into the city centre. We discovered a whole new universe of arcade entertainment centres and underutilised snooker halls. When we grew tired of playing pool and gambling away our little funds, we turned to video games. Since their humble beginnings in Space Invaders and Asteroids, they have been getting significantly more complex. Star Wars was a tremendously popular game, although it was more expensive than the other games. We ended up being R-Type, Mag Max, Galaga, and Gyruss specialists. The latter I adored since it had music from J. Bach's Toccata and Fugue in D minor, as well as a thundering electronic drum beat in the background. I could play Gyruss for hours and hours without getting tired of it, and I often did. Sometimes new kids who came to the games had no idea what they were doing, so Aksar and I would help them get through various stages before they took over, only to be slain by many aliens in a matter of seconds.

We also made it to the movies and saw the main releases of the period. Some independent theatre chains were closing owing to the entrance of US-style multiplexes and people's laziness to stay at home and watch films on television screens through VHS. *Rambo II* starring Sly Stone, *Predator* starring Arnie, and *Lethal Weapon* starring Mel Gibson were the three final films playing at the ABC Cinema on Bristol Road in 1985, and we went to watch them all one by one. They were not particularly good movies, but we were typically the only ones in the theatre, and we felt fortunate and protected. We were able to pass for eighteen on a regular basis, and we watched some intriguing art house films at the Tivoli Cinema, such as *The Realm of the Senses* or *Ai no Korda* (1976). It prompted me to seek out some curious films aired on terrestrial television, particularly those starring Isabelle Yasmine Adjani as part of BBC2's "Film Club" or Channel 4's "Red Triangle" series of dangerous foreign films (such as *One Deadly Summer* or *L'été Meurtrier*, 1983). I would keep one eye out the living room window, knowing my father was on his way home after working late on the buses. The Red Triangle film series was finally cancelled because public broadcasting officials realised that, despite the arty label, Britons' ravenous demand for sex and violence on television screens was approaching fever pitch.

❖

Fortunately, my father intervened and tried to save me from my own approaching self-destruction, even if he did not realise it at the time. The Sinclair ZX Spectrum had just been released, and it was selling like hotcakes. He saved the money, and before long, I was the happy owner of my own personal computer. Apart from playing games all day and night, I did not do anything with it. In practice, the Spectrum was only capable of one thing: shooting aliens. During the day, I would turn on the computer, and various friends from school would pop in and out for an hour or two, depending on the holes in their schedules, and we would play and play.

Obtaining games was simple. I traded on the school playground and quickly became known as the primary school gaming master. These games were traded for current games to be exchanged for new games. It meant that I could accumulate all the games, both old and new, through a type of direct trading. There was no money involved, and the only out-of-pocket expenses were blank cassettes. The worth of the games was figured out by their release date and popularity. I only ever bought two or three games at first, and then I started trading down. By trading down, I was able to get the whole portfolio, which was then traded up for the new games when someone else entered the market. It was a good system and it worked flawlessly, but I had to forsake it all because Sinclair realised how easy it was to copy games and invented a way of fast loading. It was difficult to replicate these games unless someone had access to tape-to-tape recording devices. We could not afford this new yet popular modern technology, therefore I had to gracefully resign from my post as Spectrum games master of the school. Other computers, such as the Commodore 64 and the BBC B, joined the battle. These, once again, were way too pricey for me to ever consider participating in. So, my computer gaming days were done by 1986.

While schooling had successfully evaded me between the ages of 14 and 16, and as the strikes continued, I focused all my creative energy on 48k gaming. When I finally summoned the guts to show my face in class, I felt bereft. There was also no longer a table tennis club. During basketball, Gulnawaz, the big monster that he was, practically hurled me into the air, fracturing my collar bone when I landed on my shoulder. The injury had a substantial impact on my performance and technical skills. I had missed so much that no one had even noticed I had been gone for so long. Shabir was said to occasionally mutter "yes, sir" under his breath when my name was called from the form register each morning. He even tried it once or twice when I did make it to class, much to the delight of others. Letters were never sent home since no one was available to sign and mail them. It started to affect my grades, and I began to lose confidence. I was still playing pool, going to the movies, and returning home late on occasion. Every time, the explanation was that it was for a job interview. My father thought I had spent a lot of time planning out my future, and he was mostly supportive. He had no idea I was in a pool hall someplace, trying not to get beaten up or mugged while appreciating the mechanics of urethane spheres spinning and curling on green felt as I applied changing pressures and made subtle contact on different portions of the cue ball. I once wasted my bus fare money on yet another game of pool by mistake. I had to go three miles without a coat or a scarf in the cold and rain, reaching home at 8 p.m. My pitiful explanation had been that I was attending a school career lecture. Rather, unless something drastic happened in my life, I was doomed to a bleak future.

7

Bombs, Bonds, and Boogie

Americans are the great Satan, the wounded snake,
Ayatollah Khomeini

*The point is, ladies and gentlemen, that greed, for lack of a better
word, is good. Greed is right. Greed works. Greed clarifies, cuts
through, and captures the essence of the evolutionary spirit. Greed,
in all of its forms—greed for life, for money, for love, knowledge—
has marked the upward surge of mankind,*
Wall Street (1987)

God had to create disco music so I could be born and be successful,
Donna Summer

In 1986, I was 16 years old, and my results were fast approaching. I prayed
every night before each test when I took my GCE and CSE exams, hoping to get enough passes to continue to three A-Levels, as was the traditional path. I had never begged Allah for anything before, and I was hoping
for a miracle since I did not think I would be able to get the grades I needed
without it. I knew this since I had not done any type of proper study. My
education took place in pool halls and on the streets. I needed five grade C or
above passes. I came close, but it was not to be. It was partly expected that the
scores were as poor as they were given the fact that teachers rarely showed up at
school and that when we did, there were no resources available for us to learn
from. In retrospect, I was only in school for three years.

After picking up my grades and walking back from school, I was glad to see that most of my friends had the same grades as me, if not worse. Some fared well on their tests thanks to the support of parents who were able to fill in the gaps left by the school, but the school's average scores solidified its status as a failed institution despised by parents and teachers. What would my parents say? What would the rest of the Bhattis say if they knew I would not be going to university soon? I had to dramatically reassess my stance because of the external view of how people would see my underperformance and the negative impact it would have on my parents' reputation.

When I finally told my father, he gave me a disappointed look. "Call yourself sophisticated and modern. I even have higher school-leaving credentials than you, and that was in 1957," he continued. I was at my lowest point in my whole life. My world seemed to have ended before it had really begun. Because of the importance placed on school credentials, having few or no worthwhile passes would have put me at the bottom of the food chain. I felt compelled to pursue them once more. But I had to reconsider where I needed to go to reach my full potential. The inner-city schools and institutions where I grew up lacked essential educational resources. Thousands of individuals, just like me, were doomed to be disappointed. I searched and read all I could find before deciding on a further education college on the opposite side of town. A life as a factory worker or a cab driver was simply too much for me to take. I did not talk to anyone about courses or colleges. I took command of the few remaining alternatives available to me, looked to maximise my life chances, and set off on my journey. Aksar and two more dependable friends went with me. We came to Cadbury College expecting a warm welcome and positive instruction from the teachers right away. We also discovered other people who, like us, had similarly been affected by the lack of teachers around the city. There were some intelligent and talented young people among these young people of all origins, colours, and beliefs who had just been let down, just as we had been.

My interest in economics began in the mid to late 1980s, when I became intrigued by free market ideas and the role of the individual in society. In the news on finance, money, banking, industry, and entrepreneurship, concerns like unemployment, deindustrialisation, and the continuous confrontation between miners and the state were often highlighted. Studying economics would also aid me in figuring out how to best comprehend the nature of society in terms of consumer and producer roles, as well as how growth and productivity are attained. I assumed that the "loadsamoney culture", which was prevalent in many elements of popular culture and centred on people's wealth and status, meant that studying economics would help me better understand my personal situation as well as society's larger workings. At the time, it felt like a natural extension of my existing views. Monetarism, "rolling back the state's borders," privatisation ('selling off the family silver') and miners' strikes were at the forefront of a rapidly changing post-industrial society's concerns. I wanted to learn more about Britain's political economy, and I thought that choosing this subject would help me do so.

What sparked my interest in the topic in college was the teacher who taught economics to us. Mrs Moisey, in particular, was outstanding. I was eager to impress in her class, and I always worked hard. The adulation I would receive, as well as the eagerness with which I reacted to inquiries or made inter-jections in conversations, aroused my interest. The appeal of the discipline, as well as her reactions to me, motivated me to perform well. This was a teacher who recognised that I was enthusiastic about a certain academic field. She had acknowledged my dedication and was doing everything she could to aid me in my studies. She saw how engaged I was with the subject and how well I react-ed to her teaching methods. Even if I had not raised my hand at the start, she would urge me to reply to specific responses that others would find difficult. I did not want to be known as the class nerd, since I was aware of the conse-quences that might befall people who are smarter than the rest of the group. People are always looking for ways to bring you down, and I had developed an anxiety about this.

I re-started playing table tennis, and discovered that the college was known for it. I quickly became a member of the squad and began travelling to other institutions to play away games, as necessary. To be more specific, we trav-elled around the region to compete in many tournaments. While being out of the loop for a couple of years meant that the players were quite strong and I had not gained that extra something needed to be the greatest, it gave me confidence nonetheless. But I persisted in my efforts, and my performance improved with each passing day. Soon, I was playing at the top of my game and doing as well as I had ever done in terms of winning games, defeating the opposition on a regular basis with my squad, and keeping high win-rates over a sustained period.

◇

I made new acquaintances and got along well with them all. There were several intriguing people, one of whom was Farhan. He lived at the end of my street. I would knock for him before we boarded the bus to college. He was a nice enough guy, though a little self-absorbed and eccentric. Like Aksar, he was the son of a shopkeeper. His passion was the latest technological gadgets and apparel. He did, however, have some serious personality difficulties. He once informed Aksar and me that he was a ninja in covert training to become a le-thal assassin and that he was collaborating with instructors who were semi-gov-ernmental personnel. He once dressed up like a ninja in his yard for photos he wanted me to capture, and he looked impressive, if not a little delusory.

He was also quite paranoid. He was always trying to keep his actions hidden, which irritated me. I thought he was a little crazy, if not absolutely insane. When it came to relationships, he had an especially tough time. At college, he was obsessed with a young student named Pamjit, or Pam for short, and he did everything to attract her, including sending her a three-foot tall birthday card. Farhan tried everything he could to win her over. He penned innumerable messages in his illegible scribble about his love and heart. He was absolutely obsessed with her, and at one point, he entirely lost his grounding in life owing to his fixation with Pam, who dismissed his charms despite his best attempts. Farhan was upset, and for much too long. Obsession with a woman can drive a man insane.

Farhan's fascination with the Iran-Iraq conflict was one of his most intriguing characteristics. Being of Pakistani and Shia descent, he sympathised with the Iranians who were being slaughtered in their hundreds and thousands by a well-armed Saddam Hussein and his western-backed administration. I felt sympathy for the Iranians as well, despite my reservations about the Ayatollah's theocracy. Khomeini took control in 1979, but quickly began a war with neighbouring Iraq. It was a pricey experiment that yielded no benefit at all. The deaths of up to two million men on both sides, many of whom were as young as fourteen years old, was a tragedy of epic proportions. A pointless battle with no clear goals. My worries were not ideological or sectarian in nature; rather, I was interested in studying and understanding the situation, and becoming engaged by attempting to raise people's awareness of the numerous issues at hand.

For whatever reason, I became interested in a lot of the work Farhan was doing in his community. And it was because of Farhan that I was asked to join a rally in London in 1988, which went from Hyde Park to the Foreign Office to free the Al-Aqsa Mosque from Israeli control. I had the opportunity to spend a weekend in London, which I took advantage of. It was my first memorable visit to London, and I was determined to make the most of it. We stayed in north London and slept on the floor of an Iranian Islamic centre. I found my contact with the many different Muslims to be friendly and positive, and I found it most entertaining to place pro-Palestinian pamphlets in the unsuspecting hands of Knightsbridge residents and shoppers. I grew adept at ensuring that people looked at the material and asked challenging questions without fear. Many of the locals were everyday shoppers going about their Saturday afternoon business. Despite their hasty movements, the ruckus we were creating over Israel's occupation of Jerusalem struck many individuals. My personal understanding was extremely inadequate, but I was aware that people were suffering somewhere in the equation and that I ought to act. Many political issues were developing for me here. My love affair with London had also begun. I became increasingly interested in geopolitical concerns, and

I became fascinated by the character of liberal societies and their relationship to national and international political economies.

Farhan asked me if I would join him at a local *Imambara* to help as he and I got increasingly engaged in Muslim politics and culture. He wanted to play Mustafa Akkad's *The Message* (1976), give free apples to the audience (which was my suggestion), and sell Islamic Propagation Centre books, with the revenues going to Hezbullah, which had just been founded in the aftermath of Israel's invasion of Lebanon in 1982. It was a worthy cause, given that Arabs had been slaughtered in their tens of thousands over the years. People enjoyed the movies and ate the apples, but they never bought the books. Finally, we handed them away for free, with no money passing into the hands of any Middle Eastern organisation. I took a few books home with me, but they were all incomprehensible. A lot of it was about ideological opinions on the Iranian Shia heritage, and I did not have the necessary information to understand it. In addition, I assumed that the literature was likely to be extremely pro-Khomeini, which did not pique my interest in the least.

Throughout this period, there was a lot of talk in the press about the emergence of Islamic extremism, and a lot of it was pointed at Khomeini in Iran. His outspoken opinions on the West, particularly the United States, made him a prominent figure in entertainment on political comedy shows. The caricature of Khomeini by *Spitting Image* sticks out in the mind. The TV show also targeted Libya and Gaddafi, as well as Reagan and Thatcher, who bombarded Tripoli in 1986. Reagan referred to Libya's leader as "mad dog Gaddafi." The public perceptions of Muslims were increasingly impacted by unfavourable media portrayals of their community. It often took the form of depicting individuals and groups as insane, zealots, and aggressive. Our goal in screening *The Message* was to give a historical perspective to offset the everyday damaging representations of Muslim leaders, no matter how insane they may have been in fact. Farhan and I had evening classes at another institution, and on our way up there, we would pass a "Saddam Hussein Mosque" in Birmingham's Perry Barr neighbourhood. He would stick two fingers up at it as we sped past, and he would push me to do the same. I did not since I was driving at 80 mph. This was before high-speed cameras.

❖

Cadbury College lads usually had delightful stories about dating South Asian girls to share. Because they were young males, their hormones were raging, but there were few outlets that were judged healthy overall. The dating process with other young ladies, particularly Muslim females, was a frequent narrative among many of my fellow Muslim students. Young women's sexual limits are very rigidly viewed by South Asian Muslims in the United Kingdom. Muslim

63

women dating Muslim men at college was a no-no, but it did not deter those who were guided more by their sexual instincts than by the desire to conform to a prevailing cultural framework, and this was true for both men and women. The stories we told were extremely amusing, and we had come to a general agreement on how everything always turned out the same way every time. It would take at least six dates to get a kiss. Given that income levels for young people still in college are quite low, this would be rather costly for some. Getting further, moving onto heavy petting, may take another six dates. Anything more than that was considered miraculous. Then there is a particular discourse, which is commonly shared during such interactions. "I love you," a young Muslim woman would tell her partner. "I truly adore you... But first, I love Allah, then my parents, then Imran Khan, and then, I love you more than anything else." Suffice it to say, for my college classmates who engaged in romance, it was always a short-lived affair.

Another factor in bringing together young South Asians was the Asian daytime disco phenomenon. South Asian young people were restricted in terms of how much time they could spend outside of strictly supervised hours at home. Young people, being what they are, have a proclivity to seek out relationships with people of the other sex. Some intelligent people produced the brilliant concept of conducting discos in the middle of the afternoon. South Asian kids with free afternoons or who occasionally skipped part of their courses went to these thriving discos in and around 1987. On one occasion, I was dragged along kicking and screaming, but I was also fascinated enough to find out what was going on within them. They had a strange feeling. We were heading into a disco in the middle of the afternoon, with thumping sounds from levitated speakers and dense fog from dry ice filling the stifling air. Young South Asians were busy drinking Malibu with Coke, which was many people's poison of choice. And the tunes emanating from these speakers were electronic Asian sounds that fused Bhangra lyrics with sparkling dance rhythms. Naturally, many of the young folks performing a lot of the dancing in the middle of the floor were of Sikh background, but not all of them. Everyone was swarming in, leaping up and down, and completely letting go without fear of repercussions. The lights were dim, and the air was thick. Steamy bodies brushed against one another. It was an exhilarating release of epic proportions. Finally, young South Asians have the time and energy to let all their inhibitions go. I watched from the wings, attentively observing, investigating, and comprehending the nature of young people. I tried to move my body to the music, but it was clear that I was born with two left feet and did not feel obliged to try to fix it.

It was not always, however, such a free celebration. On a disastrous Wednesday afternoon, I went to what was known at the time as the Powerhouse Nightclub. We later learnt that scenes of awful violence had happened just after we had left the disco, at approximately 4 p.m., while we were steadying ourselves and boarding our buses home. According to reports, a Sikh guy knifed a Muslim man over the head for approaching a Sikh female. There was some sexual competitiveness and some trade between South Asian men and women. It was often assumed that Pakistani and Kashmiri men, with their lighter skin tones, were significantly more appealing to South Asian ladies than Sikh and Hindu men. At the time, Sikh males were perceived to be larger and hairier, whilst Hindu men were perceived to be timid and lacking in real passion. Because of this quagmire, many Sikh and Hindu women pursued Muslim men, and Muslim men found Sikh and Hindu partners easier to attract than Muslim girlfriends.

These conflicts were already visible on the streets of inner-city neighbourhoods where opposing gangs could be found. After African-Caribbean and Irish youngsters left the area, other gangs set themselves up along South Asian sectarian and religious lines. The Black Panthers were primarily an Aston and Lozells-based Caribbean and Pakistani organisation. The Punjabi Jats were from Handsworth and Soho. And most of the Lynx and Redheads were Pakistanis and Azad Kashmiris from Small Heath and Sparkhill. There were now battles for territorial space and recognition, as well as confrontations with a sexual undercurrent. Some of these brawls broke out within the midday discos. Parents quickly realised that their young boys and girls may be attending these activities. The police were also becoming alarmed by the frequent occurrences of violence. And, considering that these were nightclubs opening in the middle of the afternoon, the authorities felt compelled to intervene. These daytime discos vanished as soon as they became national stories.

〇

Because of Black Monday, 1987 was an intriguing year. It caused a financial crisis in London and other areas of the world. Gordon Greco's "Greed is Good" years had come to a halt as the typical tax-paying citizen became saddled with the costs of neoliberalism and an exaggerated credit bubble. For some reason, the spirit of ultra-capitalism was not producing the utopian vision I had hoped for. Continued unemployment in general, as well as a weakening industrial position in the global economy, meant that Britons had to work even harder for their daily bread. Nonetheless, my interest in economics persisted, and the next year I moved on to three A-levels in economics, politics, and mathematics, and I studied hard for the next two years. I did not go out much, but I did play a lot of table tennis and see the occasional Hollywood movie when I could. Unfortunately, in the mid-1980s, ultra-violence was fashionable in Hollywood (and Bollywood). They clearly captivated an audience, as films like *Rambo III*, *Die Hard*, and *Lethal Weapon* all generated a series of sequels.

This was fast food at the movies, while *Platoon* (1987) and *A Fish Called Wanda* (1988) were thought-provoking or just entertaining.

My record in college was excellent, and I was offered a place at the London School of Economics and Political Science (LSE) to study mathematical economics. I could now attend the top university in Europe for this subject, graduate with a high-paying job, and live happily ever after. The belief was that enormous financial stability would be the only way to provide me with a specific standard of living, which was formed by the ambition to live comfortably and securely. The prevalent culture at the time swayed me. I thought this was the only choice I had to pursue my academic interests in economics; perhaps I lacked vision. I worked in my room, jumping downstairs only when I needed to eat or when the call to "come and get it" arrived. I would eat in less time than it would take others to seat themselves, and then I would be back upstairs to continue reading and taking notes.

I worked hard, but I did not receive the requisite grades to attend the LSE. It felt like a huge let-down since I thought I had made up for my losses at the age of sixteen. I would graduate a year later than normal, but the life to come would more than make up for any lost time until then. I came two points shy of the needed grade. I went to college after receiving my results, expecting to obtain some guidance because I had not investigated alternatives since I was sure I was only going to one institution. I certainly had not considered alternatives to mathematical economics, such as history of economic theory or economics and sociology, as workable choices. Dr. Hosfield gave me a pep talk about how great my progress had been in three years and how I should be pleased with how far I had come, and in the end, we secured a place at Queen Mary University of London (QMUL), for the same degree. My heart was still devastated even though it was the same institution with a different college. For a week, I did not talk to anyone. I had worked hard enough, but not smartly enough. I could have comfortably eased my way in if I had studied a few pages on mind-mapping, employed more mnemonics, learnt how to pace my essays, attended Easter break revision courses, or used privately-paid tutors. I am all too aware of this now.

Because of domestic troubles, Aksar had to drop out of college a year early. His parents were arguing and had separated. He came to London with his father and now worked as a porter at an Earl's Court hotel. He never finished his A-levels, leaving him with few educational or vocational alternatives in life other than self-employment. He presently runs six Subway franchise locations in the West Midlands. Farhan had vanished after a year of A-levels, having moved to Cricklewood in London with the hope of finishing his A-Levels there. After I moved to London in 1989, I had lost contact with both. I later learnt that he attended School of Oriental and African Studies (SOAS) and then, sometime later, completed his PhD at Cambridge on Islamic civilisation's contact with the Vikings. My other college friends only got marks that let them into the "former polytechnics," so our paths diverged, and I was alone once more. But I had spent the summer working at a well-known jewellery company's distribution centre, and I had saved quite a bit of money by working seven days a week. I was on my way to London with a full maintenance grant and a sizable sum in savings, ready to embark on the next significant chapter of my life.

8

Urgent History

The fate of our times is characterized by rationalization and intellectualisation and, above all, by the disenchantment of the world,
Max Weber

The oppressed will always believe the worst about themselves,
Frantz Franon

If you don't stand for something you will fall for anything,
Malcolm X

My time in London as a student was a bit of a purple haze. I met and spoke with people from all over the world, and we discussed a wide range of issues, with no subject off-limits. I experimented with everything at least once. Some activities were clearly more enjoyable to me than others. Everything is possible in London.

Because of the University of London's collegiate system at the time, I was allowed to pursue social psychology classes at the LSE. I had the opportunity to sample the vast resources available at all of London's main libraries, and I also got the thought of studying at the LSE out of my system. The lecturers at QMUL and the LSE were often superb, and fellow students were confident, albeit not necessarily intelligent. During my time at university, I began to see a pattern that was mirrored in some of the individuals I interacted with. Many of those who showed the highest levels of confidence did not constantly prove the same levels of skill, but they had been groomed in such a manner that they exuded an utter self-belief and an ability in the language to support the concept that they were part of a chosen few. Throughout my years of working in the proximity of elites, I kept coming back to this topic.

Even though I had completed my studies, I was not happy with all the answers. My political views were also shifting. Market economics is not the best way to distribute limited resources. Isn't there more to understanding human life than the concept of self-interest as the dominating motive? Finally, I decided not to apply for any jobs and instead return to Birmingham for post-graduate studies. As my studies in economic development and policy progressed, I found myself looking forward to attending lectures and courses, as well as spending long hours in the library. I could concentrate on my academic pursuits because I did not have to worry about rent or bills. It was clear to me that I wanted to stay in university as much as possible since the benefits of writing, thinking, and reading were too wonderful to give up.

❀

I became fascinated by the study of minority groups and the subject of ethnic studies while examining the dynamics of post-industrial cities, economic transformation, and social divisions. It appeared to me to be a beneficial synthesis of sociology, history, anthropology, political science, and religious studies. I wanted to conduct further study on ethnicity because of its relevance in understanding how we connect to one another in a complicated post-industrial society due to disparities in identity, religion, and culture. As a specific study subject, I became interested in education as a vehicle for social mobility, as well as how the experience differed due to South Asian ethnicity and culture. At the time, little was known about distinctions within the Asian category, and I hoped that my ethnographic research would reveal some of them. I decided that this would be my PhD study topic.

I joined Warwick University because they had an ethnic studies centre, while Birmingham University was frustratingly restricted in this area at the time. I had met a prominent Pakistani professor at Warwick, and after writing him a letter and investigating the possibility of cooperating with him, he was quite supportive of me. Professor Muhammad Anwar invited me to his office to meet with him. I arrived early, which gave me plenty of time to explore the vast literature in the research centre's specialised library collections. At the appointed hour, I knocked on his door.

I strode in. He was sitting in his chair, which was metres away from his door. I made for the smaller chair beside him, which seemed as if it took a lifetime for me to get to. He was dressed in a smart suit and tie with expensive brown leather brogues. He looked like a civil servant. My first impressions were that he presented himself as decidedly English. He even had a silk hand-kerchief protruding from the left lapel of his formal-looking blazer. It was also clear that he had not relinquished a thick Punjabi accent, and it took me a while to discern some of his words. He had a particular habit of pronouncing "generally" as "journal-e". Once we settled down to talk, we discussed frankly what I could do, and the ideas of political participation and representation or the education of South Asians were the ones on which I was most keen. I opt-ed for the latter as it squarely focused on the issues I was interested in, which were related to economic and social mobility, the role of different schools and domestic contexts, and the differences between different South Asian groups (i.e., Bangladeshi, Indian, and Pakistani). I also told him that I wanted to gain as much experience as I could as a social researcher and that I would like to do all the contract research I could.

He did not want to be perceived as "carrying" me as a Pakistani researcher at a prestigious research institution. At the same time, I wanted him to regard me as a leader of the future generation of intellectuals, and because he was much older than me, I could treat him like a kind uncle. That is exactly what I did. My second supervisor was Professor Mark Johnson, who specialised in health studies with an emphasis on ethnicity. He was raised in a seminary in the south of England, the son of a minister. He had an exceedingly long beard that he made little effort to keep, but he had an extraordinary sense of humour. In every sense, he was a total eccentric, and my dealings with him were always enjoyable. I liked how he calmed folks down to make them think about what they were saying. Because of the nature of the study of ethnicity, we often continue to assume that certain features of social behaviour are rooted in the culture of the individuals involved. However, much of this is based on precon-ceptions and bias, as well as specific cultural, political, and ideological factors that support such judgements, as I discovered over time.

◇

As soon as I enrolled at the University of Warwick, I was a possessed man. I realised that without riches, property, position, or even income, the only thing I could do was intellectually empower myself. I felt a little like Karl Marx. I submerged myself in the university's immense books for the first six months, and my development surprised both my intellectual masters and me. I read all I could find about history, politics, economics, and sociology of ethnicity, migration, and education. Attending some of the MA classes on this subject, I learned about the neglected tragedy that is England's past. I had studied eco-nomics and the concept of wealth creation, markets, the price mechanism, and fiscal and monetary theory, but I had not realised that the surplus labour exploited to turn a small island into one of the richest nations in the world was not strictly through the industrial revolution, commerce, and international trade, but rather through the slave trade and the exploitation of India. All these concepts were colour-blind. In truth, the fabric of society, and particularly several crucial institutions, had its origins in the sixteenth and seventeenth centuries, when Britannia ruled the waves. After it got its teeth into the business of slavery, England became the most effective slave trafficking nation in the world. After transatlantic slavery was abolished and massive compensation was provided to the traffickers rather than the victims, the focus shifted away from imperialism and toward colonialism. Before the British arrived, India was the richest country on the planet; when they departed in 1947, they left behind a country that had become one of the poorest in the world, tragically sliced into pieces.

This enraged me, and it was tough for me to process it all. Nobody taught me any of this in school, and nobody explored it in depth at university in London. It did help to understand why so many Caribbean and South Asian people in Britain today have had such a challenging time since the post-war major migration periods. Britain makes every effort to transition from a colonial to a post-colonial culture, but it has only been about seventy years since the end of the empire, and for something that was created over many centuries, a mere half-century or so would not be enough. Furthermore, I discovered that the Irish were the first peoples to be colonised by the English, and that Ireland is still colonised to some degree. The Irish in Britain suffered particularly hard in the 1950s, and little is often said about it because they were white-skinned. And, as a religious minority, Jews suffered enormously approximately a century ago. They were also demonised, stigmatised, and racialised. Fortunately, Jews in Britain have developed a strong presence in society, and it does not talk badly of this group in overt ways, even if anti-Semitism is far from defunct. The United Kingdom's experience proves that diverse ethnic, racial, and religious minorities can positively integrate into society over time, and as a result, great outcomes can be obtained for everyone if everyone buys into this vision. At the same time, it may be premature to expect that issues of diversity and equality will be overcome in the UK context. The hegemony of white Englishness continues uncontested in many respects and is strengthened by a global perspective on a society that still romanticises conceptions of empire.

All of this was thrilling for me as I learned more about the dark underbelly of what is now a nation trying to become a free and open society, accepting and appreciative of others and forward-thinking, and until recently, a leader within Europe. But it was not always like this; for much of the last five hundred years, white people have been quite disrespectful, antagonistic, uncomplimentary, and even insidious towards non-white people, and some of this has continued as part of the post-war migration and settlement process of these "others" who returned to the "mother country." I dug deeper and discovered that "old Europe," particularly the former colonial powers of the Netherlands, France, and Germany, as well as, to a lesser extent, Spain, and Italy, were founded in the same way. That is, via the exploitation of non-white labour and wealth in faraway nations, as well as the development of a cultural nationalism with an intense sense of "race," "ethnicity," and "culture". I came to oppose the widely accepted belief in society that there are many races and hierarchies among them, and that these distinctions are embedded in the genetic makeup of diverse people as well as behaviours perceived as part of people's cultural features. All of this was soon rejected after seeing how the science of racism was exploited to support imperialist institutions. There is just one "race." It is the human race. Genotypic and phenotypic variations between people are insignificant, especially in skin colour, and this was an environmental aberration rather than a biological disadvantage, as was and is often said and held by many.

Following Darwin's original ideas on natural laws governing the existence of all living species, European scientists began to classify humans as either inferior or superior, with those at the top being purely white and classically European and those at the bottom being dark-skinned and 'ape-like.' Orientals (read "Mongoloids") were somewhere in the centre. This was a major factor in convincing colonialists that their intentions were justified to cull out backward races with antiquated genetic features, thus legitimising the capture of their natural and physical resources and wealth. People of darker complexions grew to feel that there was something real about colour and so-called purity during the colonial era to underlie a sense of these power connections. As a result of "aping" the dominant white populations that ruled over them, certain indigenous South Asian and black groups developed an internalised sense of inferiority. This strengthened, if not legitimised, a symbiotic connection between oppressors and the downtrodden. Moving forward in time, the "logic of racism" is still immensely potent in how people of South Asian and African-Caribbean descent buy into the assumption that white is better and black is its opposite. This is especially true as some of these groups seek to achieve a type of social mobility associated with a desire to "fit in" with those who effectively remain powerful in society, namely the white-English, middle-England, and middle-aged (and often middle-brow) men who act as the purveyors of what is regarded as the only legitimate form of authority. In this way, the concepts of class and race are intricately linked. The desire to blend in is still crucial for people who prefer to separate themselves (blend out) from their communities of origin, which includes other visible ethnic minority groups.

It is also worth noting that there are examples in India of similar grounds. As mean wages continue to grow and living standards improve, as do the expectations and goals that come with these social world perspectives, sales of whitening creams among Indian males have skyrocketed in recent years. Exposure to the globe via the powers of global communication technology, as well as the role of Bollywood in becoming a worldwide film industry, has heightened this reality. The concept of whiteness as it is projected in Western Europe, both historically and currently, can be found in far-flung places such as India, and it supports the logic of European racism. But the issue of caste within India is also important, where skin colour and social status are also linked to the presumed superiority of whiter skin. It is no coincidence that individuals at the top of the Hindu caste structure have a lighter complexion, while those at the bottom, the so-called unscheduled castes, have darker skin. What is also worth noting about skin lightening is its inverse. It is possible to see white European women who want to curl their hair to look more exotic than they are. This is an ode to Victorian Orientalism, which saw Asian and eastern women in general as having a certain mystery and sensuality that could have eluded the Christian "memsahibs," who were considerably primmer and more proper for the English men stationed in the Indian colonies, for example. Back in Western Europe, the concept of exoticism and adventure is also associated with sun tanning, which contributes to a sense of leisure and a more luxurious lifestyle afforded to some women of certain social standing when compared to the paler English or Western European woman, who is sometimes painted as sickly or forever in despair, certainly in late Victorian "romantic" novels. All these encounters are amplified when we consider issues of power, authority, and social dominance. Despite all efforts to eradicate racism in society, increase gender equality, and foster a spirit of coexistence, the prevailing class structure has not changed. As a result, the problem of racism is as much about capitalism and class as it is about "race."

❖

Focusing more carefully on educational challenges and controversies, as this is where I chose to focus my attention on the South Asian minority, I uncovered a plethora of fascinating data. During the mid-1990s, there was little statistical data on educational gaps across groups, but there was an unspoken understanding that certain groups were undeniably surpassing others. The Indians performed the best, while the Bangladeshis performed the worst, with Pakistanis falling somewhere in between. Why is this the case, I wondered? Exploring the literature and conversations among social thinkers reveals that the three most significant parts in the mix are family, school, and society. Simply said, a stable and well-resourced household and a quality school compensate for whatever flaws or limits are seen to exist among minority groups in society. There was undoubtedly a sense that language and cultural relativism were issues, but many authors contended that this was a red herring. Isn't it the school's responsibility to guarantee that its young people learn the language and culture, especially if their parents come from poorer sending regions and have money and housing limits, which have an influence on their experience of life in disadvantaged areas? As a result, when a school claims that language is a problem, many of the professional educationalists I spoke with would argue that the schools were displacing responsibility and handing it directly back to the parents, reinforcing the idea that weaknesses within students were a function of limitations within these ethnic minority households. Similarly, when we recognise great achievement in a school for all students, is it because the school is strong? Frequently, the answer is yes. And if parents are educated, particularly to degree level, this can only be a positive factor in their children's education, regardless of the school's relative strength or the overall socioeconomic situation of other schoolchildren and parents. *Khalas*! I thought I knew how many pre-migration variables, challenges of settlement, adaptation, community development and empowerment, and the strength or weakness of schools all had an influence on educational outcomes. I was also curious about the function of religion. Is it a positive or negative factor in achieving success? Does it have an effect if the school is selective and single sex or not, as one prevalent opinion holds that males and females taught separately fared considerably better away from "distractions"?

Throughout the rest of my first year, I researched theoretical and methodological complexities and organised my research design so that I could assess all the variables to find the most prominent general patterns. In this complicated beast of a project formed of six schools and three further education colleges, I planned to conduct in-depth interviews and surveys with students, parents, and teachers from the schools and colleges. It was a daring and ambitious project that would take a long time, especially because I was the only researcher working on it. Nonetheless, I had a mission to complete, so I set to work. The incredibly difficult aspect is developing and planning a project. The rest is simply gathering data, analysing it, and writing it up. Five percent inspiration and ninety-nine percent perspiration, as the adage goes. I was utterly engrossed and in the zone.

Many intriguing findings were made on religion and education in the context of a study of South Asians. For young Muslim school and college students, paired with their working-class and lower-middle-class backgrounds, Islam was extremely important in their lives and influenced much of the educational route pursued. Young Muslims from middle-class and professional families who attended top institutions had a more complex perspective of Islam's role in their lives, which they often balanced with a secular liberal attitude to their integration process. This was also corroborated by middle-class Sikh and Hindu respondents who felt able to combine their religion and culture with their need to integrate into society. As a result, the function of religion was influenced by social class in many ways, even if the sentiments of most Muslim respondents remained stable in the face of class consciousness. Nonetheless, the spectrum of religion varied significantly across all groups, regardless of class or the impact of schooling. Culture was found to play a larger impact in deciding specific educational pathways for young Muslim women.

In the end, my research supplied the results I wanted while also opening up new avenues of intellectual inquiry, notably on broader issues of identity, religion, race, and class.

◇

During the four core years or so that I worked on my PhD thesis, I engaged in a bunch of similar research projects. I wanted to be as well-equipped and empowered as possible, and I believed that the only way to do so was to conduct as much primary research as possible outside of my core interests in sociology of education and ethnicity. I also wanted to avoid having to teach to produce revenue to support myself via my profession. Teaching seemed too time-consuming, and I needed to study more before feeling secure enough to teach others. One of the other reasons it took so long was that my wife and I had our first child in 1996, which meant that I had to do my best to be a good parent even though I was a poor father who spent far too much time focused on my work and trying to get ahead. We were still living with my parents, so we had plenty of support, but it did not change the fact that I was working much too hard.

One of my earliest projects was for the BBC *East* (1996) programme, which investigated political leadership in inner-city Birmingham. It entailed knocking on people's doors and inquiring about their Labour Party membership. It revealed the extent to which local community politics has been soiled by corruption and cronyism. This study was conducted near to where I was living at the time. The scandal broke when the current sitting MP claimed his papers had been seized from his office, and these files held a list of Labour Party members who had the right to vote on candidate selection, as well as the name of the local community elder who enrolled the specific voter. As part of my investigation, the BBC sent me this list. Later that year, I was asked to conduct research on the character of the Muslim press in the United Kingdom. It had a small social presence at the time. I conducted phone interviews with newspaper editors and managers, most of whom were based in London. Later, I discovered that the Saudi government was interested in taking over one of these magazines, especially if they had a large following. In 1996, I was significantly involved in the first part of the Runnymede Trust's Islamophobia Commission, and, together with trusted colleagues, we produced an important study report on the nature of Islamophobia in the media. The commission had a tremendous influence at the time, raising awareness of many issues affecting Muslims in the United Kingdom. With the Bosnian War lurking in the background, it was especially important that issues of prejudice, stereotyping, exclusion, and alienation be examined for what they were. My last project while still at the University of Warwick was on a nationwide initiative on political engagement. My team and I travelled throughout the country, knocking on the doors of unsuspecting homes by carefully picking certain geographical locations and asking them questions about their voting beliefs and behaviour. It was a superb chance to learn what individuals believed about the political topics that were important to them, and in the short minutes we had at each doorstep, vital knowledge about people, politics, and places could be gained. The 1997 General Election was a much-anticipated event, and as a late-twenty-something, I was ecstatic about the potential for a change in administration. I already had recollections of eighteen years of conservatism, which had to end eventually, I reasoned.

In 1998, I transferred to the University of Central England Business School, as it was known at the time, primarily because a mutual colleague who had heard of my developing prominence in the subject of ethnic studies persuaded me to seek a position as a research fellow. I also had the opportunity to concentrate on economics problems while simultaneously collaborating with an amazing scholar who has remained a valued friend and colleague ever since. At the age of thirty-six, Professor Monder Ram was appointed to a chair in small business research. As part of a team, one other research fellow and I researched issues connected to Birmingham's independent restaurant sector, many of which were South Asian and several 'Baltis': a colloquial term referring to a mini-wok-like cooking and serving utensil. It was an incredible eighteen months of rigorous study that resulted in a substantial number of globally significant publications.

During this period, my colleague Balihar and I were confined to a room together, working on various research and analytical duties. I also realised the dangers of working so closely in an office with another person, and we had many heated discussions and arguments, mostly because I would pick up his pencils to make a note while whizzing around the large office, but not always return them to their original spot on his side of the desk. Balihar was a stoic Sikh who did not practise the Sikh faith. He did not wear a turban and kept his long hair and beard open, yet his *kara* (a steel or cast iron bangle worn by Sikhs) was always striking his desk while he typed. He did not believe in buying himself lunch, and he refused my offers, but if there were leftovers from business lunches hosted by prominent finance professors, which were left outside their offices after their meetings, he grabbed as much as he could with enthusiasm. He worked hard and was a resolute sociologist, but we enjoyed debates on many theoretical and methodological matters, often just for the sake of the challenge. Soon after our employment ended, I finished my doctoral thesis and was preparing for my viva. Balihar moved to Kyrgyzstan, where he spent five years learning Russian, riding his horse, and writing about ethno-national challenges in the region. Suffice it to say that, despite our intellectual skirmishes, which usually result in positive conclusions, we are still on good terms. He is currently an established sociologist at the University of Kent.

9

Government Business

Those who tell the stories rule society,
Plato

*Men are so simple of mind, and so much dominated by their
immediate needs, that a deceitful man will always find plenty who
are ready to be deceived,*
Niccolo Machiavelli

To rule is easy, to govern difficult,
Johann Wolfgang von Goethe

After several years of intensive sociological study in Birmingham, I felt compelled to leave and pursue something else. It was too much of the same downward spiralling local area dynamics, and it was starting to frustrate me. Positive change was just not occurring, and it reinforced my research on inner cities that nothing happens to them until something catastrophic occurs, such as a riot, a disruption, or extreme societal disintegration. Birmingham saw this in Handsworth and Lozells in the mid-1980s, and if the status quo was kept, tensions would inevitably escalate to unparalleled violence and devastation again, as they did in the summer of 2001 in the North and subsequently in 2011 in parts of inner-city Birmingham. In 1999, when the project funding at the UCE Business School was about to expire, I was recommended to seek a job as a project director of a regional race equality effort based in Worcester. I was offered a Lectureship in Economics at the Business School, but I still did not want to teach. I wanted to be active—to be in the actual world—rather than simply theoretical—and I certainly did not want to face a class just yet. As my difficult interview with a nine-person panel attested, the position in Worcester was not a sure thing. But they eventually gave it to me. I was now going to be in a different section of the West Midlands, one that is lovely. To his tremendous credit, my employer, Waqar Azmi, was both hardworking and ambitious. This was all too obvious, but we rarely saw him since he was continually smooching ministers and civil workers in Whitehall. I was also enjoying my time with my colleague, Dr. Frank Reeves, who whipped me into shape with his knowledge of philosophy, sociology, and politics intertwined with his vast public service experience. He served as an academic supervisor, but I was assigned the role of his boss, which was a bizarre arrangement. As soon as I started the job, I told him how ridiculous everything was and how I still needed to finish my PhD, which was still a few months away from completion. Working with him was a fabulous learning experience, and he is a friend to this day. He still sends me a Christmas card every year.

◈

I was delighted to see that the first-term New Labour term (1997–2001) was concerned with issues of diversity and inclusion, as well as a plethora of other progressive domestic policy advances. In the year 2000, Whitehall was expanding its social research programme, and I jumped at the chance to apply. After a preliminary screening and a written examination, I was hired as a senior research officer at the Home Office. I knew I was a capable person, that my abilities would shine, and that I could soar in government, so I went for it. And the pay was also nice. After extensive security checks, I eventually joined the Home Office research unit in Whitehall in January 2001 and began the process of looking for a place to live for my wife and now two children. Everything was going well in my life at this point, personally, professionally, intellectually, and spiritually. All my "bosses" up to this point were my friends, and it was an honour to know and work with them. My life, I reasoned, was now ready for the next stage in London now that my formal education was complete. I was young, well-dressed, and ambitious, and I wanted to be effective.

I arrived on my first day of work in January 2001, having found a place to live in Woking, looking the part. I was dressed in a two-piece, two-button, double-vented navy blue Aquascutum suit, a fine Thomas Pink double-cuff white shirt with bone buttons, my usual dark purple tie, Church's shoes, and a brand new Mulberry satchel. The only thing missing was the bowler hat. When I arrived, I was introduced to Carole Willis, the Grade 5 who had interviewed me months earlier. In the months leading up to my appointment, I read every report I could find on policing and crime reduction. I was well-versed in the policy and practice of targeted policing. I found my Grade 7 boss and stepped into his office, where I discovered a tall man with a short haircut. He was dressed casually in a sweatshirt, casual pants, and a pair of Doctor Martin's shoes, with both feet resting on the end of his desk and tapping his toes as he stared out the window. I remember hearing the troops across Queen Anne's Gate practising one of their exercises as I sat down. He could see them, but all I could hear was their instruments. We chatted for a few minutes, and I found Tim to be pleasant and helpful. He then delivered the bombshell, telling me that he was going to leave the civil service and that he and his wife, both G7s, were about to leave their employment and start teaching positions in primary schools somewhere in the middle of England. He was being very polite to make me feel comfortable hearing what he had just told me. As we went out of the office, he added, "Let me introduce you to your new G7, who will take over my post in two weeks, and then we can all go to lunch." I introduced myself to a lady in her late 30s, and we proceeded to Petty France in search of a local coffee shop. My new supervisor asked me during lunch, "So why did you enter the civil service?"

"To make a difference in policy-making by contributing to its evolution via rigorous and independent social science research delivered to the greatest degree of specification and detail," I stated firmly.

At that point, Tim nearly choked on his penne arrabiata. He looked up at my new boss, Karen, and then at me and said, "I think you're in the wrong job for that." Karen added, "Yes, first, you are right in the middle of the food chain—as an SRO, you see all the grades below you and above you. Second, you are one of three hundred researchers at the Home Office alone. Third, this is a government, and so you will be at the behest of short-term policy interests. And finally, the wheels of bureaucracy grind ever so slowly." At this point, I began to feel a lump in my throat. I agreed by saying that I am merely one cog in a big machine that moves incredibly sluggishly, but I added that I have incredible energy, that I do care about making a difference to society, but that patience has never been my forte. It was a wake-up call, and I felt incredibly small suddenly.

Apart from this quick exposure to the civil service, I began my work and mostly enjoyed it. When it came to policing and crime reduction, we had a large budget and a strong political resolve to have influence. I oversaw two ROs and a batch of projects. I had authority over university professors who relied on me and my staff to respond to requests for research funds. I learned a lot about research, communications, personnel, and project management, and I was excellent at it. However, I was completely bored. I felt like a cardboard cut-out, and the prospect of performing an identical job for the next

35 years scared me to my core. Until that point, I only did what I wanted to do in terms of devoting time and attention to asking research questions that were tremendously important to me, rather than an institutional overlord. I do not think I have an issue with authority, yet authoritarianism is something to be concerned about. But New Labour was serious about equality during its first term (1997–2001), especially considering the Macpherson Report and the Human Rights Act. After inheriting a boom fostered by the former Tory chancellor, Kenneth Clarke, New Labour also had money to spend on public services. With few local or global concerns to divert attention away from the UK, New Labour was doing well, and it appeared they could do no wrong in the eyes of many at home and abroad. As a result, I stayed.

◎

A position became available in Home Office research in March 2001 to work on the first Citizenship Survey. I wanted to hone my statistical modelling abilities while also working on a topic with which I was already familiar. This proved to be a poor decision. Knowing the literature on identity, citizenship, belonging, diversity, and multiculturalism, as well as how social capital influences certain outcomes, I was squabbling with everyone. My civil service colleagues were mostly stupid and just cared about getting ahead at all costs. Outside of government, I spoke with academics who, like me, were eager for certain issues to be "examined" thoroughly. The main event happening at home, however, was the escalation of what became the worst "race riots" since the 1980s. Young British-born Pakistanis, Kashmiris, and Bengalis were rioting on the streets of their homes in five towns and cities in the north of England. I was still at the Home Office's policing research wing at the time, and I was closely watching and reading the news, as well as the reactions of police officers who had been placed under a lot of pressure following the Macpherson Report, which showed instances of institutionalised racism in London. The police had been on the back foot until then, but they now felt they could get back on track and respond to these "disturbances" with full force. These events raged on during the summer of 2001, as I finished my transfer to the Citizenship Survey unit, which was also keeping a close eye on these concerns and had been requested to deliver briefings on research and policy issues related to them.

Ethnicity is an important subject of analytical inquiry, and the significance of religion has become more widely studied, with an emphasis on Islam and Muslims. Since the end of the first Gulf War, the Bosnian crisis, and the bombings of the USS Cole and Nigeria, Islam and extremism have been perceived as synonymous. With these young British Pakistanis rioting in the streets of the north, some observers and policymakers began to equate religion with ethnicity and vice versa. I remember jumping on the tube from Waterloo to St James'

Park one morning and seeing everyone in their seats reading copies of Metro. On the main page, there was a huge photo of a young Pakistani's face. Readers of the newspapers stared at me as I scanned the top page—and I stared back. I felt almost naked, as if I were being scrutinised from every angle. It was not a pleasant sensation at all. When I walked into a meeting of white middle-aged males at the Home Office, my ethnicity was at once plain to them. It is as though my colour entered the room before I did. I would feel self-conscious, under extreme scrutiny, and as if I had to constantly prove myself and my talents to everyone. When I stepped into a conference room and spotted one woman amid a bunch of men, I felt significantly calmer and at peace knowing that I was not the only anomaly in this room. If there were minorities of all backgrounds in the room, I would feel much more at ease. The blander the colour and the homogeneity of gender of participants in meetings or different forums, the further up the food chain they are. The Home Office boasted that their workforce is diverse, with around 25% of the overall workforce coming from an ethnic minority background. What is sometimes overlooked about this number is that they are all concentrated in the bottom five grades, with only a handful getting into the top five grades, the ones with the best benefits and the most power to truly be effective. The Home Office, like many other government agencies, was organised in a quasi-militaristic hierarchical structure. My G6 could only see and hear me via my G7, and the G7 I inherited was undoubtedly less capable than he and others close to him thought and believed.

◈

Some staff had been in the Home Office for thirty years, and they were unusual. Their skin was peeling off, and they all moved slowly, ghost-like. Some were wearing the most comfortable Clark's shoes for workers, yet their feet looked completely twisted in them, indicating a fashion sense with origins in the 1970s. The younger and more recently hired researchers were all bright and devoted professionals, but there was a lot of staff turnover. The civil service fantasy was quite different from the reality of the experience. Colleagues constantly transferred to different departments and within departments. There was a culture that stifled the more innovative brains, and many looked for the more prestigious positions that included significant foreign travel and language-learning possibilities. I recall one G6 saying that the three most crucial activities for a civil servant are to "know when to keep silent, when to speak out, and when to lie."

Knowing how I am when it comes to sharing spaces with others, I knew my new boss would find it difficult to share a cramped office with me. It did not help that he was completely insensitive to many issues. He was extremely driven and ambitious, yet he could never admit to himself that he had short-comings. He once said to me, "If something goes wrong, crap on the lowest person in the food chain." I thought to myself, "Nice." And I had the impression that his comments would have a greater impact on me one day because I was his sole employee. I was trying to fit into the regime of power and control while simultaneously adhering to my intellectual ideals. I had decided that combating disparities, injustices, conflict, and outright racism was something I believed in and would stick to if I worked in government. It is a personal belief, and it should not hinder my work because most of the individuals I met were typically on the same page as me on these subjects. However, it is usually the few who cause the greatest havoc, and the Home Office and other government agencies are not immune to such consequences. Indeed, the Home Office had issues with prison personnel who proudly displayed their Combat 18 (C18) credentials at work at the time. C18 is a neo-Nazi terrorist organisation that was founded in 1992.

Many staff at the Home Office who were regarded as "deadweight losses" in labour economics terminology were often doing little more than moving around scraps of paper. They talked well and properly, but the content of their work was often hollow and constrained. Few, if any, wanted to make a difference. They only wanted a decent pension. Nobody wanted to upset the status quo, but I had met a Pakistani from Walthamstow who was working in another area of the Home Office on a training session on "motivation" one afternoon, and he proved intriguing. The fact that I was taking "motivation" training in my first six months obviously showed that I was underutilised. I started chatting with this guy via email, but it quickly became clear that he was a complete moron. Strange things were going on in Afghanistan at the time, and a group named Al-Qaida was at odds with the Northern Alliance; the former were hardliners with Arab influence, while the latter were social-democratic and from the soil. Amjad would write me emails extolling the virtues of AQ's work. I would see him walking around the buildings, clothed in a green army jacket and appearing quite combative. When AQ blew up the Baymiyan Buddhas in March 2001, he was ecstatic, and that astounded me. We did not communicate after that, but I was always interested in whether this guy had been thoroughly checked before being hired.

Problems occur for everyone in huge organisations, but it is also true that amazing individuals may be found anywhere. After joining it, I swiftly advanced to the position of chair of the Government Social Research Communications Committee. As part of that work, I was able to collaborate with social research colleagues from a variety of government agencies to explore a wide range of issues affecting the professional practice of government social research. I met folks who were a pleasure to work with. They may have an enormous impact on people's lives without even realising it. It is important for people to have some type of identifiable skill to perform their duties, but they must also have a tremendous amount of originality and personality to go with it. These people were driven by integrity, honesty, a sense of responsibility, fairness, and professionalism. It was also a fascinating class analysis lesson for me. A few people at the top of the food chain, both from Oxbridge and public schools, always regarded me favourably. This is because their personalities were formed of tremendously hilarious, clever, or very intellectually appealing interpersonal features. And I could easily be charming as well as produce a quick-witted remark when necessary. Their work ethic was the finest I had seen, as was their calmness under pressure. What I loved was the turn of phrase that could transform a crisis into an opportunity, as well as the desire to listen to others. They saw in me an inner-city-born son of an immigrant who had worked hard to reach where he was, and an opportunity to gain experience from me as I interacted with them mano-a-mano. Furthermore, in terms of class structure, I could only peer into their worlds, but I would never pose a danger to their position. Rather, I still had a lot to learn about class in England, which would be useful in supplying me with specific class tools when I needed them. In exchange, they recognised me as a committed professional whose goals would help the many rather than the few.

It was not the same for the middle classes, who were and continue to be a strange assemblage. For example, the middle classes who had gone to Oxbridge but had previously only managed grammar schools competed with the upper-middle classes. The aristocracy has all but vanished, and the landed gentry do not have the same wealth status as people with new money, who have come to dominate areas of London and the South of England. But the super-wealthy did not have much time for most of the middle classes, as it was clear to them that they were some despicable groups of liberals seeking to dismantle elite power for the supposedly good of the many, despite the fact that the middle classes would benefit the most. However, the attitudes of the middle classes toward minority middle classes are influenced not just by class but also by ethnicity. The upper classes may be more racially minded, while the middle classes are more susceptible to racism. Furthermore, the latter look down on minorities who have worked hard to reach success, because they compete for the same levels of social mobility yet come from quite diverse backgrounds. As a result, it was always going to be risky for an immigrant's son to have a Warwick University PhD by the age of thirty and to be speaking up to middle-class white colleagues. This is due to groups' proclivity to form alliances in the face of a perceived threat, as well as in-built prejudices based on pre-existing tendencies. Surprisingly, my biggest allies were those in higher positions who recognised me for the person I was and wanted to become.

I kept working, trying to make a name for myself, but I could not help but stay concentrated on my own areas of expertise. When the chance to serve as

Equalities Adviser to the Head of Research arose, I jumped at it. As part of my efforts in this respect, I oversaw an assessment of all Home Office studies to verify that equalities were fulfilled. I also analysed first-hand data on recruiting inside the Home Office's research department to ensure that it adhered to fair standards. The former entailed an expert equalities audit of more than 45 million GBP in research funding. The latter entailed statistically analysing the challenges of application, shortlisting, interviewing, and decision-making in Home Office appointments. It was extremely shocking to realise that minorities and most of all, women, were more skilled and experienced than their male white-British colleagues but were just not making it through the various stages of selection (and de-selection). Working with the Head of Research, I was confident that he, like most colleagues, looked to ensure fairness. However, the difficulties stemmed from prejudices built into the department's institutional structures that few were aware of or willing to challenge.

I recall several occasions when I would go to the restaurant at the top of 50 Queen Anne's Gate and meet African personnel from various legal, accounting, and administrative departments. As four or five 'black' guys sat together, laughing aloud at our observations of incompetence and mismanagement among our colleagues, I was conscious that those sitting around us looked at us with suspicion. It reinforced my sense of being an outsider, but I absolutely loved being (politically) black, noisy, and brawny among my African colleagues who were incredibly well-read, well-qualified, and, as it turned out, well-connected.

◈

I wanted to make a change, but the Home Office was a brick wall. Things were shifting at the same time. The disturbances in the north of England were described as an issue of identity and culture, rather than systemic and institutional racism and inequality. This had an impact on attitudes within the civil service as well. Government workers, like everyone else in society, read the popular press and watch the fabricated news. I recall attending an ACPO meeting at the Belfry and hearing how one of the top police officers wanted to "flog" these Pakistanis. This was quite upsetting. At the same time, I was at odds with my white English boss, who was younger and less qualified than me. He was afraid of me as a questioning individual, but he also had the institutional machinery behind him, and I feared him.

I took advantage of the chance to transfer to another government department entirely in late 2001, specifically the Lord Chancellor's Department, later renamed the Ministry of Justice. However, it was more likely a case of getting out of the frying pan and into the fire. My G6 took me to his room on my first day and said, "Well, thank you for joining us—we hope you will value your time here and produce good work for us—but I need to inform you that there is nothing here for you beyond this post—and when you are ready to leave, let me know and I will support you all I can." This caught me off guard, but I appreciated his candour. Even though I loved working on coordinating studies on race and ethnicity in the courts, I was nevertheless bored. I had gone from the largest government department conducting social research to the smallest. As the lone male in a crew of nine, I had an enjoyable time being pampered and looked after, but I was still jaded. I was once in a lift with a bunch of people from various racial minority origins when a white female Australian legal eagle remarked, "Well, look at this. Isn't this an excellent example of reverse colonisation?" I tried to grin, but it was very awkward.

The decision by Tony Blair to follow George Bush into Iraq, as well as the notorious "weapons of mass distraction" that were used to legitimise the allegations that Saddam Hussein was an urgent threat to the nation, occurred during this period. My colleagues and I were eating lunch in St James' Park at the time, which was something I did every day of the working week. I remember thinking to myself, almost yelling aloud, "Where are these so-called weapons ... how can we possibly embark on an unlawful war like this?" Upon hearing what I had to say, my friends looked at me as if I had committed some cardinal sin. I was truly worried and disturbed by the entire situation, and I thought it was wrong in so many ways, but Blair was persuaded, and as history has proven, he was completely incorrect. The whole country, as well as the entire globe, had been misled. The Iraqi people would be the ones who would pay the price in blood. Eventually, I resigned from the government in September 2003 and returned to my hometown university to set up a research centre devoted to ethnicity and cultural studies. I felt that by returning to the outside, I would be able to make a more significant contribution to debate and discussion, which I certainly did, up to a point.

It appeared, throughout the summer of 2001, that the issues of genuine consequence were taking place outside of the Westminster bubble, from cricket field invasions by jubilant Pakistani fans to rioting in urban areas by British-born South Asian Muslims. The issues of masculinity, violence, and conflict, as well as the identity politics of the Muslim minority, were central to my thinking. The summer of 2001 was marked by domestic upheaval, but by September of that year, something else had occurred that brought the globe to a halt. There are still repercussions from the tragedy today.

10

From 9/11 to 7/7

Governments constantly choose between telling lies and fighting wars, with the end result always being the same. One will always lead to the other,
Thomas Jefferson

It's not radical Islam that worries the US—it's independence,
Noam Chomsky

There is no moral difference between a Stealth bomber and a suicide bomber. They both kill innocent people for political reasons,
Tony Benn

On the dreadful morning of September 11, 2001, I was in my hometown of Birmingham. It was approximately 1:00 p.m., and I was in my study working on my computer, getting ready to go on a visit scheduled by the Home Office in London, which was still my workplace at the time. It was to shadow a field researcher in Coventry, a nearby city, to learn about the data collection procedure for the Home Office Citizenship Survey, which I was overseeing. A news flash disrupted the broad gamut of useless lunchtime programming as I walked downstairs from my study to enjoy my freshly made cucumber salad sandwich. The awful aftermath of what looked to be a tragic freak event in New York was unfolding before my eyes. A second plane struck the World Trade Center's second tower moments later. The impact of yet another jet crashing into a structure, this time striking the Pentagon, was seen on camera in Washington.

All these images astounded me, and I debated them with myself. Aliens are attacking the United States, but that is ludicrous. Alien invasions are a common theme in science fiction. Someone has declared war on America, but how did they get so easily into American airspace? Is there anyone on the earth with the resources, planning, or sheer "cahonas" to take on this sleeping giant? How could it have happened any other way if it were not an inside job? That is unquestionably the material of conspiracy theories. It is a group of insane so-called Muslims plotting a suicide attack against the "Great Satan." Given what was going on in the world at the time, this is the least improbable conclusion. If this is true, Muslims all around the globe are doomed. Others at once posed a battery of questions. The "why" question was easy to answer, because several countries throughout the world harboured grudges against the US for a range of fundamental grievances considered to have harmed their people, nations, and civilisations, notably during the twentieth century. The solutions to the how-question, which focused on systems and procedures, were clear in the bright light of day. Aside from these concerns, it was apparent that the impact on one global civilisation, specifically Muslims, would be disastrous. Since the conclusion of the Cold War, the Muslim world has had its own internal difficulties of democracy and development, but these were exposed when the United States and other Western European nations no longer had a single ideological opponent with which to name, namely the former Soviet empire. During the 1990s, wars in Algeria, Somalia, Sudan, Nigeria, Bosnia and Herzegovina, Chechnya, and internal disputes in Afghanistan and Pakistan drew widespread attention, signalling that these nations faced serious problems. The events of 9/11, with sixteen of the nineteen hijackers coming from Saudi Arabia, reinforced the belief that something fundamentally disturbing was afoot in the Muslim world and that the United States, as the world's "policeman," had a new imperative to address. As the days progressed, it became clear that the US was outraged and ready to strike in retaliation. With a history of militarism, the United States is prone to entering a conflict with all weapons blazing. The image of the United States as a gung-ho Texan cowboy ready to discharge his firearms at the Indians looked to be resurrected. The main architect of the 9/11 events was portrayed as a renegade Saudi millionaire with a vendetta against his own country more than anybody else. He was to be found, "dead or alive." A "war on terror" with a "coalition of the willing" began at once in Afghanistan, then two years later in Iraq, all in the name of "rooting out the evildoers" and eradicating the so-called "Al-Qaeda terror menace to the world," the world's number one adversary. Afghanistan was attacked because the country refused to hand over Osama Bin Laden, whom the Americans said was in hiding there. Iraq was targeted two years later for allegedly owning "weapons of mass destruction." Both claims were found to be overstated, if not entirely made up, to legitimise a pre-existing plan of action.

Immediately following the events of 9/11 in the United States, Tony Blair, then Prime Minister of the United Kingdom, joined forces with George W. Bush to emphasise to the world the importance of acting quickly and promptly in hunting out the worldwide menace that was eventually recognised as Al-Qaeda. Osama bin Laden and his followers, who were allegedly working out of the mountainous regions of northern Afghanistan, were now seen as the prime targets to rid the "free world" of its most immediate threat: an imminent attack on western targets, allegedly orchestrated and organised out of these hills in one of the world's most remote parts. Because of the devastation experienced by the United States and its allies, there was minimal early opposition from anywhere in the world, even the United Kingdom, which was still reeling from the aftermath of the 9/11 attacks. By November 2001, the United Kingdom was fully engaged in the "war on terror," deploying soldiers to Afghanistan as part of Operation Enduring Freedom. As people watched the news for information or read press pieces from prominent journalists in quality publications, they realised that the first victim of war is the truth, as the adage goes. Until August 2021, countless innocent individuals died in a war-torn nation for little or no reason. Osama bin Laden was not discovered until May 2011 in Pakistan, and suspicions about his eventual assassination linger. Today, we hear less about the need to eradicate the threat posed by Al-Qaeda, yet the war in Afghanistan continued for two decades. The Afghans regarded the British and other forces as invaders rather than liberators, as they did the Soviets in the 1970s and the British in the 1840s.

As the conflict in Afghanistan raged unabated, groups in Washington projected the notion that Saddam Hussein was connected to Osama bin Laden and that Iraq had "weapons of mass destruction" capable of striking western targets with impunity. War was being manufactured once again, and Tony Blair had to persuade the UK parliament of the importance of continuing military operations, this time in Iraq, in the hope that these weapons, which could hit British targets within 45 minutes, might be discovered and destroyed. After a lengthy process of cajoling and manoeuvring, MPs voted for what many consider to be an unlawful war. Baghdad was assaulted with "shock and awe" in March 2003. But soon after, many American forces were no longer looking for these weapons because none were to be found, as believed by many before the invasion began. Instead, US-led forces were striving to "modernise" Iraq, which had all its natural resources and physical infrastructure in foreign hands until recently. Iraqis were forced to pay for their own rebuilding with their own money, while profits flowed to the west. Saddam Hussain was virtually publicly executed after he was apprehended and placed on 'trial.' Iraq's power structure has inverted, destabilising the country and the region. The violence has resulted in the deaths of up to one million innocent Iraqis, as well as the displacement of many millions more. After intense public and private criticism, Tony Blair and, soon after, Gordon Brown, were obliged to withdraw British soldiers from Iraq in 2007. However, the harm had already been done to Iraq and Britain's standing as a global actor. Britain had once again allied itself too closely with American foreign policy goals, prompting accusations of being a stooge or puppet.

◊

This foreign policy disaster was making young Muslims in the United Kingdom furious, outraged, and disturbed. Nobody was paying attention to them, let alone their own community leaders, who were being wooed by New Labour to toe the line in exchange for grace and favour. I could see the problems growing in the local communities and sense the concerns about how media reporting (and misreporting) on the conflicts in Iraq and Afghanistan was generating significant anxiety. The UK saw its worst inner-city riots in almost two decades in the summer of 2001. The causes of these disturbances were entirely due to the frustrations expressed by second and third-generation British South Asian Muslims who were subjected to ongoing patterns of racism, discrimination, and prejudice, as well as a lack of education and employment that was a function of local resources rather than any direct issues of motivation or aspiration. The government's reaction, however, was to focus on the concept of communities lacking cohesion rather than on the specific resource requirements that were critical for the region, which had experienced deindustrialisation and a lack of inbound investment for the better part of the earlier three decades. However, by the end of 2001, the United Kingdom was at war. It became clear that things were getting worse for many racial and ethnic groups that were now recognised as religious and cultural groupings, particularly British Muslims. The "northern disturbances" of 2001 demonstrated that young second and third generation British Muslims were angry and resentful of the racism, intolerance, bigotry, exclusion, and vilification they faced in their communities, and this rage literally erupted on the streets in five locations that summer: Bradford, Oldham, Leeds, Stoke, and Burnley, with significant violence and physical destruction found in Bradford, Oldham, and Burnley. Since I was working in government at the time, these concerns were high on the agenda, and at meetings conducted all throughout the Home Office in London, the worry was, "What are we doing about BOB?" (BOB was an abbreviation for "Bradford, Oldham, and Burnley.") Given that the MacPherson Report labelled the Metropolitan Police Service as "institutionally racist" two years prior, it was almost as though some top police officers and other members of the criminal justice system saw a chance for "revenge." Young Muslims who flung stones at police officers as first-time offenders and were turned in by fathers and uncles after their photos were plastered all over the local media were sentenced to up to five years in jail. Many local Muslim populations were even more angry with the police forces because of this. In late 2001, David Blunkett, the incumbent authoritarian Home Secretary, set up a panel to investigate the concerns. Following a brief reporting period, the remedy was described as "communities lacking cohesiveness." In many respects, it was a total denial of the underlying concerns as well as a chance for authoritarians to revert to an assimilationist ideal proclaimed five decades earlier. The prevailing worldview emphasised beliefs, identities, and behaviours above institutional racism, discrimination, and the need to reconstruct physical infrastructure. Muslims in the north of England got an appalling deal. Their misery went unnoticed.

As these outdated and backward-looking domestic policies took effect and the unlawful war in Iraq began, the situation on the ground became even more hostile. By mid-2003, I had grown disillusioned with central government, and after speaking with a leading university in my hometown, I accepted the opportunity to set up and direct a new research centre focusing on ethnicity and culture, with a particular emphasis on British Muslims in contemporary society. As I became more concerned about the radicalisation of young Muslims in urban areas, I realised there was a tremendous intergenerational divide and a masculinity crisis, with young Muslims realising their elders were not listening. The Imams were out of touch, the media was prejudiced, the government was focused on war and external interests, and the Muslim world's elites were either sleeping or ignoring it all. What began to develop was an issue of young British-born Muslims seeking a violent political answer within a faith that is entirely peaceful and humanistic. Some of these disillusioned, alienated, and isolated Muslims became the new radicals while using the internet, clandestine study groups, and restricted Islamic literature in English. As the Madrid train bombings in March 2004 and the assassination of Theo van Gogh in November 2004 amply revealed, some second-generation Muslims were willing to engage in killing others or self-annihilation to achieve political results. The question was whether it would happen in the United Kingdom. As the April 2003 Tel Aviv Mike's Place bombing by two second-generation British Muslims proved, some young Muslims were willing to conduct "martyrdom missions." Through my work at the centre and in the media, I continued to argue that as a country, we must be cautious about what we do in the Islamic world through foreign policy and to Muslims at home through domestic policy. We were not being sensitive enough as a country, and we needed to consider the impact our policies and actions were having on people in societies that had been subjected to decades of intolerance, prejudice, violence, discrimination, and racism.

❖

On the morning of July 7, 2005, at the International Sociological Association annual conference in Stockholm, I gave a talk about British Muslim experiences after 9/11. While strolling through the book stalls late in the afternoon after my panel, which was a debate on Islamophobia and political radicalism, a colleague approached me and interrogated me. "The terror attacks in London are such a tragedy, aren't they?" she asked. "Attacks by terrorists? Which terrorist attacks?" I responded in disbelief. That morning, four second-generation Muslims from northern towns, including one as young as eighteen, attacked London at the same time. I returned to my hotel room to see video footage on BBC News and the devastation. Initial investigations and punditry all pointed to young British-born Muslims as the perpetrators. As a British citizen and a Muslim, I was very worried. There was no separation for me, yet I suddenly felt as if I had been split in half. Early July is an unusual period in Sweden since the sun does not set until the early hours of the morning. I remember trying to sleep, unable to shake the images of London from my head, frantically wishing the light would drop so the day would finish, but it did not.

When I returned to the UK a few days later, I was bombarded by media and community calls. What exactly is going on? How do we put it all together? What are our options? These were just a few of the questions posed by television crews, journalists, news reporters, analysts, and colleagues working as professionals and activists in the field. Muslims and non-Muslims, academic colleagues, community groups, and government departments were all stunned. The first reaction was to condemn the events and say that it was a dreadful act, but a few days later, certain prominent individuals, such as Lord Nazir Ahmed, ventured to openly state what everyone was thinking: that this was "Blair's blowback." Most, however, resisted the impulse to criticise government policies when fifty-two innocent people were killed and up to 700 were injured, some of them permanently scarred. Days after the occurrence, I talked live on Sky News, agreeing that it was a genuinely shocking period in the history of Muslims in Britain but saying that we needed to be cautious of overreacting or blaming Muslims alone for these conundrums.

In my judgment, this was a social issue, and in many ways, these young men were products of society in terms of the violent political resistance techniques they tried to hasten. Their reason and method were to perceive political Islamism through a restricted prism. It arose from a highly historical collection of circumstances that needed careful unpacking and comprehension. Unfortunately, many people were eager to blame Islam and Muslims in general. Because the government was not engaging with young Muslims directly or indirectly through the primary umbrella organisation with whom it had formed tight ties, especially the MCB (Muslim Council of Britain, founded in 1996), the gap widened. Opportunistic Muslims rushed to the authorities, claiming that they were the experts and could help solve the problem. All of this contributed to significant policy stagnation and polarisation of viewpoints on what the true problems were and what the genuine answers should be. It also resulted in the formation of the "Islam industry," as well as the existence of "professional Muslims," who compete within the sector at times at the request of government outreach and at other times for their own personal reasons. Disenchantment and internal conflict arose because of the process, some of which was painfully revealed in the context of participation in the media and the political process. However, it also revealed the nature of the intergenerational divide that has hampered the development of the Muslim community in Britain. Young people were no longer willing to sit back and let the elderly take the lead, and while many of the events of 7/7 were tragic, they did allow the younger generations to come out in large numbers given their demographic profile. These Muslims were astute, eloquent, professional, well-organised, and driven to convey a picture of British Islam that is integrative, developmental, and forward-thinking in every manner.

However, the characteristics of the communities also enabled them to be abused from without. Politicians and media outlets forged an unholy alliance in response to these concerns. Muslims looking to score points against other Muslims were eager to point the finger at these other Muslims. The *Wahabis*, *Deobandis*, and *Jamat-e-Islamis* were all vilified; right-wing Islamists attacked the *Brelvis* and *Tabligis*; secularist Muslims criticised all other conservative Muslims; and the *Brelvis* were the majority but the most distant from the political process. For example, through their ties with the MCB, for example, the *Wahabis*, *Deobandis*, and *Jamat-e-Islami* were the most associated with the government. In 2007, the government responded with a token gift of £140 million to be spent on localised Muslim capacity-building programmes over a three-year period to help communities in rebuilding from the ground up. This dusting of glitter, however, simply fuelled a self-serving "Islam business," with "professional Muslims" seeking access to power and privilege [police, security, and intelligence agencies received £2 billion over the same period]. The inclusion of select Muslim government workers engaged as special advisors by New Labour worsened the issue of guaranteeing effective, unbiased counsel. From 2004 to 2007, I hosted regular conferences, talks, and seminars on ethnicity, culture, religion, and politics presented by senior civil servants, House of Lords peers, senior diplomats, parliamentarians, local councillors, senior public officials, leading public intellectuals, and the most prominent academics from across the country. The debate and conversation were lively and informative, and they drew a growing audience. I was also invited to offer guidance to a variety of groups, including the government, community groups, mosques, and the media, on a variety of local, national, and worldwide levels. I was also able to reconnect with old colleagues from the Home Office now working in this field. It meant that I had access to many important government agencies working on the issue and given my background in the civil service in White-hall, I was able to make quick progress in ensuring that my ideas were conveyed properly and efficiently.

◈

The events of 9/11 were distressing, but also extremely concerning because it was clear that the US military-industrial complex would go after the criminals with all they had, and they did. Indeed, NATO soldiers were still in Afghanistan until April 2021, with the military effort there costing the United States more than $130 billion USD each year. The British military was in Afghanistan for a longer period than they were in WWII. Western European Muslims were feeling beleaguered and outraged, but some were made to believe that jihadi-terrorism would cure all their issues, from the Madrid train bombings and the murder of Theo van Gogh in 2004 to the 7/7 disaster. The events of 7/7 were terrible for a Muslim Briton. I felt torn apart – not because of a sense of divided loyalties (far from it) but because I am thoroughly British and Muslim, and I sensed that the future would be dangerous for individuals like me who would be forced to choose as if the two were incompatible. Professionally, I was smack in the middle of everything. After working in equality and believing that Britain was on the right track, the 2001 "northern disturbances" and 9/11 changed everything, and now this. Instead of receiving the critical aid I needed during a tough period, I became the target of suspicion in the eyes of those close to me who should have known better and stayed wiser. It was a soul-crunching experience. But I did not want to quit, even after the "transatlantic plot" blunder, the Forest Gate disaster, and the Danish cartoons gaffe. Every day, Muslims were labelled negatively, to the point that ordinary people and even some experts could not distinguish the difference.

I travelled everywhere and still do to reflect on these issues, speaking to audiences ranging from high-level government units to "spies" (desk security analysts in the United States, Germany, and elsewhere), community groups, university student societies, and media, and even voluntarily hosting my own show, *Politics Today*, on Raj TV, an independent satellite television channel that aired between 2005 and 2007. On my show, I spoke with local and national legislators, a former ambassador, a major international imam, professors, think tank experts, top police officers, community leaders, Israeli and Palestinian peace activists, and many others. Even if some individuals disagreed with me, I was dedicated to advancing the discussion and fostering an active discourse. Secular colleagues believed I was being too Muslim, which clashed with my identity as a British sociologist. My Muslim co-workers believed I was selling out by connecting with everyone, or that I had sold out my Muslimness as a trade-off for my involvement. I realised that these struggles were all part of the community's internal disputes and pain, as well as the piercing glare from without. It was quite simple for me to intellectualise everything. Others, on the other hand, were less considerate, and they caused me personal and professional problems. It made for a tough working atmosphere for me, which was difficult to cope with on my own.

When the banking crisis came in 2008, I had already made up my mind. This recession was unlike any other I had experienced, including those in 1980, 1987, and 1993, as well as the dot-com boom that crashed in 2000. This recession was likely to be as severe as the Great Depression of the 1930s, which was also brought on by a financial crisis. Britain had taken a turn for the worst. Even as an academic, it was no longer a place where I felt at ease. I felt constricted and under immense strain, with all eyes on me, and I wanted to flee the country. After resigning from my position at the university in 2009 and concentrating on a Foreign and Commonwealth Office-funded initiative to help solve international problems that linked England and Pakistan's de-radicalisation efforts together, I finally got the break I was searching for. I moved to Istanbul in 2010 to build my career as a professor of sociology with a vibrant vantage point from which to look both east and west. I had moved to the centre of the world.

Part II
Coming to terms with the other

11

Global Racisms
Unravelled

You can't have capitalism without racism,
Malcolm X

Racism is still with us. But it is up to us to prepare our children for
what they have to meet, and, hopefully, we shall overcome,
Rosa Parks

Ignorance and prejudice are the handmaidens of propaganda.
Our mission, therefore, is to confront ignorance with knowledge,
bigotry with tolerance, and isolation with the outstretched hand of
generosity. Racism can, will, and must be defeated,
Kofi Annan

The development of the extreme right in European society in recent years has been an intriguing phenomenon. It has been asserted that during the last three decades, particularly with the onset of Reaganomics and monetarism, western economies have been undergoing an increasingly visible shift to the right. It is also something that has occurred concurrently with the fall of socialism. However, the right's influence in society has a longer historical trajectory, much of which stems from debates about tribalism, heritage, nationalism, and ethnic identity. In 2011, there was the atrocity of the Breivik massacre in Norway, in which many young people were gunned down on an island, killing dozens. On the same day, the same culprit detonated explosives outside a government building. In England, the rise of the English Defence

League, an offshoot of the British National Party that originated in what was known as the National Front, and the earlier existence of the British Union of Fascists in the early twentieth century, all point to a problematic set of social relations centred on the idea of a nation and its peoples being pure in an absolute sense of a racial community completely distinct from others. While most of this emphasis has been focused on the preceding century, it is obvious that a sense of racial hierarchy was formed as part of the European colonial endeavour. Scientific racism substantiated the belief that there was not only a civilising mission to deliver culture to backward peoples, but also a scientific basis for a human hierarchy. The inextricable nexus between capitalism, racism, and religion was formalised and put to significant use in exploiting people in remote regions around the world.

Tribalism is an issue that arises in a variety of circumstances. It is concerned with how groups identify as having distinct types of identity from one another. There are several ways in which this genuinely bears out, ranging from local settings to experiences in specific villages or small towns to a more macro-dynamic focus on the ways in which nation-states may develop distinct types of supra-tribal identities with repercussions at various levels. As a result, the distinctions between tribalism and racism are not always clear. In many ways, we are all racialists at some level, from small-scale issues affecting, say, how elder members of a village in Azad Kashmir decide on marriage relations for certain young people to how the Nazis engaged in a holocaust that killed six million Jews, dissidents, leftists, communists, homosexuals, and so on. That is, whether in a local context or at a much larger macro-dynamic level, we define ourselves as not being the other, whatever the other may be. Race shapes people's decisions about how they connect to others and, to a lesser extent, how they treat others. This can range from the intention to destroy a race of people to the choice or rejection of specific marriage partners for young people. Both are done in the name of ideology, culture, nation-building, and a sense of exclusivity, or more particularly, the superiority of one group over another.

I recall an Anglican priest at a UN conference in Baku in 2007 making the argument that 9/11 was about tribalism, and the audience around me looked at each other in disbelief, but as the debate progressed, the good priest had a fair point, and I agreed with most of it. It is easy to get fired up over white people's bigotry toward black people when black people may be just as prejudiced as white people. There is little question that in everyday life, past or present, one ethnic group perceives another as being in some manner distinct. They may even assert that their own ethnic group is somehow superior to others due to some ideal of purity, natural intellect, cultural preservation, or moral fibre. This is common in the small local communities of Azad Kashmir, and it was common throughout the 1800s eugenics initiatives in the United States, United Kingdom, and Australia, culminating in the Nazi Holocaust of WWII. So, what is the crucial distinction? While there are many similarities and crossovers at play here, I have come to the conclusion that the essential issue is power, and it is without a doubt the primary concern.

If we can all agree that we are all racialists at some point, that is, we all categorise others as not having or owning certain norms, values, traits, characteristics, personalities, or behaviours, then how one group relates to the other is based on the power one has in competition with the other. This power can be instantaneous or a result of the long-term influence of some historical heritage linked with an earlier experience of local area tribalism that later translated into a means of empowering one group at the expense of the other. This is the significant difference. Even though we are all racialists, whether we recognise it or not, embrace it or not, it is the uneven access to power that certain groups have over others that forms the larger processes of racism and how it is mobilised. We are thus because we learn to be so through the socialisation process we engage in daily, and we often do not even realise it. Babies are not born racist or racialist; they learn it. Racialism describes race differences. Racism, on the other hand, maintains that some races are superior and others inferior, requiring differential treatment. Racism and tribalism are socially learned processes. We must unlearn and then relearn how to be anti-racialist and anti-racist to better grasp and appreciate the bigger picture and, more importantly, to wish to do something about it. A late 1970s adage iterated amongst UK anti-racist teachers who intended to alter society by using education to abolish racism was centred on the premise that "Racism = Prejudice + Power." This, I believe, still holds true in the present day.

✧

To completely understand the scope of these issues, it is necessary to travel back in time as far as possible to set up what is at the root of the problem. Racism occurs in various forms today, but it is centred on the notion of a dominating group oppressing a minority group through a process in which the dominant racial categories are improved, promoted, supported, and even reconstructed in the workings of society's institutions. As a result, minorities are oppressed, marginalised, and disenfranchised as the dominant ethnicity is reified at the expense of other ethnic groups. It is, in many respects, a cyclical process with a symbiotic link between the primary elements at play.

Much of the present malaise afflicting global ethnic relations may be traced back to colonial encounters and the way scientific racism was employed to legitimise existing structures of control and subordination. This was achieved through mechanisms of enslavement of people of darker skin complexions, who would be described as "free labour" in capital accumulation, which was the primary form of wealth creation as part of the development of European economies and societies beginning in the seventeenth century. The concept of scientific racism explains many of the reasons and aims of these wealthy Europeans who wanted a method to formalise their conduct toward individuals of darker skin tones. Scientific racism, on the other hand, is not at all scientific. It borrows some ideas from Charles Darwin, who spoke about "survival of the fittest," but it was later interpreted by European scientists and scholars to mean a hierarchical relationship between humans, with white Europeans at the top and everyone else on a sliding scale below. It progressed to the point that people with darker skin were considered the lowest of the low. It is obvious that the system is completely wrong, but it has had and continues to have an influence on the minds of lighter-skinned *and* darker-skinned individuals all over the world.

True, the Arabs engaged in some type of slave trafficking, as did the Romans and Greeks, but these slaves came from both white and darker-coloured backgrounds. Racism, as we know it now, is a product of European imperial colonialism. It existed because of the scale of its operations, how it influenced the actions of a variety of different European institutions, and how it was imported into the workings of those societies through the exoticisation of groups that were presented as variously different but, more importantly, inferior. As a result, it was the slave trade that successfully segregated people along clear lines based on skin colour. It was founded by wealthy and powerful elites whose goals revolved around the desire for wealth growth. As the few got wealthier and more powerful, the nature of oppression of those of darker colour became increasingly entrenched in the workings of those systems. This understanding was founded not just on the formation of formalised labour relations, but also on the systematic dehumanisation of those of darker skin tones in every way imaginable.

In the nineteenth century, abolitionists in both the newly formed United States and England began to have a considerable influence on the slave trade. But in the modern day, racism has found new methods to remake itself. The abolition of slavery prompted European traders to engage in forms of colonialism bolstered by notions of "the white man's burden," which was a method of imparting civilisation and culture to "primitive" peoples while also legitimising forms of colonial endeavour. Racism was reformulated to continue the process of exploiting the resources of people in distant lands in the establishment of power structures in Western European economies that became even more authoritarian, competitive, and self-serving in their approaches to these people from various parts of the world. This tendency was accelerated as European nations competed for the same profitable commerce and industry.

During the height of these colonial pursuits, which peaked in the early nineteenth century, racism underwent another evolution. It was anti-immigrant feelings among people that began to accept these exotic minorities who would now come to the "mother country," typically elites from the sending countries, to engage in business, entrepreneurship, and even education in medical schools and law colleges. In England, it began with antagonism toward Irish communities, but by the end of the nineteenth century, the tension had shifted to Jewish groups, who were facing various forms of persecution throughout Europe. However, without immigration, capitalism's progress could not continue, and shortly after World War II, all the former stronger European economies needed immigrant labour, without which there would be no genuine future for these nations. Immigrant labourers had to work in industries and economic areas that were unpopular among indigenous communities. Indigenous labourers did not want to do such unpleasant, low-paying, and undesirable jobs any longer, if they ever did. Racism was at the heart of the concept, which proposed that temporary workers might come to industrial areas in countries like England, France, and Germany to do these undesired tasks, and then return to the sending regions without more ado. Employers did everything they could to keep workers from various minority groups from banding together to formalise collective resistance strategies against systematic racism in the workplace. In many respects, it is a sort of divide and rule that marked the colonial manifestation of power that has existed since the time of the Romans. In truth, Britain was a Roman colony for four hundred years, and it was subject to the same "divide and rule" mechanisms as other Roman colonies across the world.

There is a clear association between anti-Semitism and racism in general here. In many respects, anti-Semitism is a form of blatant racism, but the distinction is that one set of opposition is directed towards people of colour, whilst the other is directed at individuals of a certain religion and race, namely, Judaism. For hundreds of years, Jewish tribes were persecuted throughout Europe, and in 1290, Edward I exiled them from England. When Isabella and Ferdinand worked together to retake Portugal and Spain from the Muslims in 1492, the Jews were expelled from the Iberian Peninsula. Many of these Jewish communities were saved by the Ottomans and sent to Constantinople and areas of Anatolia to work as architects, merchants, and scientists to strengthen the Empire. At the start of the twentieth century, there were one million Jews in a population of fifteen million people spread between Anatolia and Constantinople. Racial anti-Semitism played a significant role in how Jewish populations were discriminated against as part of the capitalist process in late nineteenth-century England. They were thought to be parasites and untrustworthy. It was also an opportunity for the working classes to fight the workings of capitalism by focusing on the Jewish population as a specific concern. What is especially significant in this context is the link between anti-Semitism and fascism, the latter of which arose in reaction to the requirements of middle-class and petty bourgeoisie factions who criticised the ways in which capitalism excluded them from advancement. In Germany, anti-Semitism developed dramatically, and the developing Nazi party, which was gaining public support, assailed the progress of Jewish organisations. The Nazi party was able to combine this with a racial purity theory that resonated in the popular imagination. In Germany, Jews faced plenty of attacks on multiple fronts, including cultural, economic, intellectual, and political assaults. It resulted in the annihilation of six million people of Jewish ancestry, as well as those of leftist, Roma, activist, dissident, gay, and communist ancestry, as well as other groups judged undesirable and unsuitable for the rising Nazi order.

◈

In today's Europe, there are a number of variants on these manipulations that persist in the guise of continuous patterns of racism. Many challenges are experienced by second, third, and even fourth generation minorities who continue to endure the hostility of racism in all its forms. Study after study continues to highlight the problem of deep-seated racism in British and other sections of European culture, and despite several legislative amendments to ban such actions and behaviours, the patterns are still difficult to change. Although the argument over race has been removed from the public realm, a focus on ethnicity has not alleviated prejudice and discrimination. Racism's rhetoric is clearly felt in politics and the media, yet little changes; rather, racism reinvents itself repeatedly. Although the terminology may change, the methods are still quite similar.

Even though primary migration has all but halted because of various developments in anti-immigrant legislation since the end of World War II, groups continue to arrive in parts of Western Europe as "asylum seekers or refugees," and they bear the full brunt of ongoing patterns of racism and discrimination. Their treatment is often cruel, and they have little to no social, civic, or legal rights. They face constant antagonism in the media, as well as in all kinds of press and television production, where depictions of the other are seen as risks to security, multiculturalism, and national group identification. Because of the embeddedness of class systems in Western Europe, the dominant groups are still the most influential at all levels of society, including academia, the media, courts, military, and government operations. Minorities face the most prejudice in these institutions, and visible everyday acts of violence are widespread, particularly in areas where minority populations are most clear due to their concentrated localised living. The concept that immigrant minority groups do not do enough to assimilate into society receives continued attention, while the workings of larger societal institutions are hardly scrutinised in this process. Nothing is said about the insecurity and lack of self-confidence that many national identities experience; rather, the risk is seen to be from the outside, and opportunities to develop from within go unnoticed as class structures are still rigid in the face of shifting patterns of industrial relations.

Transnationalism is associated with increased migrant groups, whether it is a function of indigenous established minorities with diasporas that keep links with the sending regions or new immigrant groups that move across countries to maximise returns on their human capital, which is highly skilled migrants. Globalisation has resulted in the migration of capital and labour over vast swathes of territory into the production processes of commodities and services that people take for granted. However, neither transnationalism nor globalisation has had an impact on existing class systems. Globalisation continues to help the few rather than the many, and it is an extension of existing patterns of economic development in which large international corporations gain an advantage through global economies of scale and the massive investment needed to move plants and machinery, rather than a system through which most people can improve their opportunity structures. Globalisation has concentrated wealth in the hands of fewer and fewer people through corporations, and some globalised enterprises now have more wealth and hence power than certain smaller nations. As this concentration of money, power, and authority becomes more widespread, it reifies patterns of racism and prejudice, some of which are internalised by previously conquered populations. They practise bigotry and discrimination against existing and emerging minorities in those nations, all while kowtowing to the aims of the same European corporate institutions that were once colonial masters of those same areas many centuries and decades earlier.

In many respects, Muslims in Muslim majority nation-states suffer the most animosity in the projection of a danger that is perceived to be cultural, intellectual, political, and economic. Because of several geopolitical breakdowns, much of the world's oil is concentrated in the hands of a few Middle Eastern economies, primarily Saudi Arabia, Iraq, and Iran. For well over a century, Western nations have meddled in this corner of the world. One of the reasons for the European separation of the Ottoman Empire was to keep access to this vital supply of oil. Many Western European and American economies would come to a standstill if oil were not available. As a result, China has become one of the largest consumers of fossil fuels and, as a result, one of the largest polluters of carbon emissions. Capitalism without oil appears to be an impossibility, even though the technology exists to create sustainable energy. The political recognition of the impact of carbon emissions on the ecological balance of the planet has yet to be fully internalised by the world's leading industrial powers, despite scientific and public opinion. Since the Cold War's conclusion, Muslims all over the globe have been subjected to the efforts of western nations to obtain access to and control over them. Interestingly, these tendencies have been accompanied by diverse advances in racism and prejudice at the local, national, and worldwide levels.

Locally, it is working-class communities experiencing decline in their local industrial sectors that fear immigration and people who bring a variety of diverse cultures and habits to their society the most. Given that these deindustrialisation experiences have been felt across several western economies, it is not surprising that this prejudice has been interconnected through various forms of racism that combine easily in the face of the global threat that is projected as one of radical Islamism, particularly in the aftermath of 9/11. National economies view multiculturalism as a failure of various minorities, pointing the finger at Muslims for not integrating into society, and these same minorities are now a security danger to the nation. While the Arab uprising has awoken worries about power and authority in the Middle East, worldwide attention is still focused on that area because of all the natural potential that it holds. These western countries also function in reaction to Russia's and China's projected goals, which are viewed as re-emerging threats to the European and western global order.

❖

In integrating local manifestations of racism into its worldwide dynamic, it is the stance of nationally elected authorities that causes the most disquiet. This is easily discernible in various official statements made by heads of state, which challenge the concept of multiculturalism by linking it to notions of security threats while projecting global values and notions of freedom, democracy, and liberty to the rest of the world, which appears incapable of achieving its own social, cultural, and economic development without this intervention. After one year in office as Prime Minister, David Cameron's address in Munich in March 2011 sparked widespread outrage among academics and pundits. The Prime Minister used an occasion to discuss terrorism and security challenges to make his first public remark on the topic of radical Islamism and its perils for secular liberal societies like Britain. At the time, the idea was that the fundamental problem was extreme Islamism, and that Britain could no longer accept the intolerable—that is, allegedly divisive communitarian ethno-political interests. It was a speech that was identical to one given by Angela Merkel, the former German Chancellor, only a few months earlier.

David Cameron was quick to forget that it was Michael Howard, the final Conservative home secretary of the Major era, who formalised the formation of the Muslim Council of Britain. This kicked off a process that New Labour energised with enthusiasm with the aim of favourable electoral results in Muslim-majority areas, which happened. What David Cameron wanted was to ring a familiar post-war bell – that is, to bring in a values-based assimilationist rhetoric to manage diversity concerns. This did not work in the 1950s, and it is unlikely to work now. The concept that minorities can be absorbed by an indivisible unitary notion of English society is a myth, and the idea that these minorities can be put together as an undifferentiated mass is another type of racism, if not fascism. It stood for a major rightward shift in politics that has continued unabated. This shift is the result of declining economic fortunes, but it is also the result of a narrowing sense of what it means to be European, British, and especially English, the latter of which is still entirely wrapped around the notion that it is based on Anglo-Saxon blood and could never refer to a concept that includes groups other than that explicit, exclusive definition. The speech was extremely problematic on several fronts. Following the tragic events of 7/7, real efforts undertaken by civil society and community organisations to create capacity and resilience on the ground, particularly for young people and women, were viewed as initiatives that should not be pursued further. Various key figures in New Labour, including Hazel Blears, David Blunkett, Gordon Brown, and even Tony Blair, made equally bizarre statements about the Muslim minority, identity, values, and Britishness in the years preceding this address. When other critical problems are still unaddressed, there appears to be a continuing habit among leading political players to employ the "race card." This has occurred several times, most notably in the post-war period. This new racism is fundamentally the same as the old racism. Furthermore, it is likely to grow stronger in the face of ever-increasing competition for resources in a period of austerity and cuts to public services that disproportionately affect poorer sections of society. It will embolden those like Breivik and others who believe that Europe is being penetrated not just by minorities, but also by Muslims, who pose a threat on so many levels. This threat is portrayed as one of expanding populations, security, alien values, parallel communities, and other factors.

The main concern is that all of this will influence not just how minorities are treated and perceive the social environment on a local and global scale, but also how every citizen is vulnerable to the manipulations of the security state, which promotes fear to keep control. More than ever before, the state has expanded its capabilities to check digital communications, travel, and the flow of money and people across borders. In the face of all these challenges to basic concepts of citizenship, what made Europe and Britain strong in the view of many is vulnerable to irreparable loss. The main issue is that if the residual effects of the global economic slump, with a global pandemic coming after the global financial crisis, continue to bite and many European nations insist on slashing public spending, the challenges will become much more acute. Furthermore, because of the larger socioeconomic and political-cultural framework that affects everybody, diverse minority groups will experience the combined effects of racism, discrimination, fascism, and ethnocentrism even more.

12

Classed Racisms Unchallenged

The history of all previous societies has been the history of class struggles,
Karl Marx

*Independence? That's middle class blasphemy. We are all dependent
on one another, every soul of us on earth,*
George Bernard Shaw

Money couldn't buy friends, but you get a better class of enemy,
Spike Milligan

The Office for National Statistics (ONS) released the first trench of ethnicity and religious data from the 2011 Census in late 2012. The data piqued the interest of journalists and analysts, who were eager to elucidate on the nature of the transformation that appeared to be taking place in society. For the first time since 1840, the religion question was asked in the 2001 Census, allowing population groups to be broken down by faith. Given the data from 2001 and 2011, it was possible to calculate the number of different ethnicities and their associations with various religious groupings. This major academic and policymaker opportunity contributes to more precise understandings of the nature of society as well as what is needed to maintain equality, fairness, and justice, as well as to construct effective models of tolerance, cohesion, and integration. It also tells us about the nature of ethnicity and how it is influenced by the workings of class in society, as well as how restrictive attempts to enhance mobility are both racial and classed. However, if success and performance are measured solely in terms of production, such as economic growth and capitalisation, matters will take a long time to change. The concept of GDP is insufficient to capture a nation's wealth. It only does so in strictly historical terms, as part of the trend of Western European industrial growth. Such calculations completely exclude creativity, innovation, positive externalities, and any form of formal spirituality that may have an impact on human existence. Despite the narrowing of the upper classes and the broadening of the so-called middle classes or those aspiring to be middle classes, class structure remains largely intact in terms of improving opportunities for those with less.

◈

The 2011 Census yielded several intriguing results. It informs us that Britain has become even more diverse, that more people are in mixed-race partnerships, that people's languages vary, and that there are more religious minority groups than ever before. The number of Muslims went from 1.6 million to 2.7 million, which is an increase of 2.7% to 4.8% of the total population. It may come as a surprise to some. It is, however, not a major shock. It represents the continued experience of marital migration, in which wives and husbands from the subcontinent continue to join their spouses in the UK, with as many as 10–15,000 individuals entering the UK through this process each year. It is also a by-product of higher birth rates among South Asian Muslims, who tend to marry other South Asian Muslims, whether from the UK or elsewhere. This tendency is unlikely to have shifted since 2001. People also come to the country in search of asylum and protection after fleeing persecution in their home countries. This is often because of war, conflict, and dislocation caused by political difficulties. Britain has now become a home for these people, who are more visible in the fabric of society through their diverse cultural features, as well as the visibilities of skin colour and religious norms and values.

The number of white Britons converting (or reverting) to Islam is another crucial factor in the recent growth in Muslim numbers. It is difficult to say how much of the increase in Muslims in the UK between 2001 and 2011 is due to an increase in the number of white Muslims. More data from the ONS will be available soon to support hypotheses that white Britons are dissatisfied with Christianity or that white Britons see Islam as having greater spiritual, intellectual, legal, or emotional depth than the problematic generalised media and political discourses on the subject. Another critical topic to address here is the role of white British women who convert to Islam. It is sometimes done for love and marriage. Sometimes it is done out of dissatisfaction with the patriarchal majority society, which has yet to figure out how to achieve gender equality in practice. White Britons are increasingly flocking to Islam, which can only be true, but there are a variety of reasons for them to do so. Much has also been made of the decline in the number of people who identify as Christians and the rise in the number of atheists, or those who do not believe in God. Some argue that Britain has devolved into a godless society or that it is losing its moral and ethical grip on certain societal norms as a result. This would be an overly simplified analysis. Many godless people have different moralities that promote concepts of good citizenship and humanism. This should be obvious, but in a culture where there is a feeling that the church still has an institutional function to play, the attention on the fall of Christianity is more a reaction to the institution of the church losing its grasp on people's lives.

There is a distinct impression that many individuals who would be considered different because of race or religion live mostly in the dense urban centres of older towns and cities across the UK. This implies to some that there is a lack of integration among this minority, who would rather live alone and not mix with others. This is a misleading image that entirely ignores the role of larger societal structures and organisations that hinder the lived experience as a mixed one. The word "segregation" has also been bandied about. The far right has seized on the notion that there is too much immigration to Britain and that it must be stopped. First, the issue with integration is that it is a two-way street. Minorities who are perceived as inferior, backward, alien, or plain unattractive continue to face hostility from the majority society. Second, racism is still a huge concern in society. In fact, it never went away. Colour racism is and has been one of the most pressing challenges confronting Britain in the post-war period. A culture that inherited colonial and scientific racism has been unable to escape the "ghosts of empire." Third, when looked at holistically, segregation is more likely to be seen among white British majority Britons than among minorities. Ethnic minorities are only concentrated in larger cities. In many respects, the rest of society is still overwhelmingly white. It is a simple answer for some to end immigration to improve integration. However, this is a mistaken attitude to assume. It is ideologically charged and is only ever politically expedient in the short run. There appears to be no limit to how various political actors will use the immigration issue to maximise short-term political benefits. This may be seen in contemporary times, with many initiatives made by politicians to continue to highlight the need for immigrants to improve their English or other dominant European language. This is a classic trick right out of the textbooks of post-war immigration history. Aside from the obvious, it serves no purpose for those communities; rather, it is a political manoeuvre aimed at capturing a middle ground that has shifted dramatically to the right in Europe now. As a result, it is critical to consider the political environment in which most of the conversation about diversity, race, and religion takes place. The right uses current data analysis to argue that immigration is a problem. The left emphasises inequities, racism, and prejudice.

Regardless of disparities across communities in different towns and cities across the country, individuals who control power, make crucial choices, and continue to be the purveyors of forms of hegemonic authority tend to be middle-class, English-speaking, and middle-aged males from privileged backgrounds. When I think back on the summer of 2012, the Olympics come to mind. The popularity of the games was built on diversity. A multicultural, multilingual, and multitalented variant of GB Plc was successfully disseminated across the world. Even though Britain was in the grip of a serious economic slump, the spirit of the people was raised by the games. The occasion did not, however, deter one Conservative MP from tweeting that the Olympics were some kind of "multicultural nonsense." To guarantee that diversity is recognised as a benefit, as it is, change must be found at the top of society. Greater acceptance of diversity must be included in the procedures of a wide range of major organisations that have an impact on people's lives. Parts of London, Birmingham, and Leicester are considered thriving multicultural beacons on many levels, but in the north of England, the poorest South Asian Muslim minority live side by side with the poorest white Britons, who are equally affected by deindustrialisation and a lack of inward investment. They could not be more unlike each other, however, in terms of the absence of any communal living, working, or educational environments, this "community of communities" is split in fundamental ways, and their struggle is intense, yet it is often for the crumbs of society. The workings of government departments in London are the province of the few who wield power, but they do not always consider what is happening on the ground in places such as the north-east or Midlands. As a result of the polarities in society that are a result of the economic situation, the fear is that these divisions will widen in the near future as a post-Covid world emerges among the rhetoric of a battered Britain, fuelling those who seek to divide themselves from 'less deserving' others.

There is no question that Britain is a diverse nation in which minorities live and work as proud and loyal citizens of the United Kingdom of Great Britain and Northern Ireland (as is stated on their passports). However, there is still a long way to go before these minority groups born in England feel themselves as English or are viewed as such by the mainstream English population. Being English means having Anglo-Saxon ancestors. Being British means being part of a country of immigrants. This is in effect now, but it is crucial to watch how the category of Englishness evolves in the light of broader societal changes. Muslims born in Scotland are proud Scots who feel a sense of kinship with their fellow Scots, in part in response to the Englishness that formerly colonised Scotland and may still do so to some degree. Minorities have a long way to go in English society before they are completely integrated into conceptions of Englishness, whether legally as shown on passports or as part of the lived experience.

Migration and diversity will continue to be a given in the UK and other areas of Western Europe because of globalisation and transnationalism. It is critical to understand the ramifications of these changes for society, as well as the necessity of moving beyond prejudice, chauvinism, and reactionism, which have characterised the discourse on differences in society thus far.

◈

According to the OECD, Western European economic growth will remain flat overall relative to the rest of the world, with the East taking over in 2060. Is the western economic paradigm as we know it ending? Are we all doomed, or should we reconsider and restart something that some of us have argued about for a long time?

The problem is that we judge success in terms of GDP growth. However, the issue is one of allocation and distribution rather than growth, which few people contemplate. Neoliberal economics is trapped in the abyss of economic theory. Hegel contended that "things" can only improve as "we" make "progress." But Marx, who was never wrong, only a little too enthusiastic about communism's aims, inverted Hegel and contended that "things" do not always become better. When power is concentrated in too few hands, we all suffer. This is clear from history, yet it was suggested that the UK would suffer for at least a decade when the banking sector nearly collapsed in 2008 and the recession began, which it was still feeling, and then Covid hit the world. Until then, the agony would be terrible. It might be a generation before true general prosperity returns, but it will certainly never be as we know it. Since 2007, the western model has come unstuck, the Middle East "awakened" briefly before returning to a fate worse than before, and India, Brazil, and China's position as the global economic power is becoming stronger by the day. But there is still an issue at the core of this broader global redistribution of wealth and power. All the economic success stories we hear are based on old-fashioned neo-classical economic concepts that have existed for the previous two centuries, and what is now referred to as neoliberalism in certain areas.

There is an urgent need to radically alter the way we do economics. I get the impression that this fundamental issue has not been addressed, and so we will continue to travel in circles. The other concern is whether all the doom and gloom that has infiltrated our thinking about all these problems has caused some of us to cling to the old while being unable to accept the new. We need a type of progressive welfare economics that places the elimination of social disparities at the centre of its agenda. As global differences expand, we will certainly all need a harsh awakening. There is some promise if we conceive of some type of ethical system that is based on equality and justice in terms of the drivers and mechanics of how wealth is distributed. However, until we change the notion of the profit motive at the heart of what drives them, there is little chance overall.

115

The 2008 financial crisis revealed certain underlying flaws that plague the psyches of all ostensibly liberally informed individuals and organisations. That is, the entire capitalist system is riddled with flaws because it is so inextricably linked to the current mechanisms of power and authority. Reforming the financial industry is not the only solution. I believe that we must move our focus away from production and the capitalisation of natural and physical resources entirely, as this is driven by competition. This competitive system is fundamentally unfair, and when political and economic power (the ability to compete) is concentrated in fewer hands, it causes serious issues for the many at the hands of the few. Even when systems are fully regulated, and rules are in place to keep them all in check, cronyism, nepotism, elitism, and moral and financial corruption take control.

Banks exist to store deposits made by people because of generating surplus cash via the labour they do or the businesses they run. They are also available to lend money. Lending is how banks become wealthy; they lend to individuals who need to buy a vehicle or a home, to factory owners who want to create new plants, to governments that want to build dams or airports, or, more critically, to individuals who need to get out of debt. If banks would not lend to anyone, there would be minimal capital flow and hence no opportunity for any form of activity. We would all be in the dark ages if there was no banking system, but one option would be to reorient the incentives of consumers and producers away from instant satisfaction and toward the desire to maximise long-run returns on investment.

When I was a student of economics in the late 1980s, and the monetary policies of Thatcher and Reagan pushed other nations to follow suit, there were also various Eastern European and South American economies that had variants on the command economy model. That is, centralisation of decision-making, price setting, social planning, and the provision of all public goods. Since the fall of the Soviet Union, western capitalism has dominated not just the political and global economic domains, but also people's ability to think creatively. There is a generation that has no concept of socialist ideas. We all embrace capitalism nowadays, and it has taken over our societal vision to the point that we can see no other option except to change an already dysfunctional system to make it less detrimental. Marx was correct in this regard. Only revolution can supply a solution. Workers of the world unite! However, the nightmare followed the dream. Communism has a negative side effect. Choice, liberty, democracy, and agency were all taken away and replaced with obedient, uninspired workers, with power and control still concentrated in the hands of a few, and these few did everything in their power to keep it that way. What we have now is a result of our natural evolution, but it also reveals that, as humans, we may have achieved the peak of our existence. We cannot think beyond the present, and the world's political and commercial leaders are stuck in an inward-looking circle. If the current malady is not remedied, it is likely that it will reoccur since we have lost our creativity. The true solution to all of this is to reconsider the fundamental premise of how we have the potential to do good. It entails not only root-and-branch financial reform, but also re-thinking the essence of our existence on this planet. If not, the same mistakes are repeated.

Let us not ignore the root cause of this banking catastrophe. It had to do with greed on the part of corporate banks, which rewarded people for lending money to people who had no actual means of repaying massive lifelong debts on houses bought at exorbitantly inflated prices. Banks believed that double-digit home price inflation would be an unending narrative, but this was an overestimation of the housing market's potential as well as the ability of any form of constraints on the system. Greed, in its purest form, was at the root of the problem. Banks took advantage of flaws in legislation designed to satisfy the city while also funding political parties. Any "light touch" financial restrictions that existed did little, if anything, to rein in these banks' behaviour. This nepotism, cronyism, and self-interest on the part of governing elites, whether political or economic, stood for a particular kind of class identity and an atmosphere of expectation comparable to their class values.

◈

The year 1993 appears to be in the distant past, yet few realised its significance for the British economic position at the time. Major's conservative administration was on its knees, trundling along, and eventually coming to a standstill in 1997. The Conservatives had been kicking each other over European Union membership in 1992, and to some extent, the infighting that was highlighted then still afflicts them today, now back in power after New Labour, who were effectively "New Conservatives," often lacking even the veneer of a socialist or left-oriented ideology, and the doomed Con-Lib pact (2010-2015), which gave way to Brexit. Blair and his colleagues offered Britain the "Third Way," which was neither this nor that, and certainly not one or the other, but a mish-mash of weak left and strong right ideas that fit the time. Brexit is ethnic-nationalism and proto-fascism that helps significant tax avoiders who represent extremely high levels of individual and corporate wealth in the nation.

Aside from economic and political considerations in 1993, a young Caribbean man was brutally murdered by five white English males who killed the 18-year-old Stephen Lawrence at a bus stop in a south-east London neighbourhood. The Metropolitan Police Service (MPS) conducted a dismal investigation into the murder, ignoring witnesses and confirming evidence. Nothing occurred until New Labour, led by Jack Straw, their first and least worst Home Secretary, ordered an examination into the handling of the MPS probe. The now-famous Macpherson Report, released in 1999, supplied a harsh condemnation of this police force by labelling it institutionally racist. It sparked several issues. How could a whole police force be held responsible in this case when the issues were plainly localised, or were they? If it was not a cover-up, then the entire police force was to blame, or was it? Because no proof of the latter was discovered, the term "unwitting racism" was coined to describe the experience. With no prosecutions still pending, the MPS took a beating from the media and the liberal intelligentsia, and such was the emotion and passion at the time, the country's race relations legislation was significantly strengthened by introducing some of the strongest anti-racist policies anywhere in Western Europe. The events of the summer of 2001, which saw the worst "race riots" in over two decades, and the events of 9/11 in the United States soon after, replaced the focus on racism and inequality with terrorism and problematic religio-cultural norms and values, but there were still no prosecutions for Lawrence's brutal murder. The unyielding yet restrained Lawrence family fought on for justice, but it did not arrive until 2012.

After DNA evidence was discovered 18 years after the murder, the judge in the trial of two of the original five men in court on murder charges eventually made a guilty judgement for Gary Dobson and David Norris. It was a modest success for the family, who had finally seen justice for their precious boy, and a stark message to the rest of us that racist murders would not be tolerated. However, it also proves that Britain is still a fundamentally racist country, with just two of the five suspects convicted after an 18-year trial. Racist murders and attacks are almost daily occurrences in a society where young black men are more likely to be stopped and searched, prosecuted, jailed for longer terms, and released later than others, and where colour racism, now combined with anti-Muslimism, is still one of the most serious issues confronting minorities. After the 7/7 attacks, race was withdrawn from the agenda, yet bigotry still exists. Although those who are courageous and principled enough to stand up to racism and intolerance should be admired since Britain will always produce these fighters, portions of the rest of the dominant culture have become covertly racist. No white British person would dare call a minority a "Nigger" or a "Paki" to their face these days, but that does not mean that no white British person would not want to act against someone based on some deep-seated prejudice or hatred. Justice was partially served for the Lawrence family, yet racism in the United Kingdom is still alive and well. Some things have changed, but much has remained the same, if not worse.

Racism is a big issue in the United Kingdom, but it has been removed from the agenda. However, this racism had been declining for quite some time before 9/11. The events of 9/11 brought domestic Muslim minority difficulties to the forefront, and New Labour looked to deradicalise while neglecting the true causes of the problem; foreign policy and existing domestic policy failings. The Commission for Racial Equality (CRE) was sold down the river and replaced by the Equality and Human Rights Commission, which many people find untenable. Where does a disabled black lesbian woman go to express her dissatisfaction? By the late 1990s, the CRE was faltering because of poor leadership and a lack of funding, but it at least symbolically stood for something. Racism against visible and invisible minorities is a graver issue than it has ever been. It may take twice as long for a minority to secure an interview for a job but securing an offer of employment is not guaranteed. Getting in is one thing, but there are also pay differences to consider, as well as promotion and retention issues. Despite the MPS' attempts to recruit minority personnel, however modest, retention is still a major issue. Many minorities eventually get disillusioned and are compelled to leave. These are issues in academia, government, and the media as well. Trying to be like white people to blend in has no long-term benefit for minorities and does not lessen the challenges of racism. It just makes white co-workers hostile and demeans the individual in question. In today's labour market, being able to do the job is a vital need, but the desire to regard the candidate as "fitting in" and concerns about whether they would "rock the boat" often take precedence over all other considerations.

Class and race are inextricably linked. Deep-seated class structures have appeared in the UK, and openly so, in the shape of the current administration and its ilk who sit at the cabinet table today. Race relations are prone to swings and roundabouts, and unemployment among minorities is often hyper-cyclical at these times. However, when the crisis worsens and austerity measures take root, competition for employment becomes much more difficult, and racism becomes more visible. When will it be over? Unfortunately, many more decades of effort and suffering may be needed, and even then, nothing is certain. Equality is not a given, but diversity is. In Britain, class is strongly tied to race, albeit with the many varieties of racism today more blurred than ever. That is, racism based on culture, ethnicity, or religion. At every given time, there are groups in society that are "othered" in major ways. It enables the hegemon to portray what they despise in themselves as belonging to the "other," all while preserving the dominance and subordination structures that maintain them in society.

13

Unveiling the Muslima

Women are the twin halves of men,
Prophet Muhammad

Women who seek to be equal with men lack ambition,
Timothy Leary

Male domination is so rooted in our collective unconscious that we
no longer even see it,
Pierre Bourdieu

In the contemporary age, there is a great deal of focus on questions concerning Islam or Muslims in general, but there is also a significant amount of emphasis on Muslim women. This is characterised in a variety of ways, including discussion about *hijab*, conceptions of honour-related violence, and the womanhood of Muslim women, which appears to be restrained by Muslim males. Much of the attention on Muslim women is traced back to Islam's roots. There is a widespread belief that, rather than improving the condition of Arab women in the seventh century, Islam exacerbated it. According to some historians, Muslim women became objects of Muslim males whose movements were significantly more limited than previously, their sexual liberties were constrained, and questions of property rights and succession were more open than

Islam established. Much of this critique comes from individuals who would rather argue that the rights of Muslim women were decreased rather than improved during the religion's formalisation.

For many thousands of years, especially during the Hebrew, Greek, Roman, and Persian civilisations, women were recognised as men's possessions. Women of status covered their hair when they entered the public realm during the era of the Romans and the Persians. It was more of an acknowledgement that these women were totally off-limits to the riffraff. Certainly, Roman women were barred from marrying below their station. They would be prohibited from marrying even emancipated slaves, although Muslim women were not barred from doing so. A Muslim woman, on the other hand, cannot marry a non-Muslim man, although a Muslim man can marry any woman from the "people of the book." There is a widespread belief that for extreme orthodox Islamic groups, veiling, often including the complete body covered in black clothing, including the hands, is a particular requirement of the faith. There is also a belief that Muslim men can marry four spouses, which is permissible in Qur'anic terms and many more in various cultural contexts. Indeed, the prophet of Islam had thirteen wives, eleven of whom lived to see him die. It is claimed that Aisha, the daughter of the first caliph, Abu Bakar, married the Prophet when she was only six years old. According to other sources, she was nineteen years old. What is often ignored is that Khadija, the Prophet's first wife, was a successful entrepreneur who engaged in international trading. Even though she had been widowed twice and was much older than him, it was she who offered the Prophet a proposal of marriage through an interlocutor. Polygamy was prevalent in pre-Islamic Arabia, and it still survives today in the shape of specific rituals in Arabic-speaking nations. The other concerns about the role of Muslim women in relation to men are that the former can be struck by men, that the former's evidence is worth half that of the latter, that the man can divorce his wife by declaring it verbally three times, whereas the woman must go to court to seek a divorce, and that women's witness statements are worth half that of men's.

As a result, western literature often cites polygamy, the role of women in marriage, the division of the sexes in their social spaces, especially the concept of veiling, and Muslim women's restricted influence in divorce issues as significant impediments to women's equality in Islam. In many ways, Islam enhanced existing characteristics found in belief systems, particularly monotheistic frameworks of faith, but is all this a ruse to continue focusing on problematic issues deemed undesirable, or is it a reflection of the deep Orientalism that characterises western misconceptions of Islam, particularly towards Muslim women? Without a doubt, there is a widespread belief that Muslim women's status has been constrained rather than emancipated and liberated, as some people, intellectuals and people of faith, claim. A large part of this is due to the way western Orientalism has instilled in society a variety of misconceptions about Muslim women suffering at the hands of Muslim males. There is often a lack of in-depth understanding of the religion or its application. Instead, there is an emphasis on the restricted practices of a few religious communities that want to impose customs in the name of religion, even though most Muslim women do not suffer such difficult conditions. They are more likely to have problems with patriarchy, sexism, a lack of formal education, and not being able to take part in the public arena, which is still a man's world.

◈

In Turkey, the hijab issue is the major point of contention between so-called Islamists and so-called secularists. Wearing the headscarf is viewed as a religious requirement by the characteristic, sincere, traditional Muslim woman. It signifies a type of tradition and culture, as well as the concept of devotion to the Turkish nation. Outside of liberal or secular contexts, most Turkish Muslim women virtually always wear the headscarf. Wearing a headscarf is considered an absolute no-no in many parts of Istanbul among groups that may be defined as secular liberal elites as well as those who have historically composed Turkish society's bourgeoisie. In fact, it is frowned upon and considered the behaviour of uncivilised, backward people. The political issue is that there is a heated ideological attitude taken by secular liberals that is in direct contradiction to the equally intense approach adopted by pious conservative Muslim women who rigidly adhere to these norms. Both parties have a strong feeling of Turkish nationalism and quickly unite around Turkish nationalist causes, but when it comes to this specific subject, they are strongly split and have remained so for some time.

Over dinner one evening, I had an intriguing conversation with a Turkish colleague. She had a bourgeoisie secular upbringing and still lived with her mother in one of Istanbul's posher neighbourhoods, but in recent years she had 'rediscovered Islam' and begun to engage in rituals that could be considered borderline Salafism. She, for example, refused to shake my hand when I extended it to her during my introduction. She was dressed in the hijab as well as the *abaya*, a long black robe that is a common part of women's clothing in Emirati nations in various versions. During the exchange, she would often use the terms "Alhamdulillah," "Mashallah," and "Inshallah." We had agreed to meet to explore how I might help her organisation in improving its policies to create a type of Internet-based communications gateway to unite young Muslims worldwide. I was delighted to supply my counsel, but I also saw it as an opportunity to quiz her on a few topics that piqued my interest. She was at a crossroads in her quest for self-discovery, having transitioned from a posture of secular liberalism to one of Islamic conservatism in the span of around two years. It looked like a suitable time to address a few questions that I had on my mind.

I was playing the devil's advocate to provoke a response from the Muslim woman I was speaking with. The main topic I was curious about was why there was a decision among women to wear headscarves for people who were previously not inclined to do so. Surely, is it all about symbolism since a deep personal relationship with Allah is simply that? That is, it is indeed a personal connection rather than one based on some type of physical characteristic in clothing adjustments. A profound link does not need the urge to dress up in specific clothes to show people that one is religious, or does it? I was articulating that the decision to do so is a sociological function, apart from the never-ending discussion about whether the Qur'an requires a Muslim woman to wear a piece of cloth over her head or not. I contended that it does not do so explicitly, even though I acknowledged and agreed that interpretation on this subject is broad and diverse. Much of it is also about context, with some Islamic scholars arguing that wearing a headscarf may be permissible in specific circumstances. So, by questioning this individual, I addressed a contentious issue: isn't the headscarf a simple gesture to males, especially for Muslim men who are likely to come from a patriarchal society where sexism and prejudice loom large, which is a lot of Muslim men in reality?

Her ideas were relayed over the course of a mini-lecture, which I enjoyed listening to. It was noted that there are prescriptions that may be interpreted to mean that veiling is proper, if not obligatory. It was needed for the Prophet's wives, who had the greatest rank of any Muslim woman and were known as the "mothers of the believers". This was not anything I disagreed with. She went on to clarify that, while there is mention of Arab dress and the notion of *khimar*, which is essential for women to wear over their bosoms to divert attention away from their "charms", this may be translated into the headscarf. I told her that hijab is a requirement not just for women but also for men, and that modesty is the most essential factor in this respect. We must deemphasise our "charms" while presenting ourselves to the other sex, and this applies to all sexes. I paid close attention to this woman who had spent a year living and working in New York City. I was struck by how effortlessly she held her own, her deep blue scarf gently fluttering across her face as the balmy evening air fluttered by. She sat tall and looked me in the eyes while she spoke about a variety of things. I began to change my mind and reasoned that it did not matter what I thought about why she was wearing this headscarf. She is not doing it to send a message to the dominating male world. She may wear the headscarf to express her beliefs, sisterhood, and her revealed and projected identity as a pious Muslim. There is an elaboration on the western concept of women's emancipation here. Women of Muslim origin wear the headscarf in the western setting to express who they are and what they stand for, as well as what they believe components of their faith demand them to do. Objectification by society or males in general was a social function, but hers was also an intellectual, theological, cultural, and political standpoint developed in the shape of resistance to objectification by society and men in general. As a Muslim scholar, it is obviously intriguing for me to ask such questions. Yet, in terms of the personal justification that a Muslim woman would have, I believe that what I might think and do in this respect is irrelevant. As much as I might have thought that her wearing this clothing was a reaction to broader challenges to her identity, I have come to believe that what Muslim women do is to make a statement, but more significantly, to become that message.

I am sure there are a variety of reasons why women wear headscarves: tradition, cultural expectation, societal symbolism, political opposition, identity politics, and piousness or faith per se are all acceptable individual motives and ambitions for Muslim women all around the world. As a result, making broad generalisations or finding broad trends at work is challenging. Furthermore, research can only give contextualised analytical viewpoints on diverse groups, but all of them could be important.

❁

There is a phenomenon known as "honour killings" that has evolved in Turkey and other areas of the eastern world, as well as among some elements of minorities of Muslim origin who are presently living in the West. Several high-profile examples have been documented, notably in the UK context, which have emotionally unbalanced a range of ordinarily objective commentators, journalists, analysts, and social thinkers. Naturally, there is a delicate response that reflects revulsion at the degradation of women at the hands of males, but it is also muddled by prevailing misperceptions. So-called "honour killings" are not honourable, but certain media and political discourses argue that they are yet another example of the risks that Muslims pose to the wider norms and values of majority society, which are seen as progressive, post-enlightened values that are regarded as fair and just.

The trial of British-born Shafilea Ahmed's tragic death in August 2012 resulted in the conviction of both of her parents, who were found guilty of her murder. They were each sentenced to 25 years in prison without the possibility of release. The case depicts a horrific scenario in which her school, social workers, police, doctors, and hospital all failed her, not to mention her awful parents, who functioned as though they had some cultural licence to preserve their *izzat* (respect) for what were perceived to be Shafilea's misdeeds. There is nothing in Islam that condones such acts of brutality against anyone. Several critics contended that what happened to Shafilea was a result of Islam as practised in Pakistan. That is, what these parents did is justified in some way by Islamic theory or law. That Islam granted them the right to protect the religion by killing their own daughter. Much of this was an attempt to frame the problem as one of a certain faith within a cultural setting, notably Pakistanis, who were conducting these inhumane crimes in the UK. The whole focus on the institutions that could have intervened was inexplicably removed. It also prompted many British Muslims to focus their attention on specific behaviours inside their communities, implying that the problem lay within how groups organise and see themselves. Rather, two illiterate parents, possibly both with psychological and emotional issues of their own, tragically murdered their own flesh and blood because they believed Shafilea had somehow dishonoured them among their own group in the UK or in Pakistan. Undoubtedly, there is a problem in parts of South Asia, but it is also present in South-Eastern Europe and, until recently, in the United States. It shows how women are controlled, particularly in their relationships with males who are unfamiliar to them, Muslim or otherwise, which is rooted in a deeply ingrained belief that women are at the forefront of their group's identity. When women violate these established sub-tribal identification markers, they are perceived as disrupting the social, political, and economic order. There are also sexual issues here, but more crucially, there are concerns about bloodlines, lineages, tribes, or nations, all mixed with a heavy dose of hyper-masculinity. In Shafilea's case, by displaying more understanding of westernised methods than her parents felt proper, she had pushed beyond the tribal identity. Families and communities often work through such issues in the diasporic space, but in this case, the parents were much too damaged to see the bigger picture on their own.

This concept of "honour" is strongly embedded in certain Muslim and non-Muslim societies in the Middle East. Given the centrality of group identification, it is unlikely to go away completely in the setting of diasporic transnational groups. However, it should not be confused with concerns about violence against women in general, which is a situation that is a consequence of Western Europe's history but is seldom talked about or openly acknowledged. The matter is still taboo. The criminal justice system is equally to blame for under-reporting and under-prosecuting crimes against women. Women are still afraid to come forward because of the procedures involved in taking cases to court. It is both mentally and culturally difficult. In many respects, despite how truly awful it is, violence against Muslim women committed by Muslim men is overstated, and it is easy to do so in an environment where Islamophobia is rife. At the same time, the narrative of violence against indigenous women by indigenous men, which is often tied to alcohol, drugs, and other kinds of illicit consumption, does not receive the same amount of attention. There are thus broader implications for the general focus on violence against women of all cultures by men of all backgrounds, particularly in Western Europe, where potentially more progressive legal frameworks exist in which to operationalise binding legislation and action to reduce this negative experience. Unfortunately, the civil and criminal justice systems continue to fall well short of safeguarding all women from violence.

◇

The preceding case, however, represents an important topic in how we might think about Muslim women and issues of marriage, relationships, romance, and even love. To suggest that Muslim women are unable to have loving relationships with their partners because of their faith is to return to a widely held Orientalist notion about Muslim men. However, it also allows many middle-class, middle-England men and women to continue to exoticise Muslim women as victims in need of rescue from Muslim men, via the western liberal approach. This was something that characterised the colonials' perceptions and interactions with indigenous women, which were constantly filtered through the prism of their misperceptions of Muslim men's conduct. Furthermore, the notion that Muslim women are somehow bereft of love is a total misconception, and that injecting love will end the potential for violence against them by their partners. Furthermore, if Muslim women had a greater ability to choose their partners at random from the genetic pool of humanity, it might avoid the birth of children with genetic illnesses and maladies. This is another field in which Muslims and their marital practices are being attacked in the UK context, where there is a notion that consanguinity is a major problem for communities and their integration, as well as health issues with societal cost consequences. The underlying recipe for any happy marriage is straightforward, whether individuals are madly in love before they come together or that love appears soon after. The path to success is to grow together based on some pre-existing foundation of intellectual, emotional, and physical compatibility. No marriage can be considered a success if both parties continue to be static, especially if one grows apart from the other, and much more so if an additional party or parties enter the picture. Growing together is the long-term path to marriage and relationship fulfilment.

The focus on Muslim women is also linked to the concept of genital mutilation, which is claimed to be a consequence of Muslim traditions connected to sexual control. There are Muslim groups in regions of Africa that continue to employ this pre-Islamic tradition as a means of limiting women's desire, although it is restricted and not the norm. Significant studies and public policy concerns have shown that this is a harmful action that might emotionally and physically injure a woman for the rest of her life, not to mention impair a woman's ability to deliver a healthy baby due to lasting damage to crucial reproductive systems. It is also a colossal failure in understanding young women's sexuality. Unfortunately, these actions are conducted by Muslim women who were compelled to surrender to the same throughout their adolescence. It is also true that a minority of African Muslim heritage living in the UK take their teenage daughters to parts of Sudan, Kenya, and Egypt for female circumcision on a regular basis. There is no justification in Islam for any of these activities, and they are abhorrent in the eyes of many communities in those regions and around the world. However, despite ongoing health education and the importance of awareness among these communities, the practice persists to a small but still problematic degree.

◎

When it comes to the attention that western pundits and intellectuals pay to the hair or genitals of Muslim women, there is no end in sight. Every aspect of Muslim women's femininity, sensuality, sexuality, and potential intellectual aptitude is continually re-examined in light of continuous debates about whether Muslim men treat their wives properly and whether Muslims can live in the West at all. Despite all the negative emphasis paid to Muslim women, female characters in the Qu'ran are portrayed favourably, such as the mother of Moses, the wife of the Pharaoh, Mary, the mother of Jesus, and the Queen of Sheba. Even by modern standards, the way marriage is depicted in the Qu'ran is favourable: "they [your wives] are your clothing, and you are their garment" (2: 187). Both men and women are referred to as "protective friends" (9: 71). Women are not discouraged from visiting mosques or even playing a role in the management and operation of their activities. However, this is not always the case, as many men have reverted to a more simplistic notion of authority that excludes women. There is also no sense of unfairness in terms of either sex's prospective intellectual aptitude. Following Muhammad, it was Khadija, a prosperous businessperson and one of the first converts to Islam, who stayed committed to the religion and supported the Prophet throughout his efforts to disseminate the word to the Meccan tribes and other Arabs across the Hijaz. Aisha is regarded as one of the most influential early Islamic historians. Her narrations are highly regarded. She is one of the rare people who witnessed the first four Caliphs' reigns.

There is a huge emphasis on marriage arrangements in Muslim communities and how women's rights are constrained, yet this is absolutely in contrast to the growing rates of divorce within marriages in the western environment. Most individuals prefer to cohabit rather than officially marry, owing in part to the exorbitant cost of divorce as well as the length of time it can take. The Muslim marriage contract is precise in terms of divorce stipulations and their ramifications for the man's commitment to his former wife, as well as the division of wealth among children upon death. In this case, assets are not shared between the man and the woman upon divorce; rather, they are held with whoever assumed them at the time, and further reimbursements are needed based on what is stipulated in the marital contract in the form of a *mahr* (a pre-nuptial in contemporary jargon). In actuality, the woman bears no financial responsibility for the family's upkeep, so although there may be some unequal rights, there are also uneven burdens. There is still the assumption that causes alarm among western critics that when a case is heard in court, two women's witness statements are necessary where one from a male would suffice. The reading of this is that it primarily refers to financial problems, owing to the poor education of most women at the time of the Qur'an's formalisation. When it comes to properly redeeming the value of some goods, two female statements would supply greater degrees of reliability. Rather than exclusion or misrecognition, it is a type of legal protection. The judge may also ask that several men present varied financial accounts, as such concerns are sometimes complex and need close inspection. Another old chestnut is the belief that a Muslim man can marry up to four women as told in the Qur'an. When individuals recollect the notion, the first piece of the sentence from the verse is often ignored, especially among Muslim men. 'If you are afraid that you will not be able to deal fairly with orphans, marry two, three, or four...' (3: 4). As a result, polygamy can only be justified in the context of the necessity to take women as spouses, since those with children would otherwise be left without any protection. Without a doubt, many powerful men throughout history have interpreted this to show that they can marry as many women as they see fit, including keeping women in the harem as concubines, as many sultans did during the classical period of Islamic history. However, it is expected that most Muslim marriages in the Islamic world today are monogamous.

As a result, Muslim women are in the spotlight for many western commentators, but despite all the negative attention, many Muslim men and women are in happy marriages, sometimes arranged, sometimes not, with children who are raised with the best moral and social etiquette principles, as well as a positive attitude toward learning and humility. As seen throughout Islamic history, Muslim women continue to be key influences within homes and communities, where they play an active role, sometimes behind the scenes and other times taking the lead from the front. Muslim women will wear the headscarf as a personal decision to be close to their faith, and they may also do so as a type of political statement, especially as a minority group who face prejudice on a regular basis. Gender segregation is occasionally enforced, but it is not declared explicitly. It is usually a result of cultural behaviour. Violence against women has been a concern in all communities for ages, if not millennia. This tale is not about Muslim women any less or more than it is about men. As half of the *ummah*, women have a personal stake in the future of Islam and play a vital role in its continuous growth. But there are also internal social and cultural issues between Muslim men and women that must continue to be addressed to assure a prosperous, healthy, and progressive future for all.

14

States of Pakistanis

Nations are born in the hearts of poets, they prosper and die in the
hands of politicians,
Allama Iqbal

Few individuals significantly alter the course of history. Fewer still
modify the map of the world. Hardly anyone can be credited with
creating a nation-state. Mohammad Ali Jinnah did all three,
Stanley Wolpert

In Pakistan politics is hereditary,
Imran Khan

Since the late 1970s, when I first saw a map of Azad Jammu and Kashmir on Techie Zulf's living room wall, I've been fascinated by this corner of the world. Pakistan, which was founded in 1947 following India's partition, has struggled to contain difficulties that were inherited at the time of its inception. With the displacement of ten million people, many families and communities were irrevocably affected, but strangely, a number of the present issues in Pakistan stem from the elites who migrated from India to Pakistan during this early era. This is not to say that migration was the issue, but the movement of certain elites. The lack of land reforms has perpetuated a power and patronage structure that has not evolved throughout time. Power and influence are concentrated in a small number of strong families, potentially as few as 40 or 50, who control and administer the academy, the judiciary, the media, and the military, with the latter being the most influential of the four. It instils fear in the people, who are unable to break through the feudal system owing to enormous wealth and status disparities, as well as a lack of transparency or institutional control to assure equality and justice in terms of representation and participation in society. The middle classes continue to be squeezed, unable to have a real effect on discourse or cause beneficial social or political change for many.

Pakistan is mired in a quagmire, unable to shed the legacy of the past and strangled from moving forward to the future, which, unless carefully checked, will leave one of the world's largest nations at the mercy of internal dysfunctional and narrow-minded elites or outside economic and political geo-political interests who cajole and manoeuvre the state with little active resistance from the polity. Nonetheless, Pakistan has a 5,000-year history. This era is rich in cultural and social ingenuity. Aside from its enormous natural beauty, the region is abundant in rare minerals and diamonds. The population is young and getting younger with each generation, so perhaps the true future lies in them and the role of civil society players in mobilising significant and much needed social action and change. Pakistan's population will more than double in the next 30 years, to around 450 million people. This is a significant challenge, but it is also an important chance to construct a nation that can be recognised as an example in the Muslim world. The promise persists, but the reality is less hopeful unless immense changes occur soon.

❖

In mid-2012, I had the wonderful opportunity to spend a few months as an Iqbal Fellow at the International Islamic University in Islamabad. The goal was to do research on "comparative Islamism," but also to interact with students and professors working on related fields. By the end of the first week, Ramadan had begun. Many individuals just went home, while others who stayed at work performed at an unusually sluggish pace. However, this did not stop me from enjoying a great voyage of intellectual discovery and realisation. I presented four lectures to distinct groups of students, professors, newspaper journalists, and civil society activists. All who went came to hear about my study on British Muslims and radicalism, its origins and consequences, and potential solutions. This is a topic of research that I have been working on for some time, albeit in recent times I have grown interested in the issue in geographical regions other than England, although I continue to return to questions there.

The types of inquiries that came thick and fast as I delivered my opinions formed of the typical mix of facts and clarification. One question that comes up on a frequent basis assertively questions the entire premise of my thesis on radicalisation. This is not anything new. I have been asked the same question about the role of Islam in Islamism a hundred times, and I have always replied in the same way. Islamism has nothing to do with religion and everything to do with politics. The reaction is founded on years of external persecution of the Muslim world, which has led to many kinds of resistance politics, some of which involve individuals taking out acts of self-annihilation as a means of solving individual and collective issues. This is a tremendously problematic scenario that stems from imperialism, colonialism, and continuous patterns of dominance and oppression, as well as internal fights for representation. This is a common occurrence throughout the Muslim world. In the 1960s and 1970s, it was Middle Eastern organisations, specifically the PLO, which carried out airline hijackings. In the 1980s, it was the Muslim Brotherhood that fought governmental norms. A splinter group was allegedly responsible for the killing of President Anwar Sadat in 1981. Since the events of 9/11, a variety of organisations have sprung up to try to build forms of resistance to specific issues in places including Chechnya, Sudan, Nigeria, Pakistan, and Bangladesh. This experience is about a reaction to localised reality as well as a transnational identity politics that is reified by multiple political and media discourses to become Al-Qaeda, the entity portrayed as the world's number one adversary until the emergence of Islamic State, which arose because of the fragmentation of Iraq and Syria as a result of invasion and internal conflict.

In one specific session, I presented a discussion about Islam in a UK setting, and I was chastised by one member of the audience who believed I had some kind of agenda. He implied that as a lefty, I was an apologist, harping on about US neo-imperialism without respect for the issues at hand. I let him continue while mentioning that even the MI5 report from the Behavioural Sciences Unit, which was leaked to Alan Travis, formerly of *The Guardian*, who gave me and others a photocopy in Berlin when I found myself in his company for two days in 2008, suggested that it is about grievances that affect those most vulnerable. The susceptible in this context are not only the poor, uneducated, or alienated, but all those who feel the pressures of misrecognition and antagonism toward what is perceived to be or is an illegitimate authority that has come to Muslim lands to steal, grab, or simply excavate its natural resources. The conversation between me and this person degenerated into a ding-dong. I was having none of it, so I continued putting on the pressure to a) back up my points with evidence rather than anecdotes, b) make him appear like the moron he was, and c) move the issue along since I had been speaking for two hours deep into a scorching evening with the fast's end still an hour away.

Being a Pakistani with little or no exposure to the rest of the world in general, and the massive scholarly and policymaker debate on this subject, had isolated this individual from the rest of the world. I felt motivated to teach him since no one else in the crowd felt driven to contradict what were widely accepted ideas. Because of the post-Cold War geopolitical setting, Muslim communities in the West have internal issues that put them in danger on various levels. In my research, I have emphasised that radicalisation or violent extremism among British-born Muslims has nothing to do with Islam and everything to do with history, politics, economics, and sociology. The identity gap generated among second and third generation British Muslims is worsened by social and ideological conflicts that continue to afflict the Muslim world (which still finds itself recovering from hundreds of years of imperialism, colonialism, post-colonialism and neo-colonialism).

Pakistanis in Britain confront the same exclusions and marginalisation as everyone else, but their experience is more painful given the absurdity of the worldwide "war on terror" and the debate over national cultural identity politics, i.e., are you a good Briton or a good Muslim? Locally, there is worry about "self-styled segregation," or intentional secluded life. This is fictitious, and it is no more or less of a concern than it is for Orthodox Jews living in Stamford Hill or third-generation white Britons experiencing low education, high unemployment, high teenage pregnancies, single-parenthood, and a sense of disenfranchisement and exclusion that is explained by the presence of foreign people in Britain. In the 1960s and 1970s, these "others" could have been Irish or African-Caribbean. In the 1970s and 1980s, "invading Asians" (and their potential "swamping" of our society, words famously immortalised by Margaret Thatcher in 1978, who swept into power a year later in 1979), or African and Arab "asylum seekers and refugees" in the 1990s. However, beginning in the 2000s, "Muslims," who neatly connect religion and skin colour, were seen to stand for that which is most outside of the imagined borders of Englishness or Britishness, however these may be conceptualised in reality.

In fact, class is a defining problem, particularly the downward social mobility pressures that many Muslim-Britons have been subjected to, as well as a lack of cultural, political, or spiritual guidance to keep them safe. All the rhetoric about Al-Qaida, the Muslim Brotherhood, Jamaat-e-Islami, Hizbut-Tahrir, and other Islamist organisations is meaningless when there is a simple discovery that ties every single one of the UK Muslims participating in anti-state terrorist action. They are all "British-made." After the events of 7/7, the UK government, on the other hand, was quick to place emphasis on mosques, imams, women, and the media, which is important in helping to improve the capacity and professionalisation of institutions and Islamic centres, but the huge elephant in the room was still ignored or vehemently under-emphasised: foreign policy. Having said that, my research shows that many professional Muslims working in different policy and community contexts are aware of what is going on. For all the years that these mosques, imams, and women's networks have lacked not just physical resources but also emotional and intellectual confidence, it is a critical time to engage on these fronts and when there is high-level ownership of these concerns. If the current countering violent extremism strategy can aid in developing resilient communities, they will be better equipped to oppose racism, prejudice, fascism, and vilification, and they will be more effective citizens who can look forward with confidence. It will not, however, completely eradicate the threat of violent extremism because the fundamental drivers of that are built on individualised globalised grievances that materialise in localised acts of extreme anti-state violence, with psychological vulnerabilities as the triggering factor.

Another topic I brought up was the role of the media in Pakistan, which they were quite interested in. Most people recognise the role of the western media in creating an all-encompassing adversary that poses an immediate and obvious threat to us all, as well as how an unholy alliance with politics means that one serves the interests of the other and vice versa. In my exploration of how to counter dominant media hegemonic discourses, I suggested that it was critical to supply an alternative to actively address distortion, but that this would not be simple. I once quipped that the news is like baked beans. It is available in fifty-seven varieties. The cultural allusion to Heinz marketing, which promotes the impression that there are so many variants of the original theme, was not understood by the audience. In the end, it is all baked beans, but the variety illustrates the necessity for product differentiation to appeal to minor differences in consumer desire. The news media is created with an audience in mind, and with commerciality added in, it is impossible to sidestep the market's influence in creating what the news is. As a result, the alternative is to increase commerciality, which entails assuring the quality of the product, whether it is print, broadcast, or online news. Pakistan has been opening its media in the past decades, encouraging a diversity of news mainstream and online TV channels and publications, although they still serve the interests of established media conglomerates. More must be done to lower entrance barriers, but professionalism and ethics are still critical to success.

All these seminars gave me a chance to interact with a diverse group of highly intelligent and fair-minded individuals who posed probing questions that sparked lively discussion and debate. One class was the most energising of all. I was invited to take part in an interactive seminar at an all-women's institution. A variety of young women were studying for their MPhils or writing up their PhDs around the carefully set sofas and chairs of the Critical Muslim Forum, and all were also teaching. The majority were from the English Language faculty, with a few theologians and one or two natural scientists thrown in for good measure. I was invited to speak about my work, so I began by discussing some historical challenges in the post-war migration of Pakistanis to the UK, as well as present concerns affecting UK Muslims, with Pakistanis constituting the single largest part of that group. The questions were interesting and the conversation was spirited, with plenty of allusions to Kant, Rousseau, Derrida, and Said tossed in for kicks and giggles. These students were not posturing in any way. They had been reading the literature as part of the forum's activities, all of which had been inspired by their faculty professor, the brainchild of this group. In general, these females were traditional, with two girls wearing the niqab. Unsurprisingly, they were doing most of the talking. We talked about migration, diaspora, transnationalism, Islam in Turkey, and the current situation in Pakistan, which I asked them about. We also addressed the whole foundation of western scientific knowledge and how it varies from eastern; the former categorises and divides the public and private, whilst the latter is holistic in nature, linking the person to the universe in profound and practical ways. Apart from the obvious concern about corruption, mention was made of internal challenges such as toleration of minorities and indigenous peoples' rights, awareness of Pakistan's wider history, not just in the post-independence period but also before, and the importance of Islamic awareness for cultural awareness.

◇

From the number of Pakistani taxi drivers I spoke with to the colleagues and friends with whom I discussed different issues over countless *iftar* dinners, one theme kept resurfacing. It was the topic of corruption. However, various people had different points of view based on where they were in the pecking order. The common worker struggling to make ends meet was struck the hardest by high personal taxes and growing prices compared to incomes. These folks had nothing positive to say about an issue they believed had become pervasive. As middle managers and more successful merchants spoke, they pretended as if there was a system going on around them, but as public servants and business owners, they were solely concerned with securing their own survival within it. More prominent people believed that the corruption claims were a deliberate attempt to delegitimise people to keep them in check if they posed challenging questions. Many of these charges of corruption have not been proven in court, but others have. Whatever the facts are, the beliefs are obvious, and this creates a sense of entitlement among those who view corruption as a necessary part of their existence.

One night, as my friend and I were riding his motorcycle from Islamabad to Rawalpindi, two traffic police officers stopped us for no apparent reason. I felt forced to remark, "Just give the buggers one hundred rupees and let's go on our way." Nadeem, my guide, was having none of it. The officer was about to issue a ticket for something or other when Nadeem got on his phone and called some senior friend he knew somewhere, and the phone was then passed on to the same officer, who was told in no uncertain terms that if we were ticketed, he could forget about his pension. This whole thing took less than five minutes. It was strange. During earlier travels to Pakistan, the custom for relatives ferrying me around had been to slip a note or two into the palm of a traffic police officer and be on our way. But Nadeem insisted on doing things his way. It was unclear if that traffic police officer would stop others that night in the hope of "saving up for Eid," as my companion phrased it somewhat sarcastically. My gut reaction was that these two officers would go on as if nothing had occurred and would later move on to their next victims, unconcerned about atonement. Another impression I received was that I was merely confirming the established quo, thus seemingly legitimising their behaviour, when I should have held strong.

My feelings about Pakistan were conflicted. It is the country of birth of my father and the generations before him, all as far back as memory has it. The scenery is vast and, at times, stunning. The resources are abundant in natural gas, minerals, and coal. However, the population will more than double within my lifetime. Except for those on the outside, no one is thinking that far ahead. Being immersed in internal strife serves exterior objectives. Feudalism at the top and a basic Islamic-secular education for the underprivileged masses further split society. Elites receive their education in the West and then return to use the techniques they have learnt to sustain the current system. The liberal intelligentsia has no bite since the 40-50 families that have ruled the country since 1947 have tendrils everywhere, particularly in the military, courts, media, and political process. The young want change, and many turned to Imran Khan, who became Prime Minister from August 2018 to April 2022. The president at the time of my visit in 2012 was Asif Zardari, and he was despised by everyone and everybody. Nobody had anything positive to say about him. But the system was so shadowy that little could be done to unseat him since, like many before him, he had bolstered authority via nepotism, patronage, and favour, forming a deep-state inner circle that remained securely in place. Zardari was eventually unseated in 2013.

There have been mixed political fortunes in the past when economic growth was consistent, inward investment was encouraged, foreign investment flowed in, schools, colleges, and universities were pumped with cash, physical infrastructure in the form of roads, bridges, and access to clean water and continuous electricity became more common, but the current situation is different. Fuel and food taxes are continually increasing, and inflation is out of control. Youth unemployment is on the rise. Wages have been frozen. To avoid a balance-of-payments deficit, the currency is depreciated, but this makes exports worthless. Factories that were formerly prospering, particularly the strong textile sector, have been forced to close or move their operations to the Far East. Pakistan's manufacturing industry has struggled in recent years.

◈

In 2014, I inadvertently met Imran Khan at a luxury hotel reception in Istanbul, and we talked about Pakistani concerns in the UK, Islamic issues in Turkey, and how we may learn from our past. He was a good listener, but he felt that getting rid of corruption would solve all issues. When Khan's mother died of cancer in the mid-1990s, I attended a lavish charity dinner hosted by Khan and his then-wife, Jemima Goldsmith, to collect cash for the Shaukat Khanum Memorial Cancer Hospital and Research Centre. I saw him fire inswinging yorkers at Mike Gatting and Ian Botham at Edgbaston Cricket Ground in the 1980s.

Khan, who was elected Prime Minister in 2018 and then ousted in 2022, is now all about politics, but many saw him as a military puppet ready to be controlled. On the other hand, military coups, martial law, and dictatorships have all been common occurrences in the lives of ordinary Pakistanis. Military dictators included Zia-ul-Haq in the 1980s and Pervez Musharraf in the 2000s. For better or worse, when the political class has turned corrupt, the military has often intervened. Both Benazir Bhutto and Nawaz Sharif were deposed as Prime Ministers in the 1990s. Pervez Musharraf's "enlightened moderation" helped to expand Pakistani society, but he was shortly replaced by Asif Zardari, who took over after Benazir Bhutto was slain in 2007. Sharif returned in 2013, only to be dismissed in 2017 for corruption once more, this time exposed by the Panama Papers and "fontgate." The same heinous acts of self-interest and self-aggrandisement dragged a great nation to its knees yet again.

Doomsayers and prophets scoffed at Khan's prior votes on blasphemy laws, as well as his cosying up to the military, which was said to be partnering with Khan for this 2018 campaign. According to western media, Khan's aims were an extension of his inflated ego. These are, however, overblown comments made by journalists who have no true grasp of Pakistan, its people, history, or enormous potential. I have been visiting rural and city regions since 1982, and I have collaborated with the country's intellectual, government, civil society, and political organisations. Reforming a corrupted society requires a significant amount of effort, dedication, and devotion. Khan may be the one to do it. I idolised him as an athlete in the 1980s, and he embarrassed the English cricket team on many an occasion (see my failed "Tebbit cricket test"). Imran Khan embodies the positivity that Pakistanis sorely need, but the nature of Pakistani politics, still dominated by the interest of fuedal famlies, some with links to the military, meant that his time as Prime Minister was ultimately shortlived.

In 2019, Imran Khan gave a 50-minute address to the United Nations General Assembly in New York. His remarks on Kashmir prompted major concerns about the source of anti-Muslim animosity. The recent election victory in India, based on vows to battle terrorism and promote India's splendour across the world, is analogous to victories in the United States, the United Kingdom, parts of Europe, and Turkey. It is not surprising that many governments have gained favour by demonising immigrants and minorities. The concept of the strongman versus the cosmopolitan elite is a method for winning support from less educated people who are lured to the idea of showing strength in the face of an internal danger from "others." But by decreasing taxes, setting up offshore tax havens, and avoiding public scrutiny, these political autocrats benefit only themselves and their wealthy cronies.

In India, important challenges include unemployment, regional economic growth, and inflationary pressures. As a result, people's rage and hatred are focused on "others" rather than governments, which are accountable to the entire country. Modi's rise has coincided with the demonisation of Muslims both domestically and internationally, notably in reference to Pakistan. Modi has a history of ignoring Muslim pogroms, most significantly in Gujarat in 2002. To foster a sense of Hindu purity, anti-Muslim and anti-Christian bigotry are combined with deeply rooted racism and casteism. This politicisation of religion is equivalent to the radicalism, extremism, and fundamentalism associated with similar movements across the world. In Kashmir, there have been more than 70 years of systematic persecution, marginalisation, and exclusion by several Indian governments, with over 900,000 troops stationed on Jammu and Kashmir's borders. An open prison is a good metaphor for the conditions that around eight million Kashmiri Muslims live in. Allegations of rape, human rights abuses, tens of thousands of young people imprisoned, weekly fines, and a strict curfew are rife. Even though both sides have fought three wars over Kashmir, Pakistan's stance has shifted. The right to self-determination is the only solution to the Kashmir dilemma. This is a key step and function since Kashmir is seen as a bilateral problem between India and Pakistan. Pakistan effectively silenced Kashmiris in the past, but the country is now taking a bold new approach, offering Kashmiris control over their own destiny.

Pakistan, without a doubt, has its own issues, and Kashmir has always been a source of contention. Both the United States and India accuse Pakistan of producing and training terrorists for export to other conflicts. If this viewpoint is adopted, the historical precedents for this observation are ignored. When the Soviets invaded Afghanistan in the early 1980s, Pakistan and the United States trained the mujahedeen. After the Soviets withdrew in the late 1980s, the mujahedeen were mostly on their own. During a brief period in the early 1990s, the Taliban was formed to suppress tribal massacres, rapes, and inter-Afghan violence. By the mid-1990s, the Taliban had organised around a worldwide radical Islam that extended beyond Afghanistan's borders and peoples. Following 9/11, Pakistan was lured into the "war on terror," and over 70,000 Pakistanis were killed because of Muslim attacks motivated by mistaken views about radical political Islam. Islamisation began in the early 1980s under General Zia ul-Haq, but by the mid-2000s, radicalism swept throughout Pakistan. It has had an impact on the lives of minorities of all colours and faiths, and it has led to the deterioration of the original Pakistani mosaic of language and culture. General Pervaiz Musharraf had to embrace "enlightened moderation" for himself and the country. Osama bin Laden was assassinated in Pakistan by

US special troops in 2011. People must understand how the current situation in Kashmir violates all human rights. Only diplomacy can aid after 70 years of toil and misery. To get out of this situation, Kashmiris must exercise their right to self-determination. The world must act now, before it is too late.

◇

Although much attention has been paid to the study of Pakistan's formation and the partition of the Punjab, little attention has been paid to Kashmir and the region of Azad Kashmir, which experienced its own dramatic and often violent tensions during the heady days of partition in 1947. The study of Azad Kashmiris has lately taken off, owing to the prominence of this group as part of the Pakistani diaspora, notably in North America and Western Europe, including in the United Kingdom. It is believed that there are over one million Pakistanis in the UK today, although this hides a very varied demographic group, with about two-thirds of these Pakistanis being Azad Kashmiris. The reason for this ruse is that the designation "Azad Kashmiri" is frequently merged with that of "Pakistani." However, it is clear that it is a separate ethno-cultural community distinguished by linguistic, religious, cultural, and political characteristics from others. Only in the last two decades or so has the social science literature about British Pakistanis come to the sharp realisation that when people talk about Pakistanis, they are talking about Azad Kashmiris. Furthermore, this social science literature has only recently recognised that Azad Kashmiris have specific migratory, diaspora, and transnational links to the sending regions in Azad Kashmir, making them of unique intellectual emphasis beyond that of Pakistanis. However, the literature is still woefully inadequate, and it is sometimes impossible to get a sense of what the genuine image of this vital and significant group of individuals is. Azad Kashmiris have too often been disregarded by Pakistani historians and western social and political theorists who have tended to embrace a reductionist and essentialist view of Pakistani ethnic categorisation. Regardless of existential concerns, the experience of this group in the context of migration and transnationalism research shows that some Azad Kashmiris do not perceive themselves as part of Pakistan, and some Kashmiris from Jammu do not see themselves as part of wider Kashmir either. There is a paucity of literature that focuses explicitly on the historical, social, and political aspects of Azad Kashmir, from its start in 1947 to its significance in understanding the nature of diasporic ties today. It is astonishing how little is known about this group of people's internal struggle during a painful period of political transformation. It is difficult to gain unbiased and analytical opinions on the wide variety of factors at stake, which have tugged individuals and groups in opposite ways in the decision to accede to Pakistan or India during partition. What happened at that time? What role did the key actors of the time, from Hari Singh to Sheikh Abdullah, play? How has the Azad Jammu and Kashmir regional polity evolved over the decades, and what types of consequences have there been for local people as part of the political process that can be understood in a broader historical and sociological context?

Anyone who has visited the country will remember the sincerity and devotion of ordinary people, as well as the incredible natural beauty of such a vast country. There is also the oppressive heat and never-ending dust, yet this only adds to the country's allure. Pakistan's original constitution is still one of the country's guiding lights. Muhammad Iqbal and others who followed him advocated for a liberal, tolerant, reformist, and progressive secular republic. That dream has morphed into a horror movie in some ways. The incredible energy, passion, and commitment of the younger generations, who are now more digitally connected to the world and each other than ever before, combined with the efforts of professors, teachers, lawyers, scientists, philosophers, writers, and poets who can imbue the young with a vision of Pakistan as it should have been and can still be, is the future of Pakistan. Hope may not be enough on its own, but the fact is that people are ready for change. Rather than waiting for someone to come in and address the problem from the top, ordinary people want help from the ground up. This is where civil society and the social entrepreneurship sector may play an essential role in enabling citizens to improve society. Overall, little will change in Pakistan unless the divide between the haves and have-nots is reduced, with the political process needing root and branch transformation, which will simply not happen until there is a huge sea change from within.

15

Resurgent Islamophobia

Thousands of alienated young Muslims, most of them born and bred here but who regard themselves as an army within, are waiting for an opportunity to help to destroy the society that sustains them,
Melanie Phillips

Muslims everywhere behave with equal savagery. They behead criminals, stone to death female - only female - adulteresses, throw acid in the faces of women who refuse to wear the chador, mutilate the genitals of young girls and ritually abuse,
Robert Kilroy-Silk

Clearly, something deeper is involved than these specific grievances, numerous and important as they may be, something deeper which turns every disagreement into a problem and makes every problem insoluble,
Bernard Lewis

In academic, community, and policymaker debates over the last few decades, Islamophobia has received a great deal of attention. Some have passionately opposed it, claiming that it is a method of disguising serious issues inside Muslim communities. Others have stated that this is something as ancient as Islam itself, that dread of the religion has existed since its inception and as part of the process of its growth, first across the Middle East and then across the rest of the known world. Nonetheless, the notion has achieved a level of recognition that is likely to keep it on people's lips for some time.

I initially used the concept in 1996, while I was conducting research on the subject for the Runnymede Trust. With the Bosnian war raging in the background, and various other parts of the Muslim world in flames in localised disputes that encouraged certain parties to take up more Islamist leanings, namely in Algeria and Sudan, and with the western world having moved on from the Cold War, the threat from the Islamic world appeared to be a major risk, as posited by the likes of Bernard Lewis, Francis Fukuyama, and Samuel Huntington. However, while it represents a specific period in history by reflecting on characteristics of anti-Semitism, a similar idea, there are other issues with the term Islamophobia. The definition implies an "irrational" terror of Islam, although for some this fear or dread of Islam is founded on visible, realisable, quantifiable, and empirical processes and effects. In many aspects, the phrase is a descriptive notion intended to recognise a broad sense of fear of religion rather than an analytical or theoretical category in and of itself. It reduces a wide range of different experiences into a condensed form of descriptive thinking that depicts a moment that is related to both historical encounters and modern politics. The ongoing local and worldwide repercussions of Islamophobia have ramifications for society and politics at many distinct levels. Definitions, categorisations, and debates over the nature of the notion will continue, but what is more significant are the ways it affects people's lives and the implications for how we think about the Muslim experience in the West.

❖

Islamophobia manifests itself in several ways. Part of it stems from anti-immigrant sentiment. Another factor is the perception of Muslims as monolithic, monocultural beings who are, in many respects, culturally, intellectually, and emotionally, the polar antithesis of the European self. There is also a link with the concepts of terrorism and extremism, which are viewed as problems caused by the character of Islam's religion. Many aspects of Islamophobia are perpetuated by various media and political discourses that sustain the perception that Muslims are not just a threat to forms of multiculturalism but, in more recent times, a threat to national security. The latter arose in response to the terrorism carried out in different countries of Western Europe in the 2000s, including the Netherlands, Spain, and England, and, more recently, in the wake of the decline of the Islamic State that began in 2016–2017. Another aspect of Islamophobia is that it reflects a specific circumstance in which it is tied to Empire politics, notably in the context of US foreign policy. Islamophobia in the United States is also becoming a more visible problem, causing concern in certain areas, notably the academy, but also in wider society in general. In many respects, Islamophobia is a manifestation of anti-Muslim racism in the social fabric of the United States, particularly following the events of 9/11.

Radicalisation and Islamophobia simultaneously support one another in many ways. The two have a mutually beneficial connection. They successfully feed off each other's motivation, desire, and expectations. The context within which Islamophobia and radicalism operate is primarily political, with local and global implications. To interrupt the cycle, we must first address the underlying issues. There is a perception of hatred between Muslims and others that is based on current expressions of politics, yet there have been many constructive ties between the Muslim world, the Christian world, and other civilisations throughout history. Memories, on the other hand, are selective, and emotions are readily persuaded. It is critical to contrast the experiences of European-born Muslims with those of their North American-born counterparts in this context. Much of the rise in the Muslim community in the United States occurred when the immigration system was opened up in 1965. Immigrant Muslim groups from various sections of the Muslim world flocked to America in search of greater returns on their human capital. As a result, Muslim migration to North America is vastly different from that of Western Europe. American Muslims, particularly those arriving after 1965, are highly qualified, well-integrated, and devoted to a constitutional federal republic that has established its identity on the notion that hard work leads to success. As a result, the immigrant adaptation model in the United States has been vastly different from that of Muslims who came to Western Europe as part of labour migration movements at the bottom of society. Islamophobia is a growing phenomenon in the United States, and numerous examples can be seen in a variety of current dynamics, but the issue of home-grown Muslim extremism remains an untested notion, despite the US government's various attempts to effectively intern Muslims of various backgrounds immediately following the events of 9/11, with the fear that many would engage in violent radicalisation. Even while the draconian legislation is still in effect, the latter assertion has been proven false. Theoretically, increased Islamophobia in the United States may support several types of radicalisation in the same way that it does in Western Europe, that is both of an Islamist as well as a far-right kind, but the character of North American culture is considerably different from that of Europe. Its post-1965 Muslim groups have no colonial background. And, while socioeconomic and ethnic inequalities are still large and severe, class structure is less ingrained in the workings of society.

❁

Since the 1979 Iranian Revolution, the Salman Rushdie Affair in 1989, and the events of 9/11 in 2001, the 2000s exposed a new set of Islamophobic emergencies that served to grasp the notion of Islamophobia given more current advancements in various media communication technologies. In many respects, the media plays a crucial role in generating forms of Islamophobia and then amplifying them on a worldwide scale. As much as there is a political science, sociological, cultural studies, and philosophical examination of a developing phenomenon and widely popular notion, considerable attention must be paid to the many media dynamics at work and their political ramifications.

In September 2005, Jyllands-Posten, a satirical Danish magazine, published twelve cartoons depicting the Prophet Muhammad. The goal was to show how certain artists use self-censorship to prevent a negative reaction from Muslim populations throughout the world, who they feared would respond violently to such images. When the reactions to the cartoons confirmed the concept the magazine was attempting to portray, the process became a self-fulfilling exercise. The episode became a global scandal with important ramifications for Muslim-non-Muslim relations throughout the world at a time when the Iraq war was still raging and an assemblage of instances involving torture, prisoner mistreatment, and extraordinary rendition were causing concern among a wide range of audiences.

The controversy surrounding the release of cartoons showing the Prophet in caricature in 2005 and again in 2006, lampooning and sensationalising at the same time, reinforced the underlying malaise at the core of East-West, albeit Muslim-non-Muslim, ties in Western Europe. The initial motivation for the Danish press to publish, and other European presses to reprint, these cartoons was a desire to criticise the seeming self-censorship that has seized reportage on sensitive matters concerning Muslims. Through their satire, they tried to engage in dialogue. Political cartoons have been a feature of newspapers for over a century, and they can now be seen in Muslim media as well. Using comedy constructively is a workable technique to visually illustrate and sensationalise current events. What made these twelve cartoons unique was that they caricatured the Prophet in stereotypically negative ways, including references to violence, anti-women, and regressive forms of being. Following their original release in September 2005, I was contacted by a BBC journalist who asked if I had seen the cartoons. When I answered that I did not, he did me the honour of emailing me a link to them. On that morning, I was scheduled to give a lecture to around two hundred undergraduate students enrolled in a first-year course on the depiction of Muslims in the media. I had no qualms about projecting these cartoons onto a huge PowerPoint screen in the hopes of evoking some type of reaction. A few Muslim students in the audience were uneasy, while most of the rest reacted to them in the same way that political cartoons would ordinarily be perceived.

Most of the cartoons are unfunny, but one or two may catch the viewer's attention and present a more hilarious perspective on a difficult matter without physically degrading the Prophet himself. The Prophet was not depicted in all the cartoons. Those not representing the Prophet were inclined to represent the cartoonists sympathetically. The debate, discussion, and continuous media chatter all centred on the assumption that there are two processes at work here. One argument is that artists, authors, and journalists have a right to express themselves to raise awareness about sensitive subjects, and that if an audience does not want to interact with the topic, they may just ignore it. It is akin to the idea that if someone suspects that a book may upset them, the best thing they can do is not read it at all. This was stated regarding The Satanic Verses. It is known that many of those demonstrating and participating in "book burnings in Bradford" had not read the book at all and were mostly driven by local imams and mullahs who felt obligated to react based on religious passion. Some of this may have been done with political motivations in mind. Another argument advanced by opponents of the cartoonists, and indeed of Salman Rushdie's book, is that if there is freedom to express, should there not be a restriction imposed on this to limit the freedom to offend? Is there a concept of freedom of expression that cannot be realised without some level of accountability attached to it? There is no such thing as freedom without responsibility, is there? This is something that the Danes, followed by five other European countries, did not fully understand, according to some. It is acceptable to be humorous, but what was plainly absent was the fact that favourable or negative portrayals of the Prophet are not permitted in Sunni Islam. The Danes were aware of this when they originally published the drawings in September 2005, followed by a furious response from eleven Muslim European ambassadors. What compelled several other Western European countries to follow suit? They were looking for a reaction, and one that appears to corroborate the underlying message of publishing these cartoons in the first place. Islam and Muslims are regressive, prejudiced, and aggressive. When already disillusioned and alienated young men, pumped up by frenzied regressive fanaticism, walk to the streets in angry protest, confirming the perceived assumption, reality becomes circular. Intransigent mullahs, clerics, and so-called leaders may incite their followers to rise regardless. Simultaneously, every hostile Muslim activity, no matter how minor, will be taken up by current dominant discourses and used as evidence to justify the increasingly common unfavourable views about Islam and Muslims.

In an environment of mistrust, misrepresentation, and misinformation, the publication and subsequent republication of the cartoons were an unfortunate lack of judgement on one level and a complete disregard for basic Islamic norms and values on another, possibly even a deliberate attempt to provoke already disenfranchised, isolated, and disempowered groups. Western Europe was still suffering from the aftermath of the Madrid bombings and Theo van Gogh's murder in March and November of 2004. These newspaper editors' actions amounted to the incitement of religious intolerance. They fuelled the fires that were raging over Europe without considering what it may have meant for Muslims. Western Muslims are already marginalised and isolated from ma-jority society. The way the Moroccans are viewed in France, Turks in Germany, and Somalis in the Nordic nations proves the unfavourable prejudice. Further-more, the ensuing reaction by (some radical) Muslims was a heinous, misguid-ed, narrow-minded direct shot in the foot. Neither set of activities results in real discourse; rather, it provided right-wing organisations with the ammuni-tion they wanted while forcing hesitating liberals and soft-leftists to choose a polarised position. An "us" against "them" mentality dominates, emphasising and intensifying existing social and cultural divisions. Muslims are not afraid of self-criticism, but the powers that be, with a desensitised neo-conservative mindset, twist and bend the portrayal of Islam even further. The media does not report or give a balanced picture of the world and its many concerns, but it does impact popular opinion. The outcome of their presentation in such negative terms is a shift in attitude and behaviour. Bad news travels extremely quickly, as does the preservation of current power relations between aggressor and aggressed, bourgeoisie and proletariat, exploiter and exploited, Muslims and non-Muslims. Questions of "Britishness," the "death of multiculturalism," "political correctness," and "Muslim unassimilability" resurface, causing even more concern. These, too, emphasise polarities and sharp contrasts, and a con-centration on sameness is replaced with an emphasis on difference.

A version of George Orwell's adage, "All people are different. Some peo-ple are more dissimilar than others," comes to mind. I would want to see the media focus on the positive aspects of religion and the possibilities for true inter-faith interactions. However, as recent incidents show, we are still a long way from it, and this is due to the conduct of both a minority of Muslims and non-Muslims. The bulk of Protestants in Western Europe do not want to see the obvious excesses of faith, whatever they may be. The present neo-Oriental-ist and Islamophobic discourse is supported, with Muslims falling into a trap created by neo-conservative European elites in this scenario.

❖

In early 2006, I was in Indonesia, taking part in a series of talks and discussions organised by the British Council to strengthen the image of British Islam. While I was there, I saw first-hand protests against the publication of the Danish cartoons. These gatherings were nonviolent, well-organised, and suffi-ciently focused on the message that there are limitations to free speech while being responsible. It is a widely held belief within Sunni Islam that portrayals of the Prophet cannot be perpetuated. And so, in 2012, while I was back in Indonesia, spending a month or so in the city of Jakarta conducting research, another significant Muslim media crisis arose. I was fortunate to watch yet another round of protests. This time, it was the "Mohammed film" segment, which was uploaded on YouTube on September 11, 2012.

148

Much of the local television coverage was focused on major marches, demonstrations, and violent behaviour by several Muslim communities throughout the world. In reaction to the YouTube film *Innocence of Muslims*, I watched news of violence and destruction in Pakistan on Indonesian television, leading me to believe that the entire nation was on fire. Rioting, looting, and devastation were depicted. Engaging with colleagues and relatives in Pakistan on social media and over the phone at the time, they, too, were horrified by the events and worried about the horrible state of affairs occurring in front of their eyes. Media outlets in the United Kingdom turned to moderates, questioning why Muslim leaders do not speak out at times like this to avert bloodshed. The presenter frequently asks, "But is it enough?" after delivering a thorough assessment of all methodical attempts to make a contribution. Even though this violent reaction to the now-infamous *Innocence of Muslims* film has almost nothing to do with Islam and everything to do with a response based on an accumulated set of localised frustrations, it appears never to be enough for the so-called liberal intelligentsia. The few but loudly heard Muslims channelled into violence appear to be dealing with local, national, and worldwide grievances, which are then neatly condensed into one subject. There is also a belief that the fault is with the United States in general. In a long-winded and typically selective manner, there is also a perspective on how the United States supports radical Islamism in various nations when it wishes, beginning with its foreign policy in the early twentieth century and continuing through its more recent foreign policy endeavours in the Middle East and South Asia. However, this does not excuse how Muslim-majority nation states simply allow it to happen frequently as part of a process to prop up the dominant interests of a few at the top who, in mimicking the "performance of the west," end up compromising their own people, leaving them in a state of perpetual under-development and mis-education so that they do not ask tough questions or find ways of organising in response to the hegemony they face. Pakistanis should not blame America for all their issues.

As western media news players questioned the middle ground for lack of intent while focusing on the violent agitators, media outlets in the east did the same. The primary idea is that the "moderates," or most of us, remain mute. This is obviously nonsense. The actual problem is that those in positions of authority refuse to listen. Who wants to listen to voices of reason and calm when extremism is big business (fear is sold to the populace by states; fear is sold as "news" to keep audiences gripped during advertisements while awaiting further "news updates" to calm their anxieties; and media proprietors sell newspapers and insensitive cartoon magazines)? Second, while so-called "dangerous, extreme violent Muslims" are a minuscule minority, their interests are stirred up both within and outside by the political-ideological motivations that inspire them. The subject of "Muslim extremism" is always portrayed disproportionately by a) lazy commentators, and b) those whose views are philosophically, intellectually, and, if not, organisationally consolidated.

Is it true that western nations have hit their tolerance limit? What happens when certain communities react to the constraints they face is that they reach a tipping point, at which point nation-states and their closely associated capitalist machinery mechanisms respond with even more illiberalism and intolerance, whether directed at the working classes, minorities, or disgruntled ethno-religious groups. This is true both in the west and in the east. As a result, the issues are at the state level rather than at the community level. Globalisation has undermined the territories traditionally controlled by nation-states, leaving splintered identities, tribalisms, and localisms to take their place. In such a system, the dominant few's interests take hold, the cycle continues, and arrogance triumphs. This is true at both the national and international levels. With the "base" in the west low, the intensity is amplified, and things are only going to get worse as western economies continue to struggle to compete. In the east, not so ironically, comparable forces are at work, particularly in Muslim-majority nation-states that mirror western systems of dominance and authority. Things are not as they appear. Diverse interest groups are creating various monsters. Few people think critically; instead, they become aroused and respond emotionally. However, keep in mind that emotions are easily manipulated. The mind does, in fact, pull devious tricks on itself. When people turn on the television news, they may see more trickery.

◈

In September 2020, the satirical magazine *Charlie Hebdo* reprinted the Prophet Muhammad caricature cartoons that sparked such outrage in 2005. The release came a day before the trial of fourteen people accused of assisting the shooters who struck the *Charlie Hebdo* headquarters in 2015, killing 12 people. Just over three weeks later, on 25 September, a knife assault happened outside the former *Charlie Hebdo* headquarters in Paris. In front of the structure, two people were injured. Seven people were detained, but the primary culprit was claimed to be an 18-year-old with Pakistani ancestry. Three days later, on 2 October, President Macron delivered a speech in which he claimed that "Islam is in crisis internationally." He stated that he would make "no compromises" to get religion out of schools. On 16 October, two weeks after his speech, an 18-year-old of Chechen ancestry killed Samuel Paty, a 47-year-old teacher, on his way home from work at his school in the north-west of Paris. On 20 October, the Paris Mosque was closed because it had a post on its Facebook page declaring that it did not accept the use of caricatures of the Prophet as a lesson in religious freedom. On 22 October, two Arab Muslim women were attacked repeatedly and referred to as "filthy Arabs" beneath the Eiffel Tower. Two French women were detained on suspicion of attempted murder.

Macron delivered another forceful secular address on 22 October, declaring, "We will not give up the cartoons." "He [Paty] was slain because Islamists want our future—they will never get it," he continued. On 24 October,

President Erdoğan of Turkey remarked that 'Macron needs a mental check,' and social media was flooded with calls to boycott French goods. Four days later, on 28 October, Charlie Hebdo released a cartoon of Turkey's President Erdoğan, prompting a Turkish official to declare it a "disgusting endeavour [to] disseminate its cultural prejudice and intolerance." Later that day, Erdoğan said that western countries ridiculing Islam intended to "relaunch the Crusades," and that the continued attacks on the Prophet were "a matter of honour for us." A few days later, on 29 October, a 21-year-old man of Tunisian descent massacred three parishioners in a Catholic church in Nice. On the same day, police in Avignon killed a young man who drew a pistol on members of the public, while a Saudi national was detained for assaulting and wounding a guard outside the French embassy in Jeddah.

President Macron was pivoting to the right in his address just days before the heinous murder of Samuel Paty, certainly thinking through different electoral scenarios. It coincides with President Macron's latest attempt to re-establish France's "greatness" in a far more prominent role within the EU, given that the UK has abandoned the project. It used to be a major player in the EU. With Angela Merkel's domestic popularity falling at the same time, as well as Germany's developing rightward lean, Macron had his sights set on grabbing a right-of-centre political vacuum that appears to be opening up, as well as a prominent role inside the EU. France has kept a weak stance on how it views racism within society while ramping up various neo-colonial measures in francophone Africa, particularly in Mali.

As a result, much of what has been expressed and executed by the French discourse has a neo-colonial logic that continues to perceive Muslims at home as second-class citizens and Muslims in once-colonised nations as still ripe for de-radicalisation through military operations. These incidents point to an increase in President Macron's grandiloquence, as he is seen as keeping governmental neutrality toward religion, while President Erdoğan is seen safeguarding the Sunni Muslim world from the west's recurrent cultural assault. This tit-for-tat cycle of hyperbole and counter-rhetoric conceals the truth that neither France nor Turkey feels secure about national identity problems. Indeed, France is experiencing an identity crisis, with lacité transforming from a liberal idea into a weapon to target Muslims with its disproportionate focus—which, paradoxically, contradicts the fundamental principles of lacité.

❁

As I prepared to leave Indonesia and return to Istanbul in 2012, I became aware of more media concerns that were causing shockwaves. Looking at the news on television and reading different newspaper columns and blogs on the internet, I saw that segments of the Muslim world were still enraged over a lunatic clip that had been uploaded to YouTube. It resulted in the terrible murders of a US

Ambassador and several Americans in Libya, an attack on a German mission in Sudan, and large rallies in Pakistan and Indonesia, with images of furious Muslims upset over yet another dramatic lampooning of the Prophet. However, in the latter two weeks of August, many British Muslims were dissatisfied with the contents of an 'informed' Channel 4 documentary on the early origins of Islam by Tom Holland and a BBC situation comedy called *Citizen Khan*. The first for its lack of academic independence and neglect of early Islamic texts, and the latter for being old-hat 1970s British humour partially updated for a modern audience in a farce intended to teach Pakistanis to laugh at themselves. Mr. Khan, the show's main character, was considered to depict the occasional Pakistani uncle, while Channel 4, the show's makers, and broadcasters, cancelled a private showing of Holland's documentary due to security concerns. It gave the appearance that Muslims were to blame for the restrictions on academic freedom and discussion, and that Pakistani Muslims were incapable of enjoying humour. They conjured up the vulgar innuendo that Muslims are "intolerant, prejudiced, and retrograde."

So, what exactly is going on? Why are media productions made in this manner? And more crucially, why do Muslims all across the world lose their cool so readily, frequently, furiously, and, sadly, violently? First, there is no overarching plan to demolish Muslims all over the world. Rather, there are some discredited schemes among certain anti-Islamic people who want to get some prominence from their media outputs. We had a so-called US film director who was a bit of a criminal, an academic with few relevant credentials, and a BBC executive who was out of touch. They had no relationship with one another. What was connected, though, was the number of enraged Muslims throughout the world who voiced their displeasure in a violent manner. Much of this was concerned with the many other local, national, and worldwide concerns that affect these groups. Reaching the tipping point of violence because of a Z-movie is likely to have been fuelled by a profusion of other, more immediate circumstances. Making a direct relationship between a YouTube upload and violence in Libya, Pakistan, Sudan, and Indonesia, where I was seeing the images on TV screens, was to ignore the other concerns at stake in these societies. Unfortunately, far too many journalists and pundits take the low road to ostensibly "educated" analytical insight.

The answer is straightforward enough. Muslims in diverse areas to the east and west have an obligation to act responsibly. Muslims who have the intellectual tools and organisational ability to make a difference should collaborate with others inside the system, because acting independently, particularly in a violent manner, undermines the beneficial efforts of a few. There is nothing wrong with remaining calm and organised. Everything about violence is wrong. The narrative is the reaction, and it promotes more misrepresentations of Muslim communities as well as increasing suspicion of Muslims. The issue of Muslims being portrayed unfavourably in the media is not new. In truth, it is as ancient as Islam, albeit modern forms of communication have hastened and amplified the process. Nonetheless, the difficulties are the same. When people react violently and aggressively, the story becomes about the violence and aggression, rather than how particular media outlets continue to be biased and prejudicial in their representation of certain groups in societies all over the world, which needs to be challenged head-on with intellectual might rather than brute force. It is the use of the strength of reason rather than hyperbole and literalism that is needed to design forms of peace and conciliation that have long-term effects that help everybody. The media may be a damaging tool for groups, but it can also be a catalyst for beneficial change.

16

Brexit

I've been clear that Brexit means Brexit,
Theresa May

For those who want out, Brexit remains an end in itself, regardless
of what is in the interest of our society, in terms of prosperity,
security and influence on the wider world stage,
Kenneth Clarke

The whole Brexit saga is, in my view, one big, terrifying leap in the dark,
Gina Miller

I was still in Istanbul at the time of the Brexit vote, but I was already planning to return to work in London after six years in a city unlike any other in the world. I was following the Brexit debate from a distance, confident that it would never happen. It did, much to my amazement.

Years of austerity and inequality further split an already fractured society, which had been exacerbated by the Tories since the 2008 global financial disaster. Right-wing politicians stirred up a basic fear of immigration to terrify the populace into voting for Brexit. These politicians used pre-existing fears about the emerging "other" in society and exaggerated them via outright fabrications and lies. There was a distinct feeling that the Brexit vote unveiled a dark and nasty underbelly in English culture that had hitherto gone unnoticed. The truth is that it has always existed. It is part of the character of the imagined

English nation—a cultural phenomenon arising from Anglo-Saxon history rather than one produced by waves of immigration and settlement—from the Romans through post-war "New Commonwealth" immigrant groups to 21st century EU communities. Successive UK governments tried to eliminate structural and cultural racism in Britain by enacting various anti-racist, anti-discrimination, and pro-equality policies, but the situation was only partially alleviated because the deep-seated characteristics of racism are entrenched in all aspects of society.

The question is whether racism was the root cause and immediate effect of the EU referendum, or whether there was something else to consider. From enslavement to colonialism and then to imperialism, Britain had a large empire that peaked in the early twentieth century until the rule of Britannia was destroyed by two wars with Germany. However, the end of the Second World War did not end the widespread belief that Britain is still supreme, whether among elites in London working in institutions devoted to the idea of Britain's perpetual greatness at any cost, or among working-class communities whose loyalty to the monarchy remains unquestioned. Fast forward to the EU referendum, and these working-class areas, now permanently left behind, were instructed to channel their angst against foreign influences or immigrants. They were misled by falsehoods and misinformation, while the problem has always been British government policy.

However, historically, both the metropolis of London and northern industrial towns flourished because of imperialism and colonialism. Furthermore, anti-immigrant prejudice was prevalent as early as the 1905 Aliens Act. Its main goal was to prevent Jews escaping persecution in Europe from entering the United Kingdom. In the run-up to World War II, there was anti-Semitism within the elite. During the bombing operations over Poland, although British Jewry urged Churchill's administration for acknowledgement of the Nazis' mass slaughter of European Jews, the Allies bombarded all of Poland except the extermination camps, which were purposefully overlooked. As history has shown, modern racism is about more than just skin colour.

Many scholarly studies have documented the prejudice experienced by post-war African-Caribbean and South Asian groups. From the Notting Hill race riots in 1958 to the sus laws of the 1970s, black Britons suffered the fury of colour prejudice. South Asians have been culturally feminised, while black Britons have been culturally hyper-masculinised. The "race riots" of the early 1980s, on the other hand, were typically an alliance of dissatisfied groups, all affected by deindustrialisation and economic restructuring in general, rather than merely an eruption of opposition against police violence and racism inside the criminal justice system. South Asians were quietly getting by despite all their issues until Muslim groups became politicised in the aftermath of global crises such as the Iran-Iraq war and the Soviet invasion of Afghanistan, both of which lasted into the 1980s.

Following Rushdie, the first Gulf War, and the Bosnian Crisis, British Muslims have been inextricably linked with identity politics. No acceptance of the notion of a multicultural Britain, of diversity as a positive in and of itself, could appease the white working classes or established elites. Without the elimination of structural disparities and the hurdles to social mobility imposed by a racialised class structure, multiculturalism was a liberal theory with little practical application in people's lives. Instead, it became a political football that could be used however it pleased. After 9/11 and the "War on Terror," Muslims all over the world faced an existential danger to their own lives, and they were securitised, criminalised, and imprisoned at whim. In such an environment of intolerance and discrimination, there is little talk of respecting diversity. As a result, communities are pushed inward, releasing those few who self-annihilate to self-actualise within an apocalyptic framework.

As the EU grew to include nations from South-East Europe and Eastern Europe, Britain was hit by a wave of "new racism." This was defined not by race or religion but by a fear of the "other," which was based on the belief that these outsiders were culturally undesirable, socially inferior, or politically immaterial. These groups arrived because EU legislation allowed them to. They worked hard, paid their taxes, and stayed out of trouble. Net welfare costs are low both in the short and long term since such people contribute significantly to the state's coffers. All of this, however, is lost on some in Britain, who see these new foreigners as a burden on the state and a threat to their already marginalised life chances. This is where politicians based in London take full advantage of their anxieties. This is the crux of the argument offered here. Even now, racism and capitalism are inextricably interwoven. Brexit resurrected a fear of the "other" that dates back much further in British history. Brexit awoke a sleeping dragon.

❖

In 2018, I moved to The Hague after working in London for a little over two years. Brexit was on everyone's lips, including mine, signifying that my rage had not subsided. While the Netherlands is a tiny country of around eighteen million people, it has some of the world's best universities, high levels of social and political trust, and relatively good living standards. It punches much above its weight as a renowned Western European nation. It does so not just as an independent sovereign nation-state but also as a member of the European Union, of which it is an active and capable member.

The English and the Dutch have a strange history together. Both claimed India as an important commercial partner at one point in history. However, the Dutch East India Company and the East India Company were direct competitors in sections of South Asia. Throughout the seventeenth and eighteenth centuries, they went to battle multiple times to keep a monopoly on commerce with India. The early nineteenth-century Anglo-Dutch Treaties looked to rebalance the colonial order among several European states. While the Netherlands did go on to colonise parts of South Africa and what is now Indonesia, it did not perpetrate the atrocities its neighbours did, such as the Belgians in the Congo, the French in Egypt and later in Algeria, and, more recently, the Germans in relation to their own citizens at home. Crucially, it did not become the world's largest slave-trading nation, as England did. Despite the inherent biases that come with dominant institutions, structures, and cultures within all nation-states, minority groups in the Netherlands today receive protection, rights, and opportunities following human rights law coupled with a pervasive sense of common decency. The Kingdom of the Netherlands includes the home nation, as well as Aruba, Curacao, and Sint Maarten. At the very least, all citizens of the Kingdom are treated equally under the law.

This historical tale is significant because it establishes a precedent with respect to the European Union as a club of member states, with one member now out. The end conclusion is that working together and learning to function in a way that is fair to everybody is the best way forward. However, empathy is quickly giving way to apathy. An increasingly prevalent assessment is that if Britain refuses to work collaboratively with the group in which it was a respected and valued member, having played a significant role in shaping the group's norms and working collaboratively to develop the interests of those wholly affected by the group in the past, it is a lost cause to all. Britain now wants to do things its own way, regardless of what possibly wiser and fairer members of the collective would propose, and in doing so, it is adopting narcissistic and selfish traits that preclude wider Europe from wishing to aid any more. Dutch colleagues regard British interests in Brexit as completely adrift and do not want to irritate a hostile former partner who wants to go it alone in case it causes more harm than good. There is now a pragmatic distance from a nation that desperately needs a cure but stubbornly refuses to accept it.

The Dutch remain shrewd and no-nonsense – a trait that perfectly encapsulates their attitude. British Brexit elites, on the other hand, continue to portray confidence in the expectation that this ruse will be enough to persuade others to accept their point of view. It will not, and the Dutch are aware of this, even though Brexit will have a significant impact on the Dutch GDP over a long period of time. I am discovering that the Dutch are highly pragmatic people. While there is a steady, creeping trend to the right, the Dutch have not succumbed to the populism, authoritarianism, and ethnic nationalism that have infected other Western European nations. It is a well-balanced society with high progressive taxation, a supportive welfare system, outstanding higher education, and a liberal attitude toward diversity both globally and locally (including the balance of freedom of religion vs. freedom from religion). Despite the greater global forces of illiberalism that have coincided with globalised neoliberalism, these principles continue to be upheld.

◈

The parallels between Brexit and Trump (the subject of the following chapter) are obvious. Both have displayed elements of nationalism, but they are not the same. In the case of Brexit, Britain wished to leave the European Union while still being internationally interconnected, whereas Trump wished to "put America first" and go it alone. Brexit and Trump both share populism. It is an anti-liberal revolution aimed at promoting democracy by concentrating on common fears. It strives to define the will of the people, of whole populations, while homogenising them. Populism is dictatorial, homogenising, and intellectually deficient. Its fundamental fallacy is that democracy is synonymous with popular sovereignty, even though people are neither homogeneous nor united. In effect, populism is a revolution against the liberal elite, blaming them for political failures and "turning power back to the people." For those moving further to the right, multiculturalism is framed as a yearning for separation, weakening the nation state as populism and authoritarianism collide. The 2008 global financial crisis posed serious economic problems for members of communities all around the world, particularly in areas where existing diversity and differences were considered largely unproblematic. With the advent of austerity and the implications brought by the Syrian War and the establishment of the Islamic State, illiberalism attacked the Muslim category even more, where the concentration on culture has become the dominating paradigm. The answer to the economic crisis was not to rebalance society, but to strengthen the status quo in terms of reclaiming the state's borders and giving the financial sector prominence. Brexit and Trump voters were reacting not only to their economic woes, but also to the anxieties instilled in their hearts and minds by illiberal elites.

What we are seeing now is a type of white riot in which the concept of "us" and "them" has evolved from a cultural issue impacting all parts of society to one that now has an economic component, solidifying divides, polarisations, and goals. In today's climate, there is a massive pushback against diversity. Multiculturalism was able to shock the system for a short time but owing to poor execution and mishandling in a broader political environment, it was assailed from all sides, left and right. It was eventually removed from the common language and is now regarded as "a dirty word."

Currently, the challenges of populism and the rise of far-right extremism reflect a wide range of concerns about representation and the involvement of various elements of the majority society. These worries are shared by individuals affected by Islamist radicalisation and violent extremism, but the prevalent discourse does not frame them in these terms. Far-right extremism is under-reported and given less weight than its counterpart, which is seen through the prism of religion by the organisations involved, leaving out all structural causes. It nullifies years of exploitation, racialisation, and exclusion by instilling fears and concerns about terror and violence, prompting majority populations to buckle under the weight of a powerful propaganda machine. It is improbable that multiculturalism will appear as a renewed paradigm for all in the future. The task is to establish an alternate method that embraces variety and uniqueness while still combating structural inequalities. It must also be one that is supported by a varied range of minority groups as well as dominant populations. This will need a fundamental realignment of how politics is conducted in the modern era. It will also imply ownership of the notion at both the top and bottom of society.

◇

A Brexit agreement was finalised in December 2020, and Britain left the EU on far poorer conditions than it had before its departure, despite Boris Johnson's claims of success, autonomy, and independence. He claimed to have answered a "question that has plagued politics for decades," yet this is a blatant untruth. The issue has plagued the Conservative Party for at least a decade, with David Cameron agreeing to a referendum to appease what John Major referred to as "the bastards" who were always clamouring to leave the EU. Cameron thought he was going to win, but when Leave triumphed under questionable circumstances, he walked away from politics. Theresa May was unable to appease the eighty or so members of the inaptly named European Research Group, a right-wing libertarian movement inside a party increasingly drifting to the right, and she, too, fell on her sword when she tried to navigate a middle ground between Remainers and Leavers. Boris Johnson promised and twisted his way to a late-night arrangement that lawmakers had no choice but to approve. They did not even have enough time to thoroughly scrutinise it before the withdrawal negotiating period's absolute deadline on 1 January 2021, a time that suited Boris Johnson rather than the people of the United Kingdom.

The incentives for leaving the EU have always been less about economics and more about the concept of identity, with the long-term ambition being for Britain to look beyond its nearest neighbours in pursuit of untapped markets in Asia and America once the early shocks of leaving are experienced. Britain wants to be free of the constraints of EU law and bureaucracy to reclaim its greatness, but there is more than a fragrance of authoritarian nationalism at work here. It has made the concept of disconnecting from a larger Europe appealing since it was encroaching on the sovereign rights of the UK, particularly for the very few who wanted to part company with the EU but presented it to a mostly uneducated or insular population as a matter of national identity and pride. Separation from the EU by one of the principal members of the world's greatest commercial bloc would always favour those who remained in the club, and this is the consequence today, regardless of what the British people are being told.

Many claim that Brexit favours Britain's super-rich while continuing to "leave behind" ordinary working men and women. There is a lot of truth in this. Jobs will lack the same safeguards, giving employers greater leeway to exploit workers at will. British students will be unable to study in Europe as part of the Erasmus programme. Rather, Britain will launch a standalone version while bearing the entire setup cost. It is unclear how the Horizon plan would affect UK universities after the seven-year associate membership period, which is a concern given that it is such a large source of research funding, with Britain always receiving more than it contributed. There has been much emphasis placed on fish as a potential obstacle in a settlement, even though fishing accounts for less than 0.1 percent of GDP. The fundamental difficulty was the concept of territory, which is related to ideas of sovereignty, providing further reinforcement of the symbolism associated with Brexit, which had been at the core of the project's intentions. Without a doubt, the EU has challenges, with countries in the east pushing nativist policies and states in the south suffering alignment concerns owing to the conditions of their economies. The union is far from flawless, but it continues to operate as a balancing force for all of its members, one to which Britain contributed as a leading player but has now opted to go its own way. Some people in the UK will be overjoyed. Others will bemoan what they have lost. Many people will continue to look into a dubious deal, sifting through the red herrings. It will also have ramifications for families and larger human interactions on both sides of the English Channel. In Europe, relief is likely to be followed by a tougher view that it still has everything to play for, while Britain will be on its own in a world very different from 2016, where protectionism is now the new normal, and effectively caught between the US, China, and the EU, who will always put their interests first and foremost.

I have yet to come across a single individual or a compelling argument in favour of Brexit. Instead, I sense and hear smugness, hyperbole, or a fantasy of something once grander among some English elite actors, reflecting on how Britain perceived itself in the world several decades ago. It is sheer stupidity, short-sighted, and dangerous since it cannot be perpetuated without substantial human cost, including the very real possibility of racism and exceptionalism becoming dominating themes in debates about English national identity. Despite its flaws, the EU served as a check and balance on diversity and inclusion, and it remains a political and cultural struggle. Without a doubt, this agreement, or any deal other than the one that has been in place until now, would result in far greater pain for many more people than the enormous advantages for a tiny few. Britons must brace themselves for a more unequal, polarised, and inward-looking society dominated by supporters of nationalism, nativism, and elitism. The warning flags are all too obvious.

◈

In terms of wider politics across the world since Brexit, there has been little serious criticism from politicians, but plenty of dissent from citizens. To put it another way, in many leading nations, it has been a period of ethnic nationalism, mixed with a combination of exclusive exceptionalism, relative privilege, and patronage—the reality of unaccountable elites. On the ground, however, minority communities have felt more isolated from majorities than ever before, not because they wanted to be, but because of how they have been projected due to dominant discourses that reinforce preconceptions of "others." We have lost connection and are unable to engage with each other as we may have done in the past. Following many years of efforts to bring people together via the values of inclusiveness and pluralism, this will be critical territory to reclaim. We are further away from this vision than we have ever been, despite a few "woke" gains here and there, and this is not due to our actions, but rather to the constraints that have kept us from achieving the goals of human progress.

Corruption in the form of contracts awarded to friends and party donors as a response to the Covid pandemic has exposed the lack of accountability and transparency at the top of society in the most dramatic way, particularly in the United Kingdom. However, there is no redress under the law. Although there are rumblings, these cronies are beyond the ability of the rest of us to hold them accountable. While citizens in the United Kingdom suffered greatly because of social isolation and alienation, senior political officials in Downing Street and elsewhere in Whitehall were throwing parties. These dilemmas put significant pressure on the Boris Johnson government, which rushed through the Brexit withdrawal deal in the hope that a contagious pandemic would mask some of the absurdities and injustices that it produces. Businesses are burdened by red tape. Supply chains have been disrupted. Almost one hundred thousand workers willing to drive lorries, for example, returned to the EU with no intention of coming back on temporary visas. Imports and exports now entail enormous costs, driving smaller industries such as fishing and farming to the edge. While the British government would say Covid is the bigger problem, independent economic analysis plainly shows that the cause is Brexit, which has failed. None of the promises made at the outset have come to fruition. Promises of control of borders, control of legislation, and control of capital flow have all come to naught.

Because the United Kingdom is not a member of the European Union, refugees and asylum seekers escaping the continent on dinghy boats cannot be repatriated. Trade treaties with nations such as Australia have a minor impact on the UK economy. The golden goose trade agreement with the US did not take place. Britain is still alone, adrift, and beyond the spheres of influence of Europe and the rest of the globe. Global Britain is an odd term that refers to hopes of greatness, but this "greatness" has long since passed. An arrogant and senseless unaccountable elite continues to assume that deregulation and neo-liberalisation of all aspects of the economy can result in a "better built Britain", but their assumptions are fundamentally incorrect. More and more people are becoming aware of the lies that have been told as well as the immense harm that has been done, all of which might have been avoided entirely.

However, with all the cronyism, corruption, ineptitude, and incompetence that define many ideas that emerge from the heart of political institutions around the world, there are rays of optimism. While inflation begins to rise, causing greater economic disparities, worker resistance is at an all-time high. More and more people are packing their things and saying no to their bosses. They demand that there be no more exploitation, low pay, or poor conditions. This is causing huge employment gaps in the economy, and ordinary people have had enough. It remains to be seen how this translates into changes in the law, but there are indicators that employers may well need to listen even if they do not want to.

17

White Supremacy

White supremacy is not confined to strange men in the Deep South who put on white cloaks, it is not confined to strange gatherings of the English Defence League,
David Lammy

Now, then, in order to understand white supremacy we must dismiss the fallacious notion that white people can give anybody their freedom,
Stokely Carmichael

Everything that irritates us about others can lead us to an understanding of ourselves,
Carl Jung

From Trump to the string of recent far-right killings, the spectre of white supremacy has been raised. Recent history has seen politics take a strong rightward swing, legitimising an atmosphere of white supremacy used by young, enraged white males on execution rampages across the global north. There is a visible correlation between the voices of political leaders and the acts of disaffected individuals or organisations who think they can act without impunity.

As the aftermath of the March 2019 Christchurch shootings deepens in the light of time for reflection, analysis, and conversation, it is clear that a number of significant points need to be made given what we now know but did not know at the time of those horrific attacks. Any sociological examination of the reasons for extremism and radicalisation must examine the individual's past. By examining patterns of socialisation, identity formation, and concerns of alienation and exclusion, it is possible to gain a better understanding of how an ideological viewpoint develops that causes an individual to commit atrocious acts of violence in the name of a greater cause.

We have accepted that the perpetrator in this case is a self-identified white supremacist who saw the world through a Manichean lens, viewing Islam and Muslims as a unified category of a movement and its people who are not only a blot on the landscape but should be exterminated. This is because they pose a threat to the white nation's very survival. There is no consensus on the nature of this whiteness—that is, its internal diversity or the historical legacies of class formation, colonialism, orientalism, genocide, or white nationalism—that have defined the whiteness space. However, this perspective is also an unusual combination of each of them: real anxiety is conveyed in connection to the "other," which appears to be propelled by population increase. Simultaneously, these "others" are condemned for their primitive, backward, and cruel natures, thus ostensibly legitimising racial nationalism and white supremacism.

This, some might argue, is a fact of Islamophobia. They are correct in this observation. Islamophobia is not simply a reaction to cultural degradation at the hands of some retrograde others. It also encompasses thoughts of ethnic cleansing against certain populations. There is much more to say about the nature of the killer's intentions for these assaults, which coincide with the operations of other seemingly autonomous acts of white supremacist violence. Each has committed an act of extreme violence in the name of protecting not just against the loss of advantages associated with whiteness, but also against the dread of being overrun by hordes of primitives. These kinds of views have spurred far-right radicals in several countries across the Global North in recent years, including Norway, Canada, England, and now New Zealand.

❁

Men's place in society, particularly in the labour market and education, has been significantly challenged over the last two decades. This is partly because women's positions have improved in these settings, but also because globalisation has forced the average young white man to compete harder than ever before, to the point where his privileged urban post-industrial patriarchy cannot be sustained in an increasingly interdependent world. The outpouring of hatred over the loss of dominance culminates in an expression of rage toward these newly significant "others."

In the pursuit of attention-grabbing headlines, sensationalist messaging presented as newsworthy items, and the audacious ideological motivations of certain press barons (it is unsurprising that almost all Australian news and media output is controlled by Rupert Murdoch), Islam and Muslims are demonised to the extent that being Islamophobic is considered normal. It takes a critical mind to disassociate oneself from what politicians and media sources say, yet such statements are gospel to the less-thinking individual. The Christchurch attacks were not the product of a random mentally ill person going on a rampage. They were calculating, clinical, and chilling. As he defined himself in his own writings, the assailant had a clear goal. He intended to cause terror and division around the world by publicising his acts. He referred to Eurocentric heroism, which borders on ethnic cleansing — in other words, a "kebab-removalist." The environment was heavy with Islamophobia, which provided him with the licence to engage in political violence and terrorism on a justifiable basis. Thus, the circle has been completed.

Within the broader context of global Islamophobia, these anti-Islam and anti-Muslim voices are becoming stronger at a time when politicians in Hungary, Slovakia, Slovenia, and Poland appeal to populist feelings. This is especially true given that several of these nations were directly affected by the Syrian refugee crisis that began in 2015 and resulted in the migration of over half a million refugees via the Balkans on their route to countries such as Germany. In general, Europe's far right focuses on the historical dynamics of Ottoman and Christian Europe. For example, Anders Breivik made explicit connections, imagining himself as a Knight Templar tasked with defending Christianity against the invading Muslim "other." These views appeal to young men on the margins of their society, who bury themselves in the extreme and radical right's online discourses, which are characterised by a hatred for diversity, women, and groups with various sexual orientations or leanings. All of this supports the projected inherited importance of the average white male, who must band together for a greater cause in order to a) protect the "white nation" from "invasion" via immigration and mixing, and b) eliminate these "other" undesirables, who are reproducing at an alarming rate and will completely absorb the "white nation" if left unchecked.

These ideas are tragically devoid of historical, political, or social context and are effectively ideologically instrumentalised to foment a "race war." Breivik and the white supremacist in New Zealand want a response to their terrorism that initiates this "race war".

✧

In August 2019, another weekend and another series of terrorist shootings occurred in America, perpetrated by young men driven by hatred for people who are different from them to the point of willingly killing people in public settings in mass shootings. In our haste to understand why these incidents occur on a regular basis, it would be unwise to dismiss the facts. Hate crimes more than quadrupled in counties where Donald Trump campaigned. Since 2011, almost one in every three white nationalist terrorist attacks has included a commendation for past white supremacist terrorists.

Much has been said about Trump's lack of genuine regret for blaming mental health concerns, media reporting, and internet gaming as the primary culprits of the two heinous acts in Dayton and El Paso. The reality is that Donald Trump utilised bigotry to gain support for his presidential campaign. As he prepared to run for president again in 2020, he kept his racist views and continued to foster intolerance and bigotry toward people of colour, particularly in the United States. The deaths in Dayton and El Paso marked the 250th victim of mass shootings in the United States since the start of that calendar year. By the end of 2019, 417 people were killed in mass shootings. This is an astonishing number. However, it is critical to outline the intricacies associated with these types of situations. Unsurprisingly, two-thirds of all gun-related deaths in the United States occur because of suicide. What is really intriguing, and this relates to Islamist violence as well, is that the violent perpetrators have a history of domestic abuse against women.

All of this shows that these young male killers are undoubtedly products of society, but society has not always promoted feminism or minorities at the expense of men. In America, joint-income households and diversity have always existed, but mostly from the perspective of the dominant in relation to the historically dominated. American culture as a melting pot is characterised by a high degree of flexibility in terms of gender, race, and ethnicity. However, it is contemporary cultural politics that is at the root of the malaise. Young men under the strains of globalisation and localisation might discover inspiring examples of individuals acting not only for themselves, but for others. With difficulties surrounding a crisis of masculinity among young men whose futures are unclear and insecure, the US's deregulated gun regulations make it far too easy for an angry young man to express his rage via these kinds of atrocities.

Something unsettling is occurring in British and American society, which has created the circumstances for extreme incompetence, inward-looking rhetoric, and the sheer recklessness associated with braggadocio, which has sealed these nations' fates. While condemning how these mindless elites continue to fail the rest of society might satisfy the soul, this is insufficient. Far too many individuals are still dying in vain, sometimes violently. The reasons for this are complex, but what is clear is that US gun laws, coupled with a sense of white supremacy and a deeply held belief of loss of privilege, combined with the structural realities of education and job insecurity, make these young men pliable and vulnerable to external, ideological influences. Ironically, some of this comes directly from the mouths of these same political leaders and their close allies. However, no amount of social or legal change will extinguish the fires stoked by demagogues whose callous disregard for others results in an endless spiral of misery and anguish.

These are not unique to the United States of America. The horrific attack on two shisha bars in Germany in February 2020 by a far-right extremist raised several questions about motive, activation, and impact. It was the third attack in nine months in Germany by far-right extremists, and by far the bloodiest. Eugenicism is making a resurgence in many ways. Politicians across Western Europe are increasingly comfortable voicing views that would normally be classified as racist. These ideas promoted the notion that there is an intrinsic distinction between racial groups, with white being at the top of the tree. Invariably, this hierarchy lands people with darker complexions at the bottom. The historical motivation for these efforts was to preserve the status quo on slavery and then colonialism, but it evolved into the notion of scientific racism, which reached its height with the Nazi Holocaust programme. Too many people think that Adolf Hitler instituted an extermination strategy directed against Jews, communists, leftists, homosexuals, and anybody else who rejected the Third Reich's principles. The fact is that this was only the pinnacle of what was occurring in North America and Europe for the better part of a century preceding the holocaust.

In these two shisha bars, a 43-year-old German man shot and murdered nine people while wounding five others. Most of the people were Turkish and Kurdish, with a few Bosnians, Bulgarians, and Romanians thrown into the mix. He later went to his house and shot his mother before taking his own life. This suggests a combination of issues concerning self-and other, as well as the internalisation of a particular type of racism, based on the belief that white groups are superior but are threatened by growing minority populations in particular urban areas, with their associated high birth rates and in-marriage. This man's goals were to avert the dilution of whites, as he viewed it. However, it is also obvious that the assailant suffered from mental health concerns, which is common among Islamist extremist actors, despite the media's emphasis on ideology and religion when it comes to extremists' attacks on specific religious minority groups. For far-right aggressors, the emphasis is less on ideology and more on personal worries about their mental health or other personal difficulties. This is a basic failing of reporting, particularly in the mainstream news, even though with an increasing number of incidents, such as Breivik in Norway in 2011 and Tarrant in New Zealand in 2019, it is becoming increasingly difficult to ignore what is palpably evident and obvious. Tobias Rathjen, the Hanau shisha bars attacker, released a manifesto in which he expressed dread of immigration and contempt for women.

In recent years, great focus has been placed on the concept of lone-wolf extremists to understand how far right extremists become inspired, activated, and organised. That is, people who exist on the periphery of society yet functionally act independently. It is now obvious that a considerable number of these attackers maintain an online presence, which enables them to develop their ideological ideas and gain knowledge about attack tactics and procedures. While this radicalisation happens online, it is critical to understand how it manifests in the real world. It is obvious that we live in an era in which racism toward minorities, Islamophobia, and anti-Muslim prejudice directed towards a specific segment of a minority already experiencing plenty of social, cultural, and political pressures have become the new normal. This racism stokes the flames of right-wing ideas of white supremacy, cultural superiority, and concepts of exclusivity, all of which appear to be challenged by the reality of migration and minority settlement. While politicians in the global north often demonise such groups for political benefit, individuals on the periphery of society are channelling these emotions toward far more dangerous ends. It inevitably reflects on the individuals who endure the most rapid of changes to the local economy and culture. These people are always males who have lost the trappings of privilege associated with their gender.

Three variables are critical in recognising the nature of the situation when it comes to far-right violence against Muslims. To begin with, these far-right assailants derive their ideological predilections from mainstream culture and politics. Second, the counterterrorism and counter-extremism policy frameworks that are currently receiving significant attention across the Global North are ill-equipped to deal with the growing threat of far-right extremism, owing to the historical emphasis on Islamist extremism as the most sinister form of extremism. Finally, reporting on these concerns continues to be slanted, prejudiced, or completely absent. Commentators are entirely responsible for reporting on issues fairly and obsequiously. Only then will this issue receive the attention it deserves, and that would inspire others working in this sector to see the similarities between extremism and terrorism perpetrated by various groups. And if we, as a society, focus on those issues of social development for all, we have a real chance of eliminating the threat of terrorism for all, because it is clear that there are patterns of reciprocal extremism in the current climate, and in order to break this vicious cycle, a focus on local area community development concerns and issues of social inclusion remains paramount.

◈

The world watched the tragic events on Capitol Hill on 6 January 2021, which will linger in the memory for many years after Trump has left the United States of America's political landscape. Much has been written on the role and existence of conspiracy theories among the individuals and groups that took part in that uprising, with a number of disparate groups coming together to support Trump, including the QAnon movement, white supremacists, neo-Nazis, and white nationalist groups. While this is a watershed moment in American political history, legitimate questions remain about what it implies for the country and other parts of the world where demagogues abound, and marginalised elements of the populace seek solace in the words spoken by them and purportedly for them.

Among the many conspiracy theories that have thrived in America are the notions that the CIA was responsible for John F. Kennedy's assassination; that Diana, Princess of Wales, was assassinated by the Royal Family; and that a secret cabal of Jewish financiers controls the world. Several of these concepts have deeper historical roots in antisemitism, racism, and nationalism. However, present concerns are focused on the QAnon movement, which has neither historical nor contemporary substance. Nonetheless, a sizable segment of American society believes not just in conspiracy theories, but also in the existence of a hidden organisation of paedophiles who drink the blood of their child victims while ruling the world, and that only Trump can rescue humanity from their horrors.

Around the world, rational people watched with horror as events unfolded in Washington DC on that Saturday. How could a sitting president (allegedly) incite a violent rebellion against his own administration, one that resulted in the deaths of five people, including a Capitol Hill police officer? He not only authorised these events, but also aided them through his outlandish comments, which were previously accessible to his 88 million+ Twitter followers before the private social media platform moved to permanently muzzle him.

Aside from the carnage he promised and delivered, Trump's brief but uneventful political career began with a conspiracy theory. Trump was the most vocal proponent of the President Obama birther conspiracy, contending vehemently that Obama's "missing birth certificate" proved that he was not a legal American. As a result of Obama's mockery of Trump at the 2011 Washington Correspondents' Dinner, the humiliation etched into Trump the desire to become even more brazen in his quest for electoral power. By 2016, it was clear that he was prepared to go to any length to accomplish his goals. Trump centred his campaign efforts on a racist conspiracy theory. According to historical accounts, Trump's father discriminated against New York's African American community when pursuing housing developments. Trump's grandfather's membership in the Ku Klux Klan shows a deep-seated racist heritage. In many ways, a conspiracy theorist spawned a plethora of other conspiracy theories, with the events on Capitol Hill serving as the fulcrum for the Trump agenda. His very own American carnage.

True, those who are inclined to believe in one conspiracy theory are also inclined to believe in others; this is the nature of the personality type involved in such topics. Conspiracy theories function as glue in this sense. Additionally, they may adopt cumulative forms, in which one conspiracy theory may absorb another. This suggests that there is a grand story resonating in the minds of conspiracy theorists—or that a particular type of uncritical mind is predisposed to accept them. In recognising the importance of conspiracy theories in mobilising a large movement, Trump fully exploited this opportunity structure in his pursuit of political advantage. However, many of the outlandish allegations, particularly in relation to the notion that the 2020 presidential election was stolen, were also held by other senior Republicans, who were willing to capitalise on what appeared to be a golden goose laying golden nuggets.

The issue of trust lies at the heart of this political dynamic. As a result, white middle-class Americans have lost faith in the democratic process because of their perception of being "left behind." A lack of formal education and dwindling possibilities for an already marginalised working class, along with a lack of critical thinking stoked by some media outlets such as Fox News, created a population primed for manipulation by a grand conspiracy theorist. Trump positioned himself as the white middle class's saviour. His racist leanings, suspicion of the Democrats, and particularly his enthusiastic scorn for Barack Obama's rule were all possible causes for attracting the attention of a disaffected white America, culminating in the tragic events of 6 January.

However, America is rapidly evolving. As shown by the voting experiences in Atlanta and Georgia in the 2020 Presidential Election, the country's political demographic is becoming increasingly varied. There is a growing body of educated and engaged middle-class black Americans. America's youth are significantly more receptive to and accepting of diversity than any earlier generation. However, Trump's removal does not signify the end of conspiracy theories, or the hatred and contempt expressed in a variety of current movements toward democracy. This polarisation is almost certain to intensify as the residue of the now easing Covid pandemic is increasingly felt by the poor and disenfranchised in comparison to those who have been able to avoid the pandemic's more detrimental impacts. Average white middle America is likely to pursue a Trump 2.0 unless President Biden can turn back the tide and rescue America from the precipice. While Biden is unlikely to supply all of the necessary remedies, a genuine chance exists to mend America.

This is a sizable part of the rational, sane, critical-thinking, open-minded, and intellectually transparent body of humanity worldwide that is more than happy to see the back of Trump and everything he brought to an already frail and divided society emerging from austerity measures implemented in the aftermath of the global financial crisis of 2008. However, there is still much more to be done. This means paying close attention to a post-Brexit Britain ruled by imperial ghosts. As nativism spreads across Europe, the EU's periphery is vulnerable to the unleashed forces of prejudice, hatred, and a complete lack of trust in society and politics, particularly among an adult white male population that has seen a dramatic reduction in the historical privileges associated with this segment of society, which have been shattered as a result of capital and labour globalisation—not by cosmopolitan elites, immigrants, or minorities.

Conspiracy theories come and go, but QAnon's relative influence in America and throughout Europe, as well as its ties with antisemitic, white fascist, neo-Nazi, white supremacist, and white nationalist movements and organisations, will endure. While much of the context for these conflicts is economic, especially among Democrats, it is likely to remain a significant element in determining what Biden can do. Social media's echo chamber effect also has a significant impact. This genie has escaped the bottle.

Banned from Twitter, Trump's fans will be driven underground. Conspiracy theory movements will continue to grow, and his adherents, particularly in QAnon, anti-vaxxers, and anti-5G devotees, will find new ways to deceive themselves —but the danger is that these forces will become darker, with both terrorism experts and the FBI warning of the inevitability of further violence. We wait in bemusement.

◇

In late 2015, I returned from a semester as a visiting scholar at New York University, a world-renowned institution of higher learning in the United States. Afforded the special privilege of being assigned NYU housing on West Fourth Street, the block's entrance was at the foot of Fifth Avenue, both avenues bearing major weight in New York's history. It was a combination of luck and design that led me there.

New York University is surrounded by Washington Square Park's unofficial quadrangle, with its arch honouring George Washington's inauguration as president in 1789. The arch may be seen from the Empire State Building's 86th-floor observatory with a long zoom lens. The park was not always a popular hangout for visitors, skateboarders sharpening their abilities, musicians preparing their songs, or pot users swapping vibes. From farmland until the late 1700s, the region was used as a burial spot for slaves and immigrants, at first, and then for yellow fever victims afterwards. There might be up to 20,000 dead bodies beneath the park.

It now includes a newly installed fountain that draws people's attention to the centre of the park. However, the concentric circles of individuals peering in depict both New York and the United States in miniature. Tourists and top NYU students flock to the centre. They are drinking coffee, listening to live music, and watching or taking part in the entertainment. They are buzzing, humming, and taking in the environment. The homeless, impoverished, and ostracised populate the park's four corners. They spend the day there and sleep rough at night. These visible groupings are indistinguishably black. This is, in many ways, America. At least two of the corners sell the herb late at night, reflecting the fact that in the 1960s, the park was the location to go to buy hashish and consume it in public with minimal opposition from the police. As the United States has loosened marijuana legislation in several states in recent years, New Yorkers have benefited from a more liberal attitude towards cannabis usage.

Washington Square Park was located in the centre of historic New York. Dutch immigrants and freed slaves developed a stretch of marshes into pastures in the early 1600s. It was known as Noortwyck ('north district'). This became Greenwich in the late 1600s. The cosmopolitan Greek-style townhouses on West Fourth Street were erected in the 1830s. They housed New York's upper society at the time. During the nineteenth century, Washington Square Park and Greenwich amalgamated to form Greenwich Village. It became home to intellectuals, authors, singers, painters, and designers, as well as the bohemian lifestyle associated with what became known as simply "The Village" to inhabitants and tourists. It was once home to famous performers, as well as authors and painters, before they were priced out by the ultra-wealthy. Since the 1950s, The Village has been mentioned in several films. Inside Llewyn Davis (2013), a Coen brothers' film, explores the evolution of the folk music scene, with much of the film's locales set in a representation of Greenwich Village in the early 1960s. The neighbourhood was home to Bob Dylan and Leonard Cohen. It is even the home of the fictitious heroine Wonder Woman. In 1927, Café Reggio offered the first cappuccino in America. The coffee shop can still be found on MacDougal Street.

The local Indians sold Manhattan, an island, to Dutch immigrants in 1632 for the equivalent of $1,000 USD today. However, without firing a single shot, the British seized and colonised the city in 1664. George Washington drove the British out in 1783. Following the adoption of the United States Constitution, New York was chosen as the country's first capital. Soon after, it began to prosper in industry, trade, and commerce, particularly following the 1825 building of the Erie Canal, which connected the city to the mainland of America, dramatically enhancing the city's economic prominence domestically and worldwide. Capital accumulation necessitated the use of labour. This promoted migration from throughout America but also, significantly, from around the world. Waves rolled in from Ireland, Eastern Europe, and Southern Europe. It cemented the city's reputation as a melting pot of ethnic, religious, and cultural diversity, which is still felt today. The skyline is now packed with skyscrapers, yet the minorities who work in the city's offices and towers live in the larger New York City region, which includes the Bronx, Queens, Brooklyn, Staten Island, and Manhattan. The people that make up the city are also responsible for its history. Successful entrepreneurs built magnificent structures not just to commemorate their fortunes, but also to add to the vibrancy of the city. At the request of affluent patrons, architects and designers built spectacular skyscrapers. Reaching towards the sky became a symbol of the city. When the Empire State Building was finished in the early 1930s, the country was in the grip of the Great Depression. However, this did not prevent the developers from erecting a magnificent art-deco structure in the middle of Manhattan.

As Wall Street became the financial, banking, and insurance centre, Manhattan's midtown district housed the jet set and catered to their desire for luxury goods and services. These tall structures on each side of Central Park serve as a reminder of the richness and fortune of those who came and conquered. Americans who aspired to the highest levels of society did so in Manhattan. To this day, the city exudes a vibrant vitality. It is known as the "City that Never Sleeps". For those who choose to dream, it is the stuff of dreams. The city's population is as diverse as its tourists, who come from all over the world. It is, nonetheless, a city of paradoxes. There is a dark underbelly in every major city, from London to Paris to Istanbul. Centuries of history are buried under Manhattan's streets. Long-forgotten places and people are being overwritten. There is both wealth and tradition, as well as poverty and disadvantage. New York City, like Washington DC, Chicago, and large areas of Los Angeles, is heavily racialised.

New York has long been a hotbed of political dissent. It was a key location during the civil rights campaigns of the 1960s as well as the suffrage movement. It has been at the vanguard of the struggle for LGBT rights in recent years. And, as a certain Republican presidential contender in the run-up to the 2016 elections spewed hatred and intolerance toward those considered most dangerous, from Mexican immigrants to Muslims from outside the nation, New Yorkers held firm. As swaths of American Muslims were exposed to racist and Islamophobic attacks across the country in reaction to the Paris shootings in November 2015 and the San Bernardino killings in December 2015, Jews, Christians, and individuals of no faith rallied in support of their fellow citizens.

Prominent politicians spread hate when they have both eyes on their electorate rather than on effective policymaking. They sow seeds of ignorance and bigotry. Their mistaken statements simply exacerbate the problems of Islamophobia and radicalisation. It reflects the reality that long-touted American exceptionalism has devolved into fear and contempt. Paranoia and delusion go hand in hand, from misguided politicians to uneducated everyday people. And this is the heartbreak that is America's reality. What was notable in the United States and across the world until the 1970s, especially public education, technology, science, and research, has now become the experience of the few, rather than the many. Reaganomics, like Thatcherism in Britain, abolished the welfare state and replaced it with individual achievement as the primary measure of a society's performance. It is how the rest of the world has remade itself in the twenty-first century in the absence of a workable alternative.

The DNA of the United States was created in the crucible of war and struggle. Regrettably, it is more prevalent than ever. Guns harm Americans in their own country. White police officers murder young black men, or the criminal system imprisons them arbitrarily. Obama's drones were responsible for the deaths of Afghan and Pakistani people. In many respects, New York was similarly formed from the ashes of the inferno. It became prosperous because of its diversity and opportunities. This lack of diversity among influential individuals, in elite politics, and in everyday life is causing the rest of America to be a poor shadow of its former self.

18

Accepting Differences

He who lives in harmony with himself lives in harmony with the
universe,
Marcus Aurelius

Children learn more from what you are than what you teach,
WEB Du Bois

Civilization is the encouragement of differences,
Ghandi

The idea of needing to "accept" differences in society raises an abundance of issues for those who see such distinctions as a threat or a risk to society as a whole. Others see these dissimilarities as a benefit. This is where politics enters the picture, and it is part of the reason so many people are perplexed by the concept of "multicultural societies."

There are several approaches to exploring how differences are operationalised in the context of their management of diversity in society. How Britain approaches multiculturalism in the post-war period differs from how the rest of "Old Europe" does it, for example, in France. Both had sizable empires but were forced to reach out to former colonies to assist nations suffering from labour shortages caused by the loss of men during World War II. The indigenous communities that remained or returned after the conflict had greater goals or just did not want to undertake the nasty work anymore. The United Kingdom is a conglomeration of four distinct countries, and it is undoubtedly a nation of immigrants that has evolved over the course of two thousand years. Subjects of the United Kingdom Commonwealth, formerly the British Empire, were invited, but due to various stages of anti–immigrant policy, they ended up staying permanently when it was initially assumed by both the immigrants who came and the society that hosted them that once their jobs were terminated, they would return. This did not occur. Thus, what exists now has its origins in the post-war period, when communities were seen as transitory guest-workers, as they were referred to in many parts of Western Europe. Ethnic minorities only realised they had a future in Britain once they were forced to stay and begin family reunification. However, because their employment and education levels were low, and they became trapped in mediocre jobs, poor housing, and impoverished regions, social mobility is still a pipe dream for many. Those ethnic minorities who had distinct types of social and cultural capital in the sending regions prior to migration faced all sorts of negative constraints on mobility, locking them in the same dismal inner-city areas as other minorities from less fortunate backgrounds.

In a broader sense, how the UK approaches multiculturalism differs from how several nation-states, ranging from Canada to Singapore, have constitutionalised their own models. There were several incentives at work for Canadians who wanted immigration in the 1970s to Singapore, which needed to "manage" a tremendously varied population distinguished by ethnicity and religion while also dealing with its own colonial historical heritage. These are significant advances because, even though new populations have no colonial past, integration is still a challenge. Bigotry and ethnic nationalism are problems in Canada just as much as they are in other nations. The British model is more akin to the Dutch model, which is based on the concept of "pillarisation," meaning that "we" as a state will recognise all groups, religious and ethnic, but "we" will end up doing little in terms of bringing all these groups together under the umbrella of unity within diversity. The UK makes an admirable attempt, but the words from the top are incoherent. In 1967, for example, Roy Jenkins delivered an astounding speech in which he defined integration as "not a flattening process of assimilation, but equal opportunity accompanied by cultural variety in an atmosphere of mutual tolerance." The Commonwealth Immigrants Act of 1968, on the other hand, was hurried through parliament in three days by the Labour Party of the time. The Labour Party has done more to promote anti–immigrant sentiment than the Conservatives, who have done more to promote decolonisation than Labour has ever done. In the 1980s, the increasing wave of diversity spoke of "steel bands, samosas, and saris." However, while a school in a remote backwater may have an international culinary festival on one day of the year, little is done to influence the other days of the year.

In 2011, Prime Minister David Cameron spoke of "muscular liberalism," a clear attempt to distance the Conservatives from New Labour's apparent failings, much of which was code for the belief that "Muslims killed multiculturalism." Muslims are a danger. We must kill the danger that is multiculturalism. It is possible to bring these thoughts a little closer to home by mentioning Turkey. In the contemporary period, it has few ethnic religious minorities, with no more than 100,000 out of a population of seventy-five million. Today, ethnic minorities in Turkey are regarded under a secularist system much like how the French treat theirs: everyone is a Turk first, yet Kurds endure significant prejudice. Constitutionally, Kurds are not minorities because minorities are defined solely by religious differences. However, Kurds are a marginalised, disadvantaged, and discriminated-against minority in society, fighting for legal recognition and equality. Despite its flaws, the UK performs better than most for a variety of reasons, but the main problems are a) huge regional differences, i.e., North and South; and b) enormous class differences, i.e., poor whites and poor minorities in the North are in a class struggle at the bottom of society and also divided by race. Globalisation and cosmopolitanism coexist in the South, namely London. It is a lively, challenging environment where national agenda-setters are centred. The North has seen considerable deindustrialisation and employment losses, with no workable inbound investment or regional development strategies in place. What were once booming industrial cities have been abandoned or have not been effectively regenerated into service sector economies. Since Margaret Thatcher's monetary policies in the 1980s and Reaganomics across the Atlantic, the UK economy has been dominated by the financial services industry, which is currently the largest part of GDP.

Although this may be a fascinating historical lesson, there are other levels of interpretation to consider. The first issue is one of ideology or philosophy. In other words, what type of society do we want to see in action? Is it diversity within unity or unity within diversity? Then there are the political ambitions of the multicultural society that we want to see, which are vulnerable to political manipulation. That is, short-termist dogmatic thinking that is virtually invariably tied to public opinion, such as the UK's Commonwealth Immigrants Act in 1968 or Switzerland's ban on minarets in 2010. The public is often misled by questionable newspaper reports and sensationalised television news, and while they do not trust their leaders, they mostly obey them. News propaganda has a lot to account for, but the Arab Spring and the American Autumn have taught the world that political opposition among the young is not dead, even though unabashed official repression may still rear its ugly head every now and then. In terms of economics, all multiculturalism models are vulnerable to the business cycle. We are all suffering from the impacts of the post-2008 crisis, but disadvantaged minorities are easy targets for everyone else, and with the aftershocks of 9/11 and the conflicts in the east still felt at home, Western Europe is shifting to the political right. This is not healthy for all minorities, including gays and lesbians. In terms of the social backdrop, societies need bogies on occasion. There are several examples of such vilification in the United Kingdom alone. Whether it is Jews in the 1930s, Irish in the 1950s, "the black mugger" in the late 1970s, the "Asian Gang" in the 1980s, or the "Muslim terrorist" today, these "bogies" are exploited until a new bogey takes their place. Others do come to the fore from time to time, such as "asylum seekers" in the 1990s or "hoodies" in the 2000s, but the "Muslim terrorist" or "Islamic extremist" is the one we all despise or dread the most.

When it comes to identity, there was a time when we thought of ourselves as unique, representing a specific culture, heritage, language, ethnicity, and even religion, and we defined ourselves in these terms. However, with globalisation, the internet, and 24/7 news, "who we are" is now defined more in terms of "who we are not." In a fast-paced environment, many people's senses of self have been shattered by fragmentation. Those who steadfastly keep their ethnic or religious identities do so because of the pressure placed on those identities by those who look to maintain their own in competition with them. All these conflicts are worsened during times of greatest inequity. Reducing inequality contributes to the development of coherent multiculturalism. It is not possible to acquire permanent answers by fluffing around the borders with mild touches. Equality is important for solid and stable models of multiculturalism. This is about equal chances for everyone, but it is also about an equal outcome for all. We live in a complex world, but our memories are short (what we choose to remember is also a function of what we choose to forget), our political interests are immediate, and social divisions are widening all the time, making finding the right model and applying it in the right context a huge challenge. Finally, no matter how hard we try, there is no such thing as a perfect "multicultural" society on the globe. As vital as it is to enlighten the argument and explore the competing theories and observations, how multiculturalism is operationalised remains an intellectual discourse—a "philosophical dream." Positive progressive multiculturalism is never a lasting phenomenon because it is always so readily toyed with by those in power against those seeking power.

In January of 2012, I spent a few short months in the Holy Lands, but what did I take away from my time there? I am a believer in hope. There is always hope. We must never forget that, yet there are certain misgivings that I have that tend to dampen this hope. One such source of concern is Israel. The holy lands are a strange place. They include at least five thousand years of history, mostly from the ancient Jewish, Roman, and Muslim periods, and yet, outside of the nation, most people equate Israel with a state that occupies the territories of others. For the two million Palestinian Arabs who are Israeli citizens, the sense of occupation is real. The overall trend is that they are doing the best they can, with just a small fraction doing well through commerce and trade, while the overwhelming majority feel the pressure of being walled in by a security state that is conservative, centralised, and dare I say it, racist. But it would be incorrect to paint a broad picture here. Far from it, not all Israeli Jews are the same. The ultra-orthodox make up about 15% of the five million or so people who live and work there, but they make the most noise and are heard the loudest. There are 150 separate factions within these few, and they are strongly split within them. The majority of Israeli Jews range from liberal-moderates to fervent secularists. These latter groups share so much with their Muslim counterparts, yet few recognise it. Those on the political right are the most likely to disagree with such ideas. These individuals are richer, live more exclusive lifestyles, and are better educated and well-travelled, but they are also intolerant, reactionary, and conservative (with a "small c" and a "large c"). Those on the political left are more accepting and open, but also more sceptical of authority. This is true in Jerusalem, as it is in the rest of the globe right now.

Many things bothered me as I gazed into the city. Segregation in the workplace and in the home are critical problems. Palestinians and Jews seldom share the same venues in schools, neighbourhoods, or workplaces. However, Jews are split internally by ethnicity, class, politics, and religion. For example, the inflow of Russian Jews who like vodka contrasts sharply with the Ethiopian Jews who sell coffee at Aroma or work as airport runners. Aspects of the state's machinery are also problematic: laws are discriminatory and imposed by biased judges, ranging from those prohibiting Arabs and Jews from marrying to those prohibiting Arab–Israeli political parties from being recognised if they are not openly devoted to Zionism. And the wall—that perplexing wall. Standing so close to it made me think about one thing. A prison! Arab communities that have existed for millennia have suddenly been divided. Some families now drive 90 minutes to the nearest checkpoint to visit loved ones who were formerly a 10-minute walk away on the other side of the wall.

My natural impulse is to sympathise with the oppressed, dispossessed, and marginalised and to examine social structures and all their flaws. Palestinian Arabs might always do more to show openness and acceptance, but their situation is far from ideal. From 1948 to 1967, and through two Intifadas, Palestinian Arabs have been convinced that resistance is hopeless. It just irritates the bear, who smashes the annoying mosquito with one smooth swipe of its massive claws. At the same time, Israeli Jews do not speak in unison. There is a lot of critical and progressive thinking inside the country that wants to set up long-term peace models, but it is being drowned out by the regressive tendencies of ultra-religious and neo-conservative forces that are becoming increasingly powerful. I heard reports of how an Israeli female soldier was instructed to sit at the front of a bus by the ultra-orthodox who were sitting in the rear, she refused and was assaulted by them. There have also been reports of ultra-orthodox Jewish communities where the women are referred to as the "Israeli Taliban." These women do not work, seldom leave the house, do not use contraception, and dress in layers of black clothes. No part of the body's skin is visible, including the hands and ankles. Worryingly, their seven-year-old girls dress identically. Secularists despise these groups, and they are often caricatured in the media.

In Jerusalem, I spoke to groups of graduate and postgraduate students about my research. In two instances, I reminded individuals that no matter how much we all get excited about our identities and want to defend and nurture them in the context of internal and external threats and possibilities to those identities, we are all the same as human beings. At their intersections, whether in Jerusalem or Istanbul, the emphasis is on differences rather than similarities. Remove the fanatical religious norms, the inward-looking politics, and conceptions of some type of memory centred on identity, and we're all the same.

❁

It is crucial to seek out positive components in the scriptures and the existential dynamics of real religious experience in order to come up with new ways of thinking about current challenges as a result of previous ones. The issue of absolutism, on the other hand, is one of the most pressing. We need to get over the notion that "our" faith is the only one and that the others are only supporting cast members. I am reminded of a joke I heard at an interfaith conference in Volos, Greece, when I was on a panel with a Rabbi, a Priest, and an Atheist Marxist, the latter of whom delivered it to a mixed audience of religious and community people. It is fascinating to see how atheists view theists in general and the Abrahamic faiths in particular. The joke goes like this: After a gruelling three-day symposium on interfaith dialogue and peace, a priest, a rabbi, and an imam each return home to the comforts of their loved ones, pausing to reflect on the occasion. Returning to his house, the rabbi sits in his favourite recliner with his wife, reminiscing over the events of the day. "The meal was terrific, the journey was pleasant enough, and our conversation was constructive, but you know, it's all well and good that we talk many important things to each other about our great religions, but we are still the chosen people," he remarks to her. Back at home, the priest sat on the sofa listening to his wife (this priest is an Anglican). He says, "A beautiful time was had by everybody, but, you know, although we discussed and debated, and I agree that reaching out is vital, but, you know, we still have the son of God," he remarks to her. That same night, the imam returns to his own house and says to his wife, "It was an excellent conference. We ate abundantly and discussed all manner of important topics, but, you know, while our Jewish and Christian brothers and sisters are all people of the book, and Abraham is significant to us all, we, as Muslims, have the last word."

In Birmingham, all three of my children attended an orthodox Jewish elementary school. I even served on the governing body for two years because I was interested in learning more and wanted to contribute. My son Nabeel and I were interviewed by *The Guardian* on the challenges of being a Muslim in a Jewish school. In 2007, my family and I were even mentioned in the Chief Rabbi's annual BBC Rosh Hashanah address. And there is another amusing anecdote here, which is also true. We were filming at King David School, and Chief Rabbi Lord Jonathon Sachs wanted to speak with my children about their perspectives. At the time, my son, who is a colourful character but also lives in his own world, was eight years old. He has Asperger's Syndrome, a kind of autism that can be managed. Most of the time, at least. Lord Sachs posed an intricate inquiry to Nabeel, and I could see it was not going down well. "Nabeel," Lord Sachs inquired, in his customary authoritative tone, "I notice you're a Muslim boy, and your father says you go to Arabic school on weekends, but I also see you wearing the kippah to school every day. How does it feel to wear the Jewish prayer cap every morning to school?" My son sat in his chair, dangling his legs, pondering for a few lengthy seconds that seemed to linger an eternity. He produced a slight frown before saying only one phrase clearly and accurately. "Itchy," he exclaimed. Everyone in the room tried hard not to chuckle as the Chief Rabbi looked perplexed. Curiously, this sequence did not make the final cut of the BBC television version of the show that aired in September.

❖

Over the years, I have been involved in the subject of interfaith relations because I think that by reaching out and learning about others, we may learn about ourselves. I want to dispel common misunderstandings, disinformation, and outright folly on everyone's side. Many Muslims are unfamiliar with Jews, and vice versa. It is no wonder that some individuals develop distorted perceptions of the "other" if they exclusively watch television news and read newspapers, including those we consider to be reputable media. Interconnections between communities, the academy, and policy development are a crucial axis that is not always successfully bridged in the UK since the culture of such a process is still undeveloped. The diversity paradigm in the United Kingdom has many flaws, but these may be filled by new spiritual, political, cultural, and social thought, and action. It is only a matter of connecting the dots. Building systems today is an important part of future success.

Diversity is a strength, not a weakness. People's peculiarities make them intriguing rather than a threat to who we are. Knowing others means knowing yourself. All the brightest and most well-known scientists and intellectuals from ancient and modern cultures have come to the same set of findings repeatedly. Even though we continue to make the same mistakes, it is a huge tragedy that we have not fully learned these crucial lessons. We still have the potential to do so, but as humans, we are still quite primitive. All the world's faiths have something vital to say about our human experience, and their teachings are similar in many respects, yet they have also been used in a harmful way by people with dominant interests. It is hardly surprising that so many people dismiss religion, viewing it as the source of many of the world's ills throughout history. If a member of the academy has any religious leanings, it implies that they are incapable of making reasonable decisions or exercising solid critical thinking. This could not be further from the truth since an individual can readily distinguish between a worldly and a cosmic existence. Despite what we know about the cosmos and our role within it, there is still plenty that can be done to better humanity's situation. The difficulty is still there for future generations, who will have to live with the mistakes we have made thus far and will continue making. They can proactively challenge current mechanisms. There is a lot of good will in the world. The traditional adage that "young people are our future" holds true. They live in the future, while I live in the present and will eventually disappear.

But it would be naive to believe for a moment that Muslims in the United Kingdom can continue a model of supreme guidance or truth without asking probing questions. There are a few points to bring up here as well. There are significant internal differences that are sectarian, ideological, philosophical, and political, and their permutations and combinations are acted out in many ways in the diasporic-transnational contexts where they exist. Because of disparities in attitudes towards modernity, education, integration, and gender equality, there are significant intergenerational differences. Some are strongly established and appear immovable, resisting all attempts to change, while others have obviously adapted to majority society via favourable intergenerational transmission. Some young Muslims are disempowered and disenfranchised because of the negative repercussions, while some older groups are outdated and dysfunctional. Existing leadership is ineffective, but it is rapidly changing. The events of 7/7, in fact, hastened this transformation. It had no choice but to do so, and while Muslims in general have been slammed in the media, some younger Muslims have embraced the challenge wholeheartedly. Nonetheless, more innovative thought and action are necessary.

Gender inequality continues to be a problem. There are obviously active decisions made to prioritise family obligations, such as child rearing and home management, but some Muslim women who are not in education or who are not working are not doing so by choice. Remarkably, things are moving at a brisk pace here. According to recent labour market data, second-generation Muslim women have an elevated level of education and can reach higher salaried work. They do, however, face an "ethnic penalty" when compared to most women. They are also more susceptible to the consequences of economic downturns, as proven by the 2008 recession's impact on this demographic. Even more intriguing, there is a widespread belief that Jews in Britain are universally successful and always achieve maximum returns on their investment in education and training. However, research suggests that despite being far more qualified than the average and given the group's high rate of salaried employment positions, Jews still face an ethnic penalty in the labour market. As compared to comparably qualified majority groups, more people resort to self-employment to get ahead because of discrimination. This type of entrepreneurialism is most prevalent in the financial sector. There is a significant risk to Muslim communities in the future as the number in Britain rises, especially those with firmly held localised faith-based identities. Although structural disadvantage accounts for much of this ailment, there are cultural transformations that communities could, should, and must undertake in order to realise a promising future.

19

Intellectualising Islam

Be in this world as if you were a stranger or a wayfarer,
Prophet Muhammad

For what is evil but good tortured by its own hunger and thirst?
Khalil Gibran, *The Prophet*

*The extinction of race consciousness as between Muslims is one of the
outstanding achievements of Islam, and in the contemporary
world there is, as it happens, a crying need for the propagation of
this Islamic virtue,*
Arnold J. Toynbee

Being a Muslim means submitting to Islam. The concept of Islam also includes the acknowledgement of Allah as almighty and all-knowing. Allah has bestowed upon humankind a system of beliefs, values, rites, ritualism, and spiritual philosophy through His prophets on Earth to connect human beings on Earth with their heavenly designer, chief planner, and creator-father. These are the fundamental tenets of the faith. Any attempt to say anything about a link to such a metaphysical idea needs a "leap of faith" and subsequent acceptance of all the established beliefs that go with it. As a young British-Pakistani-Englishman growing up in post-industrial Birmingham's inner cities, it became clear to me that there are many diverse religious groups where God reigns supreme. There are also several subtleties and variations on the traditional practices within every given religious community. The Islam I grew up with was inextricably linked to South Asian Berewli customs, which included a wide range of cultural events. Some of them have stayed frozen in diasporic groups that, while I was growing up, were only starting to consider permanent absorption into a rising multicultural Britain. As with many others of my generation, and even today, the teaching I got in after-school mosques was entirely inadequate for genuinely grasping the fundamental precepts of the faith, despite learning to read Arabic and mastering some Urdu. Over time, I have gained a better understanding and command of both languages. I performed Islam and faithfully followed the five pillars out of a sense of responsibility. I was not sure why I was doing what I was doing, other than the fact that if I did not, I would be accused of committing major crimes and punished by exorbitant amounts of agony and suffering. This is exactly how I took it all in at the time. However, this specific contextualisation of Islam did not sit well with me. Having travelled extensively throughout the world during my professional working years, it is clear to me that Islam is about as diverse, rich, nuanced, and profound as any religion on the planet.

The way the past has affected current views, beliefs, and ways of Islam is an ever-changing process. Learning to embrace and understand Islam has been a never-ending journey of self-discovery and enlightenment for me. Rather than adhering to a set of principles that require me to act and think in a way that is solely about acceptance, I now see and regard Islam as a far more open-ended, inclusive, and creative religion through which I conceptualise a purposeful and effective intellectual, cultural, social, economic, and political outlook (when carried out well). However, there is always a need to study and understand the entirety of Islam, as well as to critically interact with relevant debates and conversations to strengthen a cutting-edge analytical and developmental viewpoint.

❖

When it comes to social dynamics, Islam may mean a variety of things. There are clearly several essential aspects that contribute to a sense of community. They have a discernible energy, consciousness, and motive behind what current sociologists refer to as "social capital" and what Ibn Khaldun would have referred to as *asabiya* (cohesion) or *imran* (civilisation) in the fourteenth century. The concept of cohesiveness is particularly essential here. In religions and religious systems ranging from Confucianism to Taoism to Islam, the eastern world is characterised by a concept of collectivism. From extended family applications to intergenerational connectedness to ideas of raising funds among British South Asian Muslims to start up a new business venture, an element of trust, confidence, involvement, and reciprocity is inspired by a set of religio-cultural values and goals. When people in western, secular, materialist liberal cultures face difficulties, such as in the post-credit crisis environment, institutions and companies are not always there to help. Families and members of linked clan-kinship groups are sometimes there to give much-needed financial aid and support.

In expanding and linking this localised vision to society, complete conceptions of civil society begin to develop. This is a broader viewpoint in which individuals consider their actions to have an influence on larger society, regardless of whether these actions are beneficial or detrimental in their overall impact. There are many positive externalities associated with participating in civil society projects that not only assist the participant in determining a social meaning for their social actions, increasing a sense of well-being, but there is also a clear benefit to society as participatory individuals take ownership of their roles. It is an eastern philosophical perspective that is embedded in Islam and among Muslims, and elements of these methods are adopted into diaspora populations. Individuals are intrinsically linked to a larger society, and their social consciousness contributes to a sense of belonging to something bigger than themselves. As shown by recent banking crises, there are several advantages to a market-based economy, but the notion that competition and self-interest are sufficient to meet the needs and desires of all members of society is incorrect. Individualism is risky, full of danger, and it adds to the person's stress levels, which might potentially lead to more problems elsewhere. A collectivist ideal, in effect, protects the individual while also helping society in being cohesive and effective. This is not precisely communism, but rather a social democratic vision of participation and progress based on a mixed economy model.

Many social ills could be removed if a perfect collectivist system appeared in the east, but it is the combination of rural poor and less-educated masses trying to supply a basic subsistence existence for their families that is up against the self-interested materialist machinations of their land-owning, capital-rich overlords who are often trained and educated elsewhere. This transcends, for example, from a local-area environment to how semi-feudalistic systems run in local villages and towns to how Pakistan as a whole nation works. Pakistan is one such country, with a huge disparity between the ruling elites and the remaining 80 percent of the population, which is still trapped in the village system and relies on agriculture for a living. Indeed, much of the Muslim world is in a difficult position, with vast nations with widespread geographical spread and significant natural resources (e.g., Pakistan, with its enormous natural coal and gold reserves), but they are entirely reliant on ineffective political systems that are organisationally corrupt, with the powerful influence of external nations with vested interests who maintain the status quo, and without transparency or accountability to the people they are tasked with governing. In calling attention to the Arab Spring, one of the causes of the 'uprising' was an antiquated elite leadership out of touch with the needs and desires of the masses. The latter revolted against the governmental forces, launching a movement that expanded throughout the Middle East. Age-old militarist dictatorships and dynastic families ended, but it is unclear what this means for many young Arabs coming to terms with social and political change in their lives ten years on. The collectivist spirit drives many people's interests and societal aspirations, but when viewed through the lens of Islam, moral incompetence can lead to short-termism and self-interest for those at the top.

A specific example is a macro-dynamic social project based on an analysis of the Gülen Movement in Turkey and around the world, which was enormously important in Turkey until the failed coup events of 2016 resulted in its dismantling when hundreds of thousands of people thought to be associated with it were purged, imprisoned, or exiled from the country. With Fethullah Gülen at the spiritual helm of the organisation, who is now self-exiled in the United States, it inspired a global movement—sort of a *jamaat*—of devoted followers, members, activists, entrepreneurs, and communitarianists with the express desire to find a set of actions to improve trust, cooperation, dialogue, and coexistence in Turkish society and beyond. It is estimated that there were up to six million sympathisers, followers, and active members of a tight-lipped operation that sought to propagate a spiritualistic and cultural message. It was enriched by Turkic-Sufi theology as expressed in Said Nursi's writings, but it was also ideological and political in that it actively promoted a soft pan-Turkism around the world and a deeper understanding of the Ottoman past. Many staunch Turkish secularists despised the movement and saw it as political in how it "placed" people in society, but many traditionalists and conservatives saw the movement as beneficial because it allowed them to take part in an organisation that supported their entire social, economic, and political outlook. True, since 2002, there has been a considerable emergence of the "Islamic bourgeoisie" in Turkey, helping it to become one of the world's strongest economies and the most stable polities in the Middle East. This rising group of people looks to preserve portions of their cultural, spiritual, and religious history while also taking part in a network of others with similar goals for Turkey's future. Understandably, Islam deeply influences the Gülen Movement, but it is also a practical and socially-oriented initiative that remains primarily inclusive and outward-looking. Many different critiques have been levelled against the movement, one of which is that it is male-dominated, hierarchical, lacks transparency, or is ideological. In Turkey, such accusations are taken seriously. Nevertheless, if we extend our perspectives, we may see that many secular, liberal, and even irreligious institutions share these qualities. When I asked one student what it was like to be part of the movement, to be taken in, supported, motivated, and perhaps "placed" in society once his studies were through, he replied, "If you are a Muslim, it is easy."

Social capital is vital in constructing types of social collectivism within the family as well as how an entire society may look to organise itself. However, there are some restrictions to consider. Social connections with people who are too like each other can be a source of negative social capital. Immediate within-in-group self-interests take precedence, putting greater aspirations of outreach, with inclusivity and tolerance at risk. Members of the group are supported, but non-members find it difficult to join due to various barriers to entrance. Furthermore, while members of a group enjoy some liberties, there are also rites and obligations that bind the individual to the group, which may or may not appeal overall. Islamic movements do not have to operate in this manner. Although "there is no compulsion in religion," certain localised group formations may become constrained by even more localised ethno-cultural and socio-political goals, jeopardising the aims of the larger movement. It then leads to many conflicts for authenticity, representation, and authority, as well as the power struggles that arise because of such challenges. The Gülen Movement struggled on some levels, yet its progress exceeded its setbacks. However, the risks persist, just as they do in wider society, when collectivist fervour can lead to excessive ethno-nationalism characterised by selective historical memory, political aspirations, or even religio-cultural passion. Islam teaches us ordinary humans to see beyond ourselves and engage with our human brothers and sisters as "peoples, tribes, and nations that we have yet to know better." Narrower ethnic, cultural, and political motivations, on the other hand, can drown the essence of the message behind the rhetoric of a broader social appeal. It also ends the possibility of creative individualism or autonomous critical inquiry, both of which can be harmful to everyone. A healthy balance must be supported at all levels, and Islam has numerous precepts to ensure that it is achieved in practice.

❖

In many ways, Europe would not exist if it were not for Islam. Because of increasing power from the Islamic world, particularly the Ottomans, as late as the eighteenth century, an assortment of nations that were, and still are, at odds with each other were grouped together. During and after their colonial heydays, and following the tragedy of World War II, they have more recently organised as a union of quasi-Christian states keeping certain principles, freedoms, and rights, as well as a neoclassical economic hegemony that protects their own primarily. Historically, as Islam spread beyond Arabia at once after the Prophet's death, partly due to the division of the Christian Empire, this same Western Europe became exposed to external assaults. To safeguard an identity as well as a religious system that was dependent on and formed by Islam, Islam was portrayed as a monolithic and immediate Arab-Muslim plague. It resulted in the establishment of the Crusader worldview, which portrayed the Arab as a licentious Saracen, if not an infidel. The Crusades were unsuccessful, although there was significant cross-fertilisation of literature, art, architecture, and culture in general, as well as massive demonisation on both sides. Following the establishment of colonial European powers in the aftermath of their respective industrial revolutions, and following a period of intellectual renaissance, enlightenment, and reformation, economic and political dominance migrated to the west. The east became dependent on the west over time, which taught the east that it was inferior, tyrannical, and untrustworthy. In many aspects, the east now regards the west as decadent, selfish, immoral, and corrupt. Contemporary Islam and Europe are, in fact, functions of one another in terms of how each is perceived and interpreted. Istanbul, known as Constantinople until less than a century ago, is truly the bridge of civilisations, surrounded by 10,000 years of Persian, Greek, Roman, and Ottoman history. However, one rapidly realises that the notion of cultures that can be separated into two is somewhat of a fallacy. The visible contrasts across civilisations here are less prominent than the wide range of similarities that unite a large population. Certain political projects are given licence and then credibility by emphasising differences rather than commonalities. The truth is that there are few cultural distinctions. More troublesome are broader differences that are the result of political and economic forces.

Parts of the Islamic world are currently suffering as a result of various internal issues relating to development at various levels, but what made it strong in the eyes of many, with the world's leading educational institutions in places such as Baghdad, Samarkand, Isfahan, and Cordoba, to name a few, was the concept of Islam. The Qur'an can and is interpreted in a variety of ways by individuals who study and learn from it, and all these viewpoints had a significant role in constructing Islamic civilisations that were world centres, from the Mughals, Ottomans, Saffavids, and Andalusians. The intellectual stream of learning and wisdom that flows from the Qur'an inspired these civilisations, and in response, a European project arose. Islam inspired the likes of Ibn Khaldun, Ibn Sina, Ibn Rushd, and Al-Ghazali, whose writing and thinking had a tremendous influence on the newly formed Europe. Today, though, Europe has forgotten that its nearest neighbour was also its closest teacher. As the United States is still the world's greatest geopolitical force, Pax Americana has achieved its pinnacle, having been established only 250 years ago following a violent civil war in which the South was supported by the English. Scientific racism, which appeared in the nineteenth century and culminated in the Nazi holocaust programme, ensured that the darker-skinned people of the so-called backward civilisations of the east remained so in popular literature, mainstream culture, high politics, and the media both then and now. These inclinations gradually faded because of the west's era of self-discovery following the devastation of World War II, as well as the robust civil and human rights movements that arose in a progressive late-1960s time period in certain western contexts. Western Europe is currently stalling as a political and economic project, with significant social and cultural disparities among the major participants in European politics. However, Islam is still a source of concern for many people. It has had a tremendous impact on Turkey's admission into the EU and will continue to do so. In the current period, the western neoclassical economic hegemonic mode is ineffective in finding broader social stability and cohesion for the people, institutions, and structures that comprise these nations and governments. Too reliant on the financial services sector, with manufacturing often outsourced to third-party providers in the Far East, the economic foundation is fragile and highly susceptible to price-inflation bubble effects, erratic business cycles, and geopolitical advances to the east that always backfire. The world now is different from it was after the end of World War II.

All these concerns have resulted in the creation and then entrenchment of the problem of Islamophobia, which is a re-establishment of pre-existing Orientalism but enhanced to include an array of new characters in the negative construction and imagination of Islam or Muslims. This Islamophobic experience may be found all over Western Europe and, increasingly, in the United States. There are issues in the media, politics, popular culture, film, journalism, literature, and even computer games; however, there is also the issue of Occidentalism. Muslims across the world are guilty of simplifying, reducing, objectifying, and maligning non-Muslims, especially when the premise is European or Christian. This is where Muslims' Muslimness must be strengthened by becoming more open, active, and tolerant of others. We are all human beings, and there is only one race—the human race. It is possible to have unity within diversity as well as diversity within unity.

◇

Thinking about the linkages between the social and the cultural leads to a spiritual perspective: What is the spirit of a sociologist who studies social and cultural relations in communities and economies? Is it the subconscious of those who cannot separate their heads from their hearts and view them as one—even as the soul? Is it a rudimentary biologically-evolutionary psychological trick to keep us simple humans from becoming nihilistic while also providing us with a feeling of purpose and direction in our otherwise "nasty, brutish, short" existence that we all have on this physical earth? How can we be optimistic about religions when historians, archaeologists, anthropologists, and modern psychoanalytic thinkers argue that religion is a mere invention of human need in a struggle for existence where resources are limited, possibilities are limited, and our existence is transient? Although modern hypothetico-deductive science undoubtedly aids in asking fundamental questions about who we are and what we must all do, enormous gaps exist. Regardless of how much public intellectuals try to demystify the concept of God by confusing ordinary people with science and philosophy, religion, especially in this case, Islam, clearly delivers to its thriving band of global adherents. These are instruction manuals on how to think about responsibilities and roles in life and in expectation of a life beyond death, however that may be perceived or imagined. There are moral rules, ethical principles, and philosophical concerns that go beyond our immediate and obvious needs and desires. Being a social thinker who is critical of all parts of society is consistent with being a critical-thinking Muslim if we have an open view of the world and are not afraid of being challenged about what we believe about ourselves and who we are or are not. Islam encourages us to be critical thinkers who ask probing questions and look for equally probing solutions. Furthermore, it provides us with the energy and space to focus on an intellectualism defined by many experiences and perspectives, rather than being trapped in specific worldviews or ideological dogmatism. Every advancement in our social and cultural existence poses new obstacles and needs a deeper examination of what humankind must achieve well. Islam is not about ceremonies and rituals, though these are significant aspects of the religion's codification for certain people, but about what people do and how they relate to one another as part of the struggle for (co)existence and comprehensive human development.

We all live in the same world and have a common history. We are also on a single planet in a single universe. I am reminded of a trip I took to Western Australia in late 2007. Our car was stopped on the way back from a farm around ninety kilometres inside the mainland from Perth, and the driver urged us all to get out. I was half asleep and unaware of what was going on around me. My French, Indian, and Australian colleagues were as perplexed as I was. We were instructed to gaze up as soon as we went outside. I discovered a gorgeous night sky with an unlimited number of sparkling stars glistening in the darkness. I had never seen the sky like that before, and as I peered at the Milky Way, I felt as if I could reach out and touch this hovering twisted cloud. It made me feel quite insignificant. A small speck in the scheme of things vastly grander than my meagre life. For religionists, the origin of our cosmos is no accident of atoms, and while theories of human evolution or the Big Bang are not un-Islamic, there are few observable and quantitative differences between religion and science. These are not distinct routes to information, knowledge, or wisdom. Others who employ pseudo-science to "prove" the Qur'an are just as guilty as those who want to use science to completely reject the concept of God. Both have been significantly influenced by the other. If we separate what are instruments for survival from what are tools for thinking about the cosmos in which we live, we can see how religion may inspire and encourage thinking minds. However, if we are too intricately connected with a single knowledge system that leaves no room for ambiguity or uncertainty, there is a risk that we may accept too easily and think for ourselves too infrequently. But, no matter how much one can wax lyrical about the virtues of religious faith, and in this case Islam, which is viewed by some as a complete system of economic development, education, governance, justice, and equality in an ideal world, Islam has been politicised by all, including Muslims, particularly those who still suffer from an inferiority complex based on years of colonialism and its aftermath. We must all find a happy medium.

◈

There are still considerable challenges in the field of social research. With all the attention paid to Muslims by think tanks, policymakers, research councils, and even individual academics, little or no research is being conducted on the role of society. In certain situations, there is still an Orientalist gaze that supports the idea of Muslims as objects rather than people in this context. As a result, the primary research questions are inverted. The issues are not always about Islam and Muslims, but how dominant western nations manage minorities, which include Muslims. The fascination with the exotic minority serves to support the status quo. It has persisted despite all contemporary anti-discrimination initiatives. Leaving out the whiteness in modern anti-Muslimness completely misses many of the genuine issues. Instead, Islam is homogenised as a single worldwide religion, with a focus on terrorism, extremism, gender problems, and cultural dynamics, all of which are a result of minorities being treated as if they are still temporary visitors in a nation far apart from anything they could know. It is a modern-day manifestation of age-old Orientalism and a function of post-imperial civilisations.

Over the years, I have had the opportunity to thoroughly consider the nature of my admiration for Barelwi Islam, which is what the majority of traditional British Pakistanis, particularly the Azad Kashmiri people, follow, and apply. My relationship with Islam is such that some would describe me as a "Muslim," in that I fully value the global religion's various intellectual contributions as well as the richness and diversity of Islamic traditions as important sources of knowledge and inspiration, but I am lapsed in my ability to support it fully. I keep a level of association with my community of origin, mostly to keep certain cultural relationships. I am open to all Islamic traditions because they all have something to offer humanity in terms of increased Islamic consciousness. I am also open to different religions as systems of personal belief or activity, as well as how they reflect on learning, knowledge, and action for the greater good of humanity. Many people, however, are not always able to discern their pathways with any precision or clarity. And this is often the source of the ailment. Many Muslims have moved away from their cultural roots in search of a more radicalised form of Islam that provides them with an individual and collective political purpose as a means of figuring out answers that are local, global, and cosmic. We have seen all too clearly how these violent and self-destructive effects affect us all. Other young Muslims secularise to the point that their appreciation of Islam becomes so watered down that it borders on apostasy for hardliners. In some situations, these individuals may be referred to as "cultural Muslims." Intolerance and bigotry are huge issues for all of us, and they are not limited to "angry dark-bearded men" or "apparently submissive tent-clad women." I will continue to value the merits of being open-minded while still being a critical believer in the reasoning of faith(s) in dynamic cultures.

20

The End of History
(Again)

*Civilized society is perpetually menaced with disintegration through
the primary hostility of men towards one another,*
Sigmund Freud

*A country is considered the more civilised the more the wisdom and
efficiency of its laws hinder a weak man from becoming too weak
and a powerful one too powerful,*
Primo Levi

*Islam's borders are bloody and so are its innards. The fundamental
problem for the West is not Islamic fundamentalism. It is Islam, a
different civilisation whose people are convinced of the superiority of
their culture and are obsessed with the inferiority of their power,*
Samuel P. Huntington

There is a big emphasis on the idea that humanity has reached a tipping point. One of the bloodiest centuries in history was the twentieth century. As the old European powers turned their attention to each other, great world wars erupted, killing tens of millions of young men. As the same old European empires lost their grip on distant areas, they often left behind shattered regimes. Today, as I look around the world, I feel as though I am surrounded by an incessant clamour of strife and turmoil, with only a few true instances where there is still hope. Social differences are deeper than they have ever been, both globally and inside most of the world's countries. Politically, there has been a shift toward economic marketisation, and we are now all consumers. This consumer culture pervades both a sense of personal identity and a concept of how life should be lived.

In early 2011, I had the enormous pleasure of spending five or so stimulating days with a range of bright graduate students and professors from the more well-known east coast universities of the United States, namely Harvard, Princeton, Cornell, and New York University, at a conference in the Swiss Alps. I was invited because I was acquainted with the husband of the director of the institution that hosted the event. The two-day intensive discussions focused on history and religion in history. I realised, towards the end of the last session, that I had been missing a trick. Grand gestures and strong remarks received a lot of attention, but little or none of it was supported by empirical study. As a social scientist, the "variables" of history and religion mean distinct things to me in that people who see religion do so by personal choice of a belief system or because they are driven to it for ethical and moral reasons. From my perspective, a religious person is still a category. They have limited agency outside of the manner of individual and communal religious behaviour conditioned and contextualised by an opportunity structure that rationalises the consequences of status, organisation, and authority in satisfying the requirements of a community. Some researchers were concerned that I was solely sociologically motivated and influenced by scholars such as Marx, Weber, and Durkheim, and that I was only interested in social facts, status, and class structure. When I started thinking about history, I gave myself even more headaches. Surely, all of history is the historian's subject because we can never know all of the facts surrounding an event or a person at any given time. History is about remembering but also about forgetting. Furthermore, if we go to the past to obtain lessons for today, we typically find that we humans are a restricted set of people, even though we occasionally produce magic, at the heights of civilisation. The Greeks, Persians, Romans, Arabs, Ottomans, and others carried out incredible things for humanity at their pinnacle, but on the way down, many of these same civilisations fell from within or without, frequently leaving a path of destruction and exploitation in their wake. So, what do we genuinely learn from our past for our human existence now when we, as a species, continue to make the same mistakes repeatedly? If religions are viewed as social organisational forces in the context of the obstacles faced by civilisations across millennia, a great deal about the physical lived experience of history can be deduced. Religion, on the other hand, means a lot more to people whose lives are shaped by it in so many complicated and profound ways. One thing is clear: self-serving religionists will rewrite history to confirm certain assertions. Historians constantly rewrite history.

My own motivation for attending the conference was to illustrate how things are currently growing a lot worse for a variety of previously marginalised ethno-religious minorities, who are increasingly being identified as the all-encompassing problems for sophisticated secular liberal post-modern nations. My point was that this was a fact that represented the hyper-cyclical nature of these countries' migration, citizenship, identity, and diversity issues. In times of wealth, multiculturalism is regarded favourably. Differences across populations are not considered a good thing at times of major risks to society, which could have a negative economic impact for a decade or more. Indeed, they are viewed as more than just a burden, but as the primary cause of the downturn.

◈

Although it is necessary to try to focus on a larger global perspective, the role of the United States is of particular significance. While the "clash of civilisations" theory has been played out over the last two decades or so, we have also seen the development of the eastern world now returning to worldwide domination, as it was many thousands of years ago. The so-called Asian tiger economies were thriving in the 1990s, with Indonesia and Malaysia, for example, experiencing unprecedented economic expansion and growth. While the western world was engrossed in the "war on terror" and global stagnation followed in the latter part of the last decade, China and India have appeared as superpowers to compete directly with the economies of the United States and Western Europe. As a result of the western world's economic crisis, the Chinese hold a huge part of the United States' debt. This provides them with enormous power over specific currency and trade issues. Furthermore, nations such as Brazil and India can compete on a global scale, putting significant pressure on the western economic paradigm. This shift in the global economic order is likely to continue, and India, China, and Brazil will be among the world's main economies over the next 20 to 30 years. What it does is put pressure on the United States in its role as a global policeman, which it emphasises through its activities as a member of the United Nations, the International Monetary Fund, the World Bank, and NATO, as well as through its cultural influence over the world through institutions such as Hollywood and the impact of its global media outreach potential.

If anything, the last several decades have shown the erosion of the United States' worldwide economic supremacy. It is an ironic twist that the United States has found itself unable to compete in its efforts to spread freedom, liberty, democracy, and capitalism to the rest of the globe. What is more important is that inside the United States, there are certain inequalities that are profoundly entrenched. It leads to the dominance of a few who work tirelessly to further their own interests while becoming more disconnected from the rest of American society and the rest of the globe. With other economies throughout the globe increasingly showing their potential for efficiency, marketisation, and ingenuity, what was viewed as the basic Americanisation of global society has receded. There has been a lot of attention focused on Joe Biden finding a more open-ended geopolitical strategy, but there is still a lot to be done to undo most of the harm done by American foreign policy over the previous two decades, particularly after the fall of the former Soviet empire. It is true that the United States has been reaching into the Middle East for the better part of the twentieth century for a variety of reasons, including the need to keep market penetration as well as to ensure the availability of fossil fuels as reserves in the United States become increasingly vulnerable to depletion. But what comes next?

Much of the 2000s were focused on the United States' efforts to bring freedom and democracy to various parts of the world, but for a brief moment, the events of the Arab awakening demonstrated that Arabs throughout the Middle East were not willing to accept any further abuse of power, injustice in society, illegitimacy of authority based on years of undemocratic rule, and the huge social divides that had been created between elites and the masses. It resulted in a demographically youthful Middle East, effectively dethroning powerful rulers who had been in power for more than four decades in certain cases. What this meant for the United States is that the Middle East was no longer in the hands of chosen leaders but is instead in the hands of local interests. Rather, it was due to the whims of the people (or at least temporarily). The end of history thesis advanced by several neoconservative scholars at the close of the 1980s has ironically exposed the end of American history. Much of this is due to dissatisfaction with American foreign policy as well as a function of the media, which I refer to as information and communication technology, particularly the liberalisation of satellite and television in many Muslim-majority countries. Citizens now have greater access to many sources of media than ever before, including social media. This has resulted in a level of awareness that would not have been possible in the past. People can critically interact with a wide range of themes by taking part in the creation of that media, for example, through formats such as Twitter and Facebook, as well as visual manifestations such as YouTube and the emergence of independent broadcasting. Hegemony is predicated on the concentration of economic, military, political, and cultural power in the hands of a few, but the availability of the media in all its forms has also had an impact on the collapse of US influence. The western economic neoliberal framework's institutions and procedures have provided opportunity structures for the eastern part of the globe to respond to the issues that they have presented.

However, it should be noted that America is still a young country. The United States of America as we know it today arose as a result of the influx of Puritans from England and other European discoverers who set about eradicating the land's indigenous native people. Imperialism and colonialism are embedded in the DNA of its people, from those who were oppressors and through their rule and authority, to those who have been subject to its forces directly and indirectly because of the ongoing forces of racism and discrimination that affect the lived experiences of various minority groups. Although it is easy to show the decline in the extent of American economic hegemony in the context of how the country's foreign and domestic policy is used to maintain its position, there has also been a range of important and valuable contributions made from which the rest of the world has benefited. Whether we like it or not, the greatest universities in the world are unquestionably found in the United States. This is defined by the enormous resources available in these institutions to offer the best opportunities for academics and scholars to conduct research, ask independent probing questions, and work within the realms of others whose goals are to advance all matters of the human, social, and physical sciences. They still have enthusiasm, passion, and a devotion to technology and understanding the world. There are also many people who advocate for fairness, justice, tolerance, and liberty as ideals that are beneficial to humanity rather than the opposite. We must remember that the labour of the good is often overlooked and undervalued in comparison to the work of the wicked, who are few but can also be among the most readily heard. When there is a lack of cohesiveness, the extremes are heard loudest.

❁

In reaction to challenges to their collective hegemony, various nations have had to discover means to organise. This response was political, ideological, and cultural in nature. The tables have shifted over the years as the Islamic world has declined and the Western European model has risen. The Muslim nations suffer from a sense of inferiority acquired as part of the colonial endeavour, whereas Western European economies became strong and galvanised together to create the globe in the eighteenth and nineteenth centuries. With the experiences of international migration and transnational communities, as well as the forces of globalisation and the role of technology in bringing people together and speeding up forms of communication between them, the old distinctions of East and West, Europe and Asia, or Christianity and Islam, are now weaker than they have ever been in history.

Although regional boundaries have faded and the global economy is more intertwined than it has ever been, injustices persist within these linkages. There is little question that a worldwide polity of empire persists, part of which lingers in the psyche of the Western European imagination, while other parts pertain to how the United States has seen its place in the globe up until recently. This worldwide imperial game is heavily influenced by the European Enlightenment and its sequel, European Romanticism. The exoticisation of the eastern world resulted in Orientalism and scientific racism. This legacy lives on in the migration of Muslim minorities to Western Europe today. Nonetheless, the image of Islam in the minds of European constructionists persists, influencing how Europe views the "other" and, more crucially, how Europe sees itself. The United States, as the twentieth century's preeminent global hegemon, rationalised the eastern world through the same prism that characterised European beliefs of the eastern world. It is still present in elements of academia, as well as government institutions, global governance, multinational enterprises, and attitudes toward immigrant groups and ethnic minorities.

Despite these issues, some pundits and intellectuals continue to advocate for Europe to remain a Christian entity. Because Europeans were heavily involved in murdering each other during the twentieth century, economic unification in the face of Pax Americana was unquestionably needed to remain competitive locally and worldwide. Historically, the concept of an enlightened Europe arose when it effectively abandoned fundamentalist religion in favour of science and industry. But it was also about individualism supplanting collectivism and forgetting its long shared history with Islam, which formed in response to perceived challenges from this Islam, where the age of discovery was more about slavery and where colonisers took over Muslim lands and exploited every last drop of goodness from them, leaving newly-created, artificially constructed nations in complete disarray.

Today's Europe requires immigration. The facts, whether liked or disliked, speak for themselves. Without immigration, Europe's future is dubious. Despite the challenges, Muslims in Western Europe continue to try contribute. When they are confined by bigotry and violence, they build communities that mostly contain their own, becoming more visible in the process and confirming notions that they not only do not belong, but are in fact foreign to us. The language of lazy politicians who would rather outlaw headscarves—a piece of fabric—is "they are not us" and "we are not them." Ironically, the finest of progressive Islamic and Christian ideas originated exactly when the two shared the most, but by pushing apart for self-interested and inward-looking motives among the dominant and subjugated, Islam and Christianity have been split, possibly forever, unless we are all wiser.

◈

What do contemporary civilisations' experiences, Europe's origins and growth, and the advancement of western capitalism have to say about the essence of humanity? Hegel first proposed the concept of history as a dialectical process, which Marx later expanded on. There is little new in the work of Francis Fukuyama, who sprang to prominence in the late 1980s with his "end of history" theory, which claimed that western capitalism, which had championed the old-age fight between communist and market economies, was no longer relevant. In the fourteenth century, an important figure in classical Muslim history, Ibn Khaldun, wrote about the emergence and collapse of civilisations. The Islamic world was in decline at the time, both within and outside. Because of Mongol invasions from the East and Christian powers from the West, several Islamic countries began to crumble from within. Even though Ibn Khaldun is frequently removed from the canons of sociology that are taught in departments across the western world, there is no question that he is one of the most influential thinkers in the social sciences. Sociology, as we know it now, was primarily founded by a group of European scientists around the turn of the twentieth century. Many people consider Marx to be a philosopher, political scientist, and sociologist, yet it was Max Weber and Emile Durkheim who set up sociology as a distinct study within the social sciences. Many of these European writers conducted their studies during the heights of European empire and colonialism, as well as near the conclusion, when the ill effects of capitalism could be seen at home. The negative impacts of industrial societies have a wide range of consequences for considerations of class structure, status, consciousness, mobility, and religion. These sociologists also formalised many methods of conceptualising the social world via the perspective of methodologies such as positivism, rationalism, and empiricism, as well as their connections to policy. In the study of the social world, sociology has a nineteenth-century background, although its scientific analysis dates back far deeper into classical history. Spencer, Pareto, Rousseau, and Comte were all influential thinkers, but no one contributed more to the study of the social world than Ibn Khaldun.

His broad idea posits that the essence of humanity decides human wants. They are the fundamental necessities that humankind has around it. A man needs to eat food to survive, but a man also needs clothing on his back and a shelter over his head. These are some basic requirements for human survival. As these fundamental desires are satisfied, man looks for more. His aspirations shift to supporting his mental growth through the acquisition of information and skills. As a result, a set of secondary requirements appears. Tools are created to increase humanity's ability to create the commodities needed to sustain life. The next phase is to construct a method that leads to the development of civilisation. However, to attain civilisational growth, humanity would have to give up its need for luxury items. A shift is made away from immediate consumption and toward furthering the development of civilisational instruments. Great civilisations can advance through these mechanisms. Members of society must fulfil reciprocal commitments to meet the demands of production as part of the process of constructing civilisations. This can lead to specialisation and reliance among humans. This also happens in a cyclical dynamic when individuals from rural cultures migrate to the urban domain, which later concentrates on specialisation and interdependence. All of this encourages greater intellectual and organisational growth, and a cyclical equilibrium is kept by the methodical leadership of the people. However, when the leadership loses touch with the masses by indulging in increasingly lavish commodities, a breakdown in human-to-human interactions arises, which can lead to resistance and, finally, rejuvenation. According to Ibn Khaldun, there is a spiritual connection that links individuals together to guarantee that the greater good is realised. These spiritual commandments may come from an Islamic perspective, but they might apply to any religious group. He was able to figure out that societies are forms of ecological existence in which living creatures undergo forms of birth, development, degeneration, and finally death, for a multitude of universal in-nature reasons. He was able to formally correlate the pinnacles of any specific social existence with the balance of luxury and necessity products, but with decline beginning at the point at which immigrant groups would be necessary to supply the labour demands of nations reluctant to give up their desire for luxuries. His fundamental purpose in his study was to characterise the variety of economic, environmental, social, and psychological elements that exist in the progress of human life. The ties between groups and group sentiments, known now as social cohesion (*asabiya*), set the circumstances for the birth of new upgraded civilisations (*imran*) and the power structures that accompany them.

There are significant connections to be seen between Ibn Khaldun's thinking on civilisation and how we would think of European or western culture today. As a result of the colonial enterprise, Western European countries evolved a distinct set of refined tastes and preferences. Part of this was due to the consumption of unusual cuisines, but it was also due to a desire for luxury items such as fine clothes, better housing, and other material desires. Even though the Western European model began to erode around the beginning of the twentieth century, the necessity to give up the desire for luxury items has not evolved. Given the existing inequities throughout the world and the unique power structures that were centred in the West, the authorities chose to retain existing levels of consumption and use the physical and human resources of the previously colonial world to sustain existing patterns. The fundamental paradigm has not altered, and the rest of the world has joined it. This distinctive way of life has its drawbacks, causing worry inside nations owing to deep-seated disparities and class warfare, while beyond nations, huge international firms use competitive techniques to push nation against nation in the search of profits. One of the ongoing reasons for certain sections of the world's persistent underdevelopment is the behaviour of huge international corporations that engage with governmental authorities to decide preferential treatment while abusing human capital.

This "machine brain" concept of economic growth and development is still trapped in the late nineteenth century. Even the names used to describe the functions reflect a mentality that arose because of the reliance on industry. We talk about "overheating" economies, the need to "gear" finance, or fiscal "pumping." There is a lot of talk about the "oiling" of the industry's "machinery." In many aspects, there is a need to return to Ibn Khaldun's notions about communities being like gardens. Large trees in one corner may make the garden appear attractive, but they draw most of the water in their roots while the rest of the garden remains lifeless. The concept of a progressive tax system may be applicable here. Weeds must be pulled out sometimes because they are toxic to the growth of other plants in the garden. This might be interpreted as a type of corporate regulation. Furthermore, there is an aesthetic impact owing to the diversity of many shrubs, plants, and flowers, each producing their own dynamic. A garden requires continual care and balance. The world's gardens are in full disorder under the current environment. One of the primary causes of this is the persistent emphasis on economic rather than social, cultural, or spiritual elements of human existence. Therefore, some think that the western world has achieved its pinnacle. It has devoured the rest of the globe, which has remained servile rather than critically assessing its state. As a result of this process, internal divisions become more pronounced. Those who have more desire even more. Meanwhile, those who do not have much have less than they have ever had.

Dramatic adjustments in how we think about what is vital for the welfare of humanity are needed, yet creativity is severely lacking, and the effects are such that the wider world suffers. It's as though humanity hasn't accomplished anything more than the bare necessities. A sea change is required, and it must happen soon since time is running out. Despite rapidly advancing technical knowledge and ability, as well as the continual discovery of new natural resources, the world's population is growing at an alarming rate, and the resources accessible to us all are becoming increasingly limited. Civilisational crises are a manufactured phenomenon. They are not an unavoidable conclusion. It is up to the rest of humankind to realise that the end of history is still a long way off.

Postscript

The hardest thing of all is to find a black cat in a dark room,
especially if there is no cat,
Confucius

Don't be satisfied with stories, how things have gone with others.
Unfold your own myth,
Rumi

Learn from the mistakes of others. You can never live long enough
to make them all yourself,
Groucho Marx

Concerns about what were believed to be problematic inclinations on the part of Muslims in the west, particularly in Britain, were increasingly viewed as a consequence of religion per se in the mid-2000s. The "war on terror" began in late 2001, the war in Iraq began in early 2003, there were challenges concerning veiled women in Turkey, and the Cartoons Affair sparked widespread worldwide outrage. Much of the Muslim reaction to a perceived sense of Islam under attack was to resurrect more archaic notions of Islamic identity, which historically arose in response to physical, psychological, and political attacks on Islam from the religion's start to the period when European colonialists gradually began to overrun Islam in Africa and Asia. However, while this response on the part of Muslims is based on some gut reaction to perceived and actual persecution, the larger issue is Islamophobia in wider society and the convergence of several fears about differences in society that focus on the immigrant-outsider, the demolisher of multiculturalism-cohesion, and the terrorist-security threat, all conveniently packaged into a single narrative.

The Rushdie Affair of 1989 exposed wider fears about identity, the law, blasphemy, and the devotion of British citizens, whether it be to the Qur'an or to the monarch, to put it simply. Muslims, on the other hand, feel completely British, are more likely to have non-Muslim friends and relatives than non-Muslims, and are willing to work hard to integrate into society, valuing education, technology, and freedom. Muslims in the United Kingdom view themselves as a lot more British than common perception would imply. Having a feeling of Britishness is not the issue, nor are ideals linked with "loyalty" or national identity in general. Muslims are consumers in society, from visiting high-street supermarkets, shops, and fast food chains to buying German and Japanese cars, tweeting, blogging, or generating internet content. They are producers in society, ranging from manufacturers to industrialists, designers, and innovators. British Muslims, who are divided along ethnic, social, and sectarian lines (as are other religious communities), are as integrated as they might be, at least among younger British-born generations.

However, integration is a complicated subject. Briefly, it is the idea that minorities respect the rule of the country and contribute to and engage in the national social model to the best of their abilities. In exchange, the state provides protection against discrimination and human rights breaches while acknowledging and accepting diversity. It is a two-way street, not a cul-de-sac, as some may perceive assimilation to be. When a lack of integration is paired with societal pressures, the conditions for radicalism are created. This is not only regretful, but also terribly distressing for individuals who consider themselves to be fully British and entirely Muslim. Most Muslims, on the other hand, are law-abiding, peace-loving, hardworking, and religiously balanced while being ardent and loyal subjects of His Majesty. The most obvious difficulty is that, while Muslims feel British and wish to be British as much as they can, the true concern is whether Muslims feel accepted as British. This inquiry is likely to indicate that minorities may strive to fulfil all of the aspirations of wanting to integrate into society, and they almost always do, but they are not always accepted. Granted, it is far better in the United Kingdom than in most other parts of Western Europe, but it is far from ideal.

❦

In terms of sociological research, a subject that developed after 9/11, and notably 7/7, was the question of "who speaks" for British Muslims. The underlying concern is whether Muslims can be regarded seriously by the academy in terms of their reputation for doing "excellent" research on Muslims. It is one of the themes that could only be discussed in the UK or even the US, the latter of which has recently developed its own Islamophobic connotations by "keeping an eye" on Muslims in academia. Muslim-on-Muslim social research raises myriad concerns for both the researcher and the research subject, centred on power, subjectivity, and identity. However, in the end, it comes down to the questions of integrity, transparency, and ontology and epistemology. That is how a Muslim social researcher figures out their position based on their personal experiences, the nature of their relationship with the research, the larger socio-political milieu, and how researchers and the research conceptualise and rationalise it all. More recently, the notion that Muslims cannot conduct research on Muslims has been used as a rod to beat Muslim academics in the UK higher education (HE) sectors in the present atmosphere, owing to various concerns about security, fear, and even academic envy. Without a doubt, Muslim academics must work harder to advance, and even when they succeed, they are easy targets due to their visibility. Even 'white Muslim' academics work in the UK academy but do not notify their Muslim colleagues in various research groups that they are Muslim for fear of retaliation within the ethnic category or from HE institutions. There has been a lot of research done on Muslims who face various disadvantages in the UK HE labour market (the HE sector is extremely competitive, and they have to be good, but these "good" Muslims tend to be better qualified, work harder, have more and higher quality outputs, but they also have to juggle more balls than most). There is no scarcity of non-Muslims who do research on Muslims. Do they know or do more since they are further removed from the situation? Is it true that Muslims conduct more research on Muslims than non-Muslims? The response is that it simply relies on how the study is conducted, the honesty of the researchers, and the nature of the research project's contribution to a broader knowledge of the case being reported on. Nonetheless, there is no shortage of "senior" white academics who hire "junior" (non-white) Muslims to be their "eyes and ears" in the research process, only to be quickly forgotten, allowing senior white academics to gain the upper hand and ensure the perpetuation of a racialised academic power structure. The issues surrounding Muslims in the academy are all about institutional biases, existing prejudices (people with PhDs can still be prejudiced), power (middle-aged, middle-class, English men), authority (production and ownership of the machinery of HE as well as the structures of inclusion and exclusion within it), and extensive networking (within self-selecting elitist groups), rather than a focus on the individual and their apparent ability to conduct research on Muslims. The researcher's abilities are just as crucial as how they communicate their views. The tools are the same for everybody, yet the game is not fair, let alone the means or the ends.

◇

We are, undoubtedly, living in interesting times. But what do we know about these challenges on a local and global scale, and how can we prepare for the repercussions of these tremendous changes that appear to be occurring before our eyes? The Organization of Islamic Cooperation (OIC) Member States now have approximately 338 million young people aged 15–24, accounting for 17.9% of their total population. As a result, OIC Member States host 28 percent of the world's total youth, a figure that is expected to rise to 30.7 percent by 2030. In the Middle East, North Africa, and South Asia, half of all Muslims are under the age of 25. They face several fundamental issues, including development, education, gender equality, intercultural and religious relations, leadership, law and human rights, dialogue and coexistence, a general lack of coherence, and the presentation of constant conflict in domestic and international media. These unresolved issues must be addressed to ensure regional stability and coherence, as well as a confident, articulate, and engaged youth. This should be obvious, but what happens to young people in the Muslim Arab world reflects the continuous pressures from current difficulties, the consequences of which will have substantial ramifications for policy, the economy, and society.

One specific issue that is the importance of ICT (internet communication technologies) in youth involvement, participation, and development cannot be viewed as the sole realm of current politics. When access to ICT is restricted, there are constraints to its use as a tool for change. If some states so want, Facebook and Twitter may be taken down in an instant. Nonetheless, there is no doubt that these localised forms of political mobilisation have had a worldwide influence. We must not overlook the events surrounding the "American Autumn," in which young people organised aggressive challenges to the current dominant order by "taking over" public areas and demonstrating in huge numbers, despite crackdowns or violent retaliation by several governments. Similar concerns exist in parts of South Asia. In Pakistan, there has been social unrest and political turmoil for an extended period. Democracy, political involvement, and participation continue to face obstacles. This is being evaluated, but what is still crucial in the current moment is the character of the media environment in which many of the complicated disputes are aired and analysed, as well as the involvement of a wide range of diverse interest groups and political manoeuvres. In Pakistan, the urban elite read English news, while the rural majority read Urdu news. Critical journalists are in grave danger of harming their own safety and security. Pakistan has long been regarded as one of the most dangerous locations in the world for journalists, both domestic and international. Most Pakistanis are under the age of twenty-five, as is the case across the Muslim world. The importance of ICT in influencing young political, cultural, and social action and mobilisation will become increasingly essential in shaping Pakistan's future.

There are complicated difficulties at play in Western Europe, where over 30 million Muslims live as minorities. Islamophobia and anti-Muslim discourse are prevalent in a variety of new and conventional media outlets. They take many forms, including anti-immigrant sentiment, the persistent projection of conflict and bloodshed, a concentration on fundamentalist strains, the ongoing "othering" of the existing Orientalised "other," misogynism, and the belief that Muslims are anti-human and anti-universalist. These are substantial exogenous reasons, but there are also endogenous difficulties of internal intergenerational alienation, which lead to expanding cultural divides, economic immobility, and societal pressures because of the worldwide "decline of masculinity," both inside and beyond. Nonetheless, there is potential for constructive transformation. Young Muslims in the Arab world and South Asia demand demilitarisation, de-tribalisation, and an end to quasi-feudalism. They advocate political empowerment for all, regional autonomy, deregulation and liberalisation of the media, inward investment and entrepreneurial development, including micro-financing, and a net decrease in wealth disparities through active and effective social policies. Young Muslims in Western Europe desire equal opportunities to take part in society as equal citizens of the countries in which they live and work. Furthermore, given the space afforded to liberal critical discourses, Western Europe is an opportunity to help define the nature of a forward-thinking Islam at peace with benevolent capitalism, democracy, the rule of law, and human rights, with lessons for both the eastern Muslim world and Muslims in the west. However, the importance of technology and political investment for economic and social progress in the Muslim world cannot be overstated. The problems in the current era are tremendous, yet every struggle is an opportunity. Significant efforts are needed to create social infrastructure, boost access, and guarantee that journalists and authors do not participate in self-censorship. The stability of the whole MENA and South Asia area for future decades is at stake, as the US economy maintains stability, maybe never completely rebounding at all given China's, India's, Brazil's, and other huge nations' massive rise.

However, the situation in the United Kingdom could not be more unpleasant. At the time of writing, there is a genuine risk of a recession because economic growth is low, inflation is high, wages have frozen, unemployment remains high, business confidence is low, and people are genuinely concerned about their jobs and livelihoods in general following Brexit and given the ongoing impact of the global Covid pandemic that has hit Britain harder than its European counterparts. There is also a wild beast of white supremacy, which claims authority over an English-ism that has crumbled in the face of alleged threats from multiculturalism and violent Islamic radicalism among a few young Muslims. The fascist far-right is growing in several other Western European countries, and the challenges are still significant at present, with a political vacuum for a beleaguered white working class cementing the political centres of nations out of touch with the rest of their populations. During an economic slump, tensions, disputes, and discrimination will rise. Meanwhile, societal differences expand, and extremes clash even more. One thing is certain. Europe is confident, but Britain will continue to trundle along with its own deep-seated problems of class, elitism, bourgeois racism, and a definition of Englishness that may be obsolete and even dysfunctional in the current moment.

❖

This book reflects on a half-life journey from my earliest recollections to studying themes that influence me emotionally and intellectually, as well as how I work now as a professor in a nation far from my birthplace. What I provide are my perspectives as a radicalisation studies academic and a Muslim in the West. I say this as a British-born person with Azad Kashmiri parents who is currently teaching and studying in The Hague, the international city of peace and justice. Civilisations rise and fall. Wars and conflicts continue to burn over perceived or actual conceptions of identity or belonging in opposition to those who are viewed in less human terms. Growing up in a hostile environment raises several problems about identity, loyalty, and belonging that continue to trouble us all to this day. Identity, transnationalism, diaspora, and migration are all topics of interest to me, and it is in response to these concerns that I authored this book. That is, to reflect, re-learn, re-think, and enlighten others about the difficulties of life. However, these concerns will not be remedied quickly. As I write, the impact of a devastating global pandemic is still being felt. White supremacy is on the rise. Islamophobia is a huge problem in the global north. My own ancestral village in Azad Kashmir is fast vanishing, with only a few Bachlakran-born people in existence while the adjacent dam raises its waters higher and higher. Backhlakrans in Birmingham flourish as a community within communities, integrating, professionalising, and taking part in society as active citizens as best they can.

Questions of ethnic identity, cohesiveness, and conflict will never go away. We humans are still reasonably primitive and self-interested enough to keep these kinds of difficulties in play all the time. As a social scientist, I am fortunate in that I can identify with specific study issues and debates because of where I come from and what I have seen and experienced. It allows me to have a better understanding of what is going on inside communities and on the ground inside the towns and cities where many people like me still live and work. However, I have seldom written about myself as part of the "story." It has never been about me. This book is an unusual deviation from a well-trodden path. My identity is muddled in the sense that I am a mash-up of everything and nothing. But, to a considerable extent, it does not matter what I think of myself. Instead, who I am is decided by what I do and hence represent. Being a Muslim is more about intent, humility, and character than anything else. My Muslimness provides me with an intellectual perspective on the world and its many unique and intriguing people. Diversity is not a threat. It is an advantage. The sooner we all realise this, the better for all of us.

I hope that this work may aid others on their own path to enlightenment and self-discovery, especially considering the continuous challenges to individual identities and collective belonging.

Further Reading

Chapter 1

Ali, N. (2009). The making of Kashmiri identity. *South Asian Diaspora*, *1*(2), 181-192.

Ali, R. N., Khan, A. A., & Iqbal, A. (2019). Political Consciousness of the Muslims in Jammu and Kashmir State 1846-1947. *Journal of the Research Society of Pakistan*, *56*(1), 15.

Anwar, M. (1979). *The myth of return: Pakistanis in Britain*. Heinemann Educational Publishers.

Ballard, R. (1991). Kashmir crisis: view from Mirpur. *Economic and political weekly*, 513-517.

Bolognani, M. (2014). Visits to the country of origin: how second-generation British Pakistanis shape transnational identity and maintain power asymmetries. *Global Networks*, *14*(1), 103-120.

Choudhury, G.W. (1968) *Pakistan's Relations with India, 1947–1966*, New York: Praeger.

Ellis, P., & Khan, Z. (1998). Diasporic mobilisation and the Kashmir issue in British politics. *Journal of Ethnic and Migration Studies*, *24*(3), 471-488.

Institute of Race Relations (1985). *How Racism Came to Britain*. Institute of Race Relations.

Kalra, V. S. (2019). *From textile mills to taxi ranks: Experiences of migration, labour and social change*. Routledge.

Khan, V. S. (1976). Pakistanis in Britain: perceptions of a population. *New community*, *5*(3), 222-229.

Lamb, A. (1967). Pakistani Kashmir since the 1965 war. *Journal of the Royal Central Asian Society*, *54*(2), 151-155.

Schofield, V. (2021). *Kashmir in conflict: India, Pakistan and the unending war.* Bloomsbury Publishing.

Shaw, A. (2001). Kinship, cultural preference and immigration: consanguineous marriage among British Pakistanis. *Journal of the Royal Anthropological Institute, 7*(2), 315-334.

Snedden, C. (2012). *The Untold Story of the People of Azad Kashmir.* Columbia University Press.

Snedden, C. (2015). *Understanding Kashmir and Kashmiris.* Oxford University Press.

Sökefeld, M., & Bolognani, M. (2011). Kashmiris in Britain: A Political Project or a Social Reality? In *Pakistan and its Diaspora* (pp. 111-131). Palgrave Macmillan, New York.

Tharoor, S. (2018). *Inglorious empire: What the British did to India.* Penguin UK.

Visram, R. (1990). *Ayahs, Lascars and Princes: Indians in 1700-1947.* Pluto.

Chapter 2

Anwar, M. (2002). *Between cultures: continuity and change in the lives of young Asians.* Routledge.

Chambers, C. (2015). Myth of Return Fiction of the 1970s and 1980s:'A bit of this and a bit of that'. In *Britain Through Muslim Eyes* (pp. 189-217). Palgrave Macmillan, London.

Charsley, K. (2013). *Transnational Pakistani connections: Marrying 'back home'.* Routledge.

Dahya, B. (1974). The nature of Pakistani ethnicity in industrial cities in Britain. *Urban ethnicity, 77*(118), 116-128.

Dudrah, R. K. (2006). *Bollywood: sociology goes to the movies.* Sage.

Hussain, S. (2020). Kashmiri imaginings of freedom in the global arenas. In *Kashmir and the Future of South Asia* (pp. 116-138). Routledge.

Khan, V. S. (2017). *Minority families in Britain: support and stress.* Macmillan International Higher Education.

Moore, R., Shuttleworth, A., & Williams, J. (1967). *Race, community and conflict: a study of Sparbrook.* Oxford University Press.

Patterson, S. (1964). *Dark Strangers: A Sociological Study of the Absorption of a Recent West Indian Migrant Group in Brixton*, South London. Indiana University Press.

Rex, J., Moore, R. S., Shuttleworth, A., & Williams, J. (1967). *Race, community and conflict: a study of Sparkbrook*. Oxford University Press, USA.

Rex, J., & Samad, Y. (1996). Multiculturalism and political integration in Birmingham and Bradford. *Innovation: The European Journal of Social Science Research*, 9(1), 11-31.

Rex, J., & Tomlinson, S. (1979). *Colonial immigrants in a British city: a class analysis*. Routledge.

Samad, Y. (2004). Muslim youth in Britain: Ethnic to religious identity. *Muslim Youth in Europe: Typologies of Religious Belonging and Sociocultural Dynamics, Edoardo Agnelli Centre for Comparative Religious Studies, Turin*.

Shaw, A. (2001). Kinship, cultural preference and immigration: consanguineous marriage among British Pakistanis. *Journal of the Royal Anthropological Institute*, 7(2), 315-334.

Wolffe, J. (2012). Fragmented universality: Islam and Muslims. In *The Growth of Religious Diversity-Vol 1* (pp. 133-172). Routledge.

Chapter 3

Bano, S. (2012). *Muslim women and Shari'ah councils: Transcending the boundaries of community and law*. Palgrave Macmillan.

Begg, M., & Brittain, V. (2011). *Enemy Combatant: My Imprisonment at Guantánamo, Bagram, and Kandahar*. The New Press.

Bowen, I. (2014). *Medina in Birmingham, Najaf in Brent: Inside British Islam*. Oxford University Press.

Breen, D. (2018). Critical race theory, policy rhetoric and outcomes: The case of Muslim schools in Britain. *Race Ethnicity and Education*, 21(1), 30-44.

Halstead, M. (2004). An Islamic concept of education. *Comparative education*, 40(4), 517-529.

Hussain, A. (2004). Islamic education: Why is there a need for it?. *Journal of Beliefs & Values*, 25(3), 317-323.

Iqbal, M. (1977). Education and Islam in Britain-a Muslim view. *New Community*, 5(4), 397-404.

RUMINATIONS

Parker-Jenkins, M. (1991). Muslim matters: the educational needs of the Muslim child. *Journal of Ethnic and Migration Studies, 17*(4), 569-582.

Sarwar, G. (1982). *Islam, beliefs and teachings.* Muslim Educational Trust.

Shah, S. (2012). Muslim schools in secular societies: persistence or resistance! *British Journal of Religious Education, 34*(1), 51-65.

Shah, S. (2014). Islamic Education and the UK Muslims: Options and Expectations in a Context of Multi-locationality. *Studies in Philosophy and Education, 33*(3), 233-249.

Shail, R. (Ed.). (2019). *Seventies British Cinema.* Bloomsbury Publishing.

Walker, J. (2017). Rewind, playback: re-viewing the "video boom" in Britain. In *The Routledge Companion to British Cinema History* (pp. 344-353). Routledge.

Werbner, P. (2004). Theorising complex diasporas: purity and hybridity in the South Asian public sphere in Britain. *Journal of ethnic and migration studies, 30*(5), 895-911.

Chapter 4

Bagley, C. (1979). A comparative perspective on the education of black children in Britain. *Comparative Education, 15*(1), 63-81.

Carrington, B. (2010). *Race, sport and politics: The sporting black diaspora.* Sage.

Cole, M. (2004). 'Brutal and stinking' and 'difficult to handle': the historical and contemporary manifestations of racialisation, institutional racism, and schooling in Britain. *Race Ethnicity and Education, 7*(1), 35-56.

Gilroy, P. (2013). *There ain't no black in the Union Jack.* Routledge.

Haley, A. (2016). *Roots: The saga of an American family.* Hachette UK.

Lorna, C. (2017). *From immigrants to ethnic minority: Making black community in Britain.* Routledge.

Maguire, J. A. (1988). Race and position assignment in English soccer: A preliminary analysis of ethnicity and sport in Britain. *Sociology of Sport Journal, 5*(3), 257-269.

Malcolm, D. (2001). 'It's not cricket': Colonial legacies and contemporary inequalities. *Journal of historical sociology, 14*(3), 253-275.

Nayak, A. (2010). Race, affect, and emotion: young people, racism, and graffiti in the postcolonial English suburbs. *Environment and Planning A*, *42*(10), 2370-2392.

Phoenix, A. (2009). De-colonising practices: Negotiating narratives from racialised and gendered experiences of education. *Race Ethnicity and Education*, *12*(1), 101-114.

Race, R. (2005). Analysing the historical evolution of ethnic education policy-making in England, 1965-2005. *Historical Social Research/Historische Sozialforschung*, 176-190.

Tomlinson, S. (1980). The educational performance of ethnic minority children. *New Community*, *8*(3), 213-234.

Tomlinson, S. (2008). Race and education: Policy and politics in Britain: Policy and politics in Britain. McGraw-Hill Education (UK).

Vincent, C., Ball, S., Rollock, N., & Gillborn, D. (2013). Three generations of racism: Black middle-class children and schooling. *British Journal of Sociology of Education*, *34*(5-6), 929-946.

Chapter 5

Ball, S. J. (2012). *Politics and policy making in education: Explorations in sociology*. Routledge.

Bhavnani, R., Mirza, H. S., & Meetoo, V. (2005). *Tackling the roots of racism: Lessons for success*. Policy Press.

Galbraith, J.K. (1963). *Economic Development in Perspective*. Harvard University Press.

Gillborn, D. (1997). Racism and Reform: new ethnicities/old inequalities? *British educational research journal*, *23*(3), 345-360.

Gillborn, D. (2005). Education policy as an act of white supremacy: Whiteness, critical race theory and education reform. *Journal of education policy*, *20*(4), 485-505.

Hall, S. (2021). *The hard road to renewal: Thatcherism and the crisis of the left*. Verso Books.

Jackson, P. (Ed.). (2003). *Race and racism: essays in social geography*. Routledge.

Jacobs, S. (1985). Race, empire and the welfare state: council housing and racism. *Critical Social Policy*, *5*(13), 6-28.

Little, A., & Westergaard, J. (1964). The trend of class differentials in educational opportunity in England and Wales. *The British Journal of Sociology*, *15*(4), 301-316.

Phillips, D. (2006). Parallel lives? Challenging discourses of British Muslim self-segregation. *Environment and planning D: society and space*, *24*(1), 25-40.

Skellington, R. (1996). *'Race' in Britain Today*. Sage.

Solomos, J. (1989). Urban Politics and Racial Inequality. In *Race and Racism in Contemporary Britain* (pp. 83-98). Palgrave, London.

Thomas, H. (2004). *Race and planning: the UK experience*. Routledge.

Troyna, B. (1990). Reform or deform? The 1988 Education Reform Act and racial equality in Britain. *Journal of Ethnic and Migration Studies*, *16*(3), 403-416.

Troyna, B., & Carrington, B. (2011). *Education, racism and reform* (Vol. 123). Routledge.

Whitty, G., & Menter, I. (1988). Lessons of Thatcherism: education policy in England and Wales 1979-88. *Journal of Law and Society*, *16*(1), 42-64.

Chapter 6

Wolf, M. J. (Ed.). (2008). *The video game explosion: a history from PONG to Play-station and beyond*. ABC-CLIO.

Vinen, R. (2013). *Thatcher's Britain: the politics and social upheaval of the Thatcher era*. Simon and Schuster.

Sutton, J., & Keogh, E. (2000). Social competition in school: Relationships with bullying, Machiavellianism and personality. *British Journal of Educational Psychology*, *70*(3), 443-456.

Skelton, C. (2001). *Schooling the boys* (pp. 199-217). Buckingham: Open University Press.

Orwell, G. (2008) *Nineteen Eighty-Four*, London: Penguin.

Griffiths, M. (1997). Computer game playing in early adolescence. *Youth & Society*, *29*(2), 223-237.

Griffin, C. (2000). Discourses of crisis and loss: Analysing the 'boys' underachievement debate. *Journal of Youth Studies*, *3*(2), 167-188.

Farrall, S., Gray, E., & Mike Jones, P. (2020). The role of radical economic re-structuring in truancy from school and engagement in crime. *The British Journal of Criminology*, *60*(1), 118-140.

Cooper, B. S. (1988). School reform in the 1980s: The new right's legacy. *Educational Administration Quarterly*, *24*(3), 282-298.

Coleman, R. (2004). Images from a neoliberal city: the state, surveillance and social control. *Critical Criminology*, *12*(1), 21-42.

Blatchford, P., & Sharp, S. (2005). Research on children's school playground behaviour in the United Kingdom. In *Breaktime and the School* (pp. 22-42). Routledge.

Ball, S. J. (2012). *Politics and policy making in education: Explorations in sociology.* Routledge.

Chapter 7

Beeson, M. (2014). *Regionalism and globalization in East Asia: politics, security and economic development*. Macmillan International Higher Education.

Dudrah, R. (2011). British bhangra music as soundscapes of the Midlands. *Midland History*, *36*(2), 278-291.

Gopinath, G. (1995). "Bombay, UK, Yuba City": Bhangra Music and the Engendering of Diaspora. *Diaspora: A Journal of Transnational Studies*, *4*(3), 303-321.

Gretton, J., Harrison, A., & Beeton, D. (1987). How far have the frontiers of the state been rolled back between 1979 and 1987?. *Public Money & Management*, *7*(3-4), 17-25.

Huq, R. (2003). From the margins to mainstream? Representations of British Asian youth musical cultural expression from bhangra to Asian underground music. *Young*, *11*(1), 29-48.

Massey, D., & Meegan, R. (2014). *The Anatomy of Job Loss (Routledge Revivals): The How, Why and Where of Employment Decline*. Routledge.

Masulis, R. W., & Ng, V. K. (1995). Overnight and Daytime Stock-Return Dynamites on the London Stock Exchange: The Impacts of "Big Bang" and the 1987 Stock-Market Crash. *Journal of Business & Economic Statistics*, *13*(4), 365-378.

McEwan, C., Pollard, J., & Henry, N. (2005). The 'global' in the city economy: multicultural economic development in Birmingham. *International Journal of Urban and Regional Research*, *29*(4), 916-933.

McNeill, P. (1991). Loadsamoney? myth of the affluent teenager. *New Statesman and Society*, *3*, 29-29.

Parker, D. (2004). Lessons from Privatisation. *Economic Affairs*, *24*(3), 2-8.

Parker, D., & Martin, S. (1995). The impact of UK privatisation on labour and total factor productivity. *Scottish Journal of Political Economy*, *42*(2), 201-220.

Schotter, A. (1985). *Free market economics*. St. Martin's Press, Incorporated.

Sharma, S., Hutnyk, J., & Sharma, A. (1996). Dis-orienting rhythms: The politics of the new Asian dance music.

Zohlnhöfer, R., & Obinger, H. (2006). Selling off the "Family Silver": the politics of privatization. *World Political Science*, *2*(1).

Chapter 8

Carter, B., & Virdee, S. (2008). Racism and the sociological imagination. *The British Journal of Sociology*, *59*(4), 661-679.

Cole, M. (2007). *Marxism and educational theory: Origins and issues*. Routledge.

Cole, M., & Maisuria, A. (2009). Racism and Islamophobia in post 7/7 Britain: Critical Race Theory,(xeno-) racialization, empire and education–A Marxist analysis. In *Class in Education* (pp. 126-145). Routledge.

Gabriel, J., & Ben-Tovim, G. (1978). Marxism and the Concept of Racism. *Economy and society*, *7*(2), 118-154.

Gabriel, S. (1990). The continuing significance of race: An overdeterminist approach to racism. *Rethinking Marxism*, *3*(3-4), 65-78.

Miles, R. (1987). Recent Marxist theories of nationalism and the issue of racism. *British Journal of Sociology*, 24-43.

Miles, R. (1988). Racism, Marxism, and British Politics. *Economy and Society*, *17*(3), 428-460.

Rex, J. (1982). Racism and the structure of colonial societies. In *Racism and Colonialism* (pp. 199-218). Springer, Dordrecht.

Solomos, J. (1986). Varieties of Marxist conceptions of "race", class and the state. A critical analysis.

Solomos, J., & Back, L. (1995). Marxism, racism, and ethnicity. *American behavioral scientist*, *38*(3), 407-420.

Virdee, S. (2019). Racialized capitalism: An account of its contested origins and consolidation. *The Sociological Review, 67*(1), 3-27.

West, C. (1989). *Toward a socialist theory of racism.* New York: Institute for Democratic Socialism.

Wilson, C. A. (1996). Racism: From slavery to advanced capitalism (Vol. 17). Sage.

Wilson, C. A. (1996). *Racism: From slavery to advanced capitalism* (Vol. 17). Sage.

Winant, H. (2017). Is Racism Global?. *Journal of World-Systems Research, 23*(2), 505-510.

Walvin, J. (1983). *Slavery and the slave trade: A short illustrated history.* Macmillan International Higher Education.

Fanon, F. (2008). *Black skin, white masks.* Grove press.

Du Bois, W. E. B. (1903). *The Souls of Black Folk: Essays and Sketches.* Chicago: AC McClurg and Co.

Chapter 9

Alam, Y., & Husband, C. (2013). Islamophobia, community cohesion and counter-terrorism policies in Britain. *Patterns of Prejudice, 47* (3), 235-252.

Amin, A. (2003). Unruly strangers? The 2001 urban riots in Britain. *International journal of urban and regional research, 27*(2), 460-463.

Bagguley, P., & Hussain, Y. (2006). Conflict and Cohesion: Official Constructions of "Community" Around the 2001 Riots in Britain. In *Returning (to) Communities* (pp. 347-365). Brill.

Birt, J. (2006). Good imam, bad imam: Civic religion and national integration in Britain post-9/11. *The muslim world, 96*(4), 687-705.

Jackson, L. B. (2018). Good and Bad Muslims in Britain: Community Cohesion and Counterterrorism Discourse. In *Islamophobia in Britain* (pp. 31-58). Palgrave Macmillan, Cham.

Kalra, V. S., & Kapoor, N. (2009). Interrogating segregation, integration and the community cohesion agenda. *Journal of ethnic and migration studies, 35*(9), 1397-1415.

Kapoor, N. (2013). The advancement of racial neoliberalism in Britain. *Ethnic and Racial Studies, 36*(6), 1028-1046.

Kundnani, A. (2007). Integrationism: The politics of anti-Muslim racism. *Race & Class*, *48*(4), 24-44.

Kundnani, A. (2008). Islamism and the roots of liberal rage. *Race & Class*, *50*(2), 40-68.

Kundnani, A. (2012). Radicalisation: the journey of a concept. *Race & Class*, *54*(2), 3-25.

Mandaville, P. (2009). Muslim transnational identity and state responses in Europe and the UK after 9/11: Political community, ideology and authority. *Journal of Ethnic and Migration Studies*, *35*(3), 491-506.

Samad, Y. (2013). Community cohesion without parallel lives in Bradford. *Patterns of prejudice*, *47*(3), 269-287.

Thomas, P. (2013). From petrol bombs to performance indicators: the 2001 riots and the emergence of 'community cohesion'. In *Rioting in the UK and France* (pp. 101-113). Willan.

Thomas, P., & Sanderson, P. (2011). Unwilling citizens? Muslim young people and national identity. *Sociology*, *45*(6), 1028-1044.

Chapter 10

Abbas, T. (2007). Muslim minorities in Britain: Integration, multiculturalism and radicalism in the post-7/7 period. *Journal of Intercultural Studies*, *28*(3), 287-300.

Croft, S. (2006). *Culture, crisis and America's war on terror*. Cambridge University Press.

Durodié, B. (2013). War on Terror or a Search for Meaning?. *This report represents the views and opinions of the contributing authors. The report does not represent official USG policy or position.*

Featherstone, M., Holohan, S., & Poole, E. (2010). Discourses of the War on Terror: Constructions of the Islamic other after 7/7. *International Journal of Media & Cultural Politics*, *6*(2), 169-186.

Halliday, F. (2010). *Shocked and Awed: A dictionary of the war on terror*. Berkeley and Los Angeles: University of California Press.

Hiro, D. (2002). *Iraq: A report from the inside*. Granta.

Jarvis, L. (2008). Times of terror: Writing temporality into the war on terror. *Critical Studies on Terrorism*, *1*(2), 245-262.

Kundnani, A. (2014). *The Muslims are coming!: Islamophobia, extremism, and the domestic war on terror*. Verso Trade.

Lynch, O. (2013). British Muslim youth: Radicalisation, terrorism and the construction of the "other". *Critical Studies on Terrorism*, 6(2), 241-261.

Macpherson, W. (1999). *The Stephen Lawrence inquiry* (Vol. 1). London: Stationery Office Limited.

Miah, S. (2013). 'Prevent'ing Education: Anti-Muslim Racism and the War on Terror in Schools. In *The state of race* (pp. 146-162). Palgrave Macmillan, London.

Morgan, G. (2016). *Global Islamophobia: Muslims and moral panic in the West*. Routledge.

Poole, E. A. (2011). Change and continuity in the representation of British Muslims before and after 9/11: The UK context. *Global Media Journal*, 4(2), 49-62.

Qurashi, F. (2018). The Prevent strategy and the UK 'war on terror': embedding infrastructures of surveillance in Muslim communities. *Palgrave Communications*, 4(1), 1-13.

Spalek, B., Lambert, R., & Baker, A. H. (2009). Minority Muslim communities and criminal justice: stigmatized UK faith identities post 9/11 and 7/7. *Race and criminal justice*, 170-87.

Chapter 11

Bhattacharyya, G., Gabriel, J., & Small, S. (2016). *Race and power: Global racism in the twenty-first century*. Routledge.

Bonnett, A. (2006). The Americanisation of anti-racism? Global power and hegemony in ethnic equity. *Journal of Ethnic and Migration Studies*, 32(7), 1083-1103.

Castles, S. (1995). How nation-states respond to immigration and ethnic diversity. *Journal of Ethnic and Migration Studies*, 21(3), 293-308.

Castles, S., & Davidson, A. (2020). *Citizenship and migration: Globalization and the politics of belonging*. Routledge.

Castles, S., & Kosack, G. (1973). *Immigrant workers and class structure in Western Europe*. London; New York: published for the Institute of Race Relations, London, by Oxford University Press.

Cox, O. C. (1945). Race and caste: A distinction. *American Journal of Sociology*, 50(5), 360-368.

Law, I. (2013). *Racism and ethnicity: global debates, dilemmas, directions*. Routledge.

Lorna, C. (2017). *From immigrants to ethnic minority: Making black community in Britain*. Routledge.

Miles, R. (1984). Marxism versus the sociology of 'race relations'?. *Ethnic and Racial studies, 7*(2), 217-237.

Peach, C. (1997). Postwar migration to Europe: reflux, influx, refuge. *Social Science Quarterly, 78*(2), 269-283.

Phizacklea, A. (1984). A Sociology of Migration or Race Relations'? A View from Britain. *Current sociology, 32*(3), 199-218.

Pilkington, A. (1984). *Race relations in Britain*. University Tutorial Press.

Winant, H. (2006). Race and racism: Towards a global future. *Ethnic and Racial studies, 29*(5), 986-1003.

Winant, H. (2017). Is Racism Global?. *Journal of World-Systems Research, 23*(2), 505-510.

Younge, G. (2011). *Who are We--and Should it Matter in the 21st Century?*. Bold Type Books.

Chapter 12

Anthias, F. (1999). Institutional racism, power and accountability. *Sociological Research Online, 4*(1), 143-151.

Balibar, E. (1997). *Class racism* (pp. 318-329). Cambridge: Polity Press.

Balibar, E., Wallerstein, I. M., & Wallerstein, S. R. I. (1991). *Race, nation, class: Ambiguous identities*. Verso.

Bonnett, A. (2005). *Anti-racism*. Routledge.

Bourne, J. (2002). Racism, postmodernism and the flight from class. *Marxism against postmodernism in educational theory*, 195-210.

Cashmore, E., & Jennings, J. (Eds.). (2001). *Racism: essential readings*. Sage.

Fekete, L. (2001). The emergence of xeno-racism. *Race & Class, 43*(2), 23-40.

Fenton, S. (1999). *Ethnicity: Racism, class and culture*. Rowman & Littlefield.

Gabriel, J., & Ben-Tovim, G. (1978). Marxism and the Concept of Racism. *Economy and society, 7*(2), 118-154.

Gillborn, D. (2015). Intersectionality, critical race theory, and the primacy of racism: Race, class, gender, and disability in education. *Qualitative Inquiry, 21*(3), 277-287.

Gillborn, D., & Kirton, A. (2000). White heat: Racism, under-achievement and white working-class boys. *International Journal of Inclusive Education, 4*(4), 271-288.

Gilroy, P. (1990). The end of anti-racism. In *Race and local politics* (pp. 191-209). Palgrave Macmillan, London.

Mason, D. (1994). On the dangers of disconnecting race and racism. *Sociology, 28*(4), 845-858.

McVeigh, R. (1992). The specificity of Irish racism. *Race & Class, 33*(4), 31-45.

Meer, N., & Nayak, A. (2015). Race ends where? Race, racism and contemporary sociology. *Sociology, 49*(6), NP3-NP20.

Rattansi, A. (2000). On being and not being brown/black-British: Racism, class, sexuality and ethnicity in post-imperial Britain. *Interventions, 2*(1), 118-134.

Sarup, M. (1991). *Education and the Ideologies of Racism*. Trentham Books.

Sivanandan, A. (1983). Introduction challenging racism: Strategies for the '80s. *Race & Class, 25*(2), 1-11.

Virdee, S. (2014). *Racism, class and the racialized outsider*. Macmillan International Higher Education.

Williams, J. (1985). Redefining institutional racism. *Ethnic and racial studies, 8*(3), 323-348.

Chapter 13

Afshar, H., Aitken, R., & Franks, M. (2005). Feminisms, Islamophobia and identities. *Political Studies, 53*(2), 262-283.

Ahmad, F. (2003). *Turkey The Quest For Identity*, Oneworld.

Brown, K. (2006). Realising Muslim women's rights: The role of Islamic identity among British Muslim women. *Women's Studies International Forum 29*(4): 417-430).

Dwyer, C. (1999). Contradictions of community: questions of identity for young British Muslim women. *Environment and Planning A, 31*(1), 53-68.

Dwyer, C. (2000, July). Negotiating diasporic identities: Young British South Asian Muslim women. In *Women's Studies International Forum* (Vol. 23, No. 4, pp. 475-486). Pergamon.

Göle, N. (1997). Secularism and Islamism in Turkey: The making of elites and counter-elites. *The Middle East Journal*, 46-58.

Göle, N. (1998). Islamism, feminism and post-modernism: Women's movements in Islamic countries. *New Perspectives on Turkey, 19*, 53-70.

Haddad, Y. Y., Smith, J. I., & Moore, K. M. (2006). *Muslim women in America: The challenge of Islamic identity today*. Oxford University Press.

Islam, M. K., & Kavakci, M. (2010). *Headscarf politics in Turkey: a postcolonial reading*. Springer.

Kadioğlu, A. (1994). Women's subordination in Turkey: Is Islam really the villain? *The Middle East Journal*, 645-660.

Khan, T. S. (2006). *Beyond honour: a historical materialist explanation of honour related violence*. Oxford University Press.

Lockhat, H. (2004). *Female genital mutilation: treating the tears*. Libri Publishing Limited.

Mardin, S. (2006). *Religion, society, and modernity in Turkey*. Syracuse University Press.

Mirza, H. S. (2013). 'A second skin': Embodied intersectionality, transnationalism and narratives of identity and belonging among Muslim women in Britain. *Women's Studies International Forum, 36*, 5-15.

Sardar, Z. (2017). *Reading the Qur'an: The contemporary relevance of the sacred text of Islam*. Oxford University Press.

Tekeli, S. (1992). Europe, European feminism, and women in Turkey. In *Women's Studies International Forum, 15*(1): 139-143.

Chapter 14

Ali, T. (2008). *The Duel: Pakistan on the flight path of American power*. Simon and Schuster.

Bano, M. (2007). Beyond politics: The reality of a Deobandi madrasa in Pakistan. *Journal of Islamic Studies, 18*(1), 43-68.

Binder, L. (1961). *Religion and politics in Pakistan*. University of California Press.

Freeman, J. (2010). *Granta 112: Pakistan*. Granta.

Khan, A. (2005). *Politics of identity: ethnic nationalism and the state in Pakistan*. Sage.

Khan, I. (2011). *Pakistan: A Personal History*. Random House.

Khan, Y. (2008). *The Great Partition: the making of India and Pakistan*. Yale University Pres.

Leiven, A. (2012). *Pakistan: a hard country*. Penguin.

Malik, I. H. (2008). *The history of Pakistan*. Greenwood Publishing Group.

Maniruzzaman, T. (1966). Group interests in Pakistan politics, 1947-1958. *Pacific Affairs*, *39*(1/2), 83-98.

Moghadam, V. M. (1992). Patriarchy and the politics of gender in modernising societies: Iran, Pakistan and Afghanistan. *International Sociology*, *7*(1), 35-53.

Roy, A., Mishra, P., Bhatt, H., Chatterji, A. P., & Ali, T. (2011). *Kashmir: The case for freedom*. Verso Books.

Shafqat, S. (1996). Pakistan under Benazir Bhutto. *Asian Survey*, *36*(7), 655-672.

Shaheed, F. (2010). Contested identities: Gendered politics, gendered religion in Pakistan. *Third World Quarterly*, *31*(6), 851-867.

Shaikh, F. (2018). *Making sense of Pakistan*. Oxford University Press.

Talbot, I. (2009). *Pakistan: A modern history*. Hurst.

Yilmaz, I. (2016). *Muslim laws, politics and society in modern nation states: Dynamic legal pluralisms in England, Turkey and Pakistan*. Routledge.

Chapter 15

Abbas, T. (2019). *Islamophobia and Radicalisation: A Vicious Cycle*. Oxford University Press.

Allen, C. (2016). *Islamophobia*. Routledge.

Cesari, J. (2009). *Muslims in the West after 9/11: Religion, politics and law*. Routledge.

Cesari, J. (2011). Islamophobia in the West: A comparison between Europe and the United States. *Islamophobia: The challenge of pluralism in the 21st century*, 21-43.

Esposito, J. L., & Kalin, I. (Eds.). (2011). *Islamophobia: The challenge of pluralism in the 21st century*. OUP USA.

Klausen, J. (2009). *The cartoons that shook the world*. Yale University Press.

Klug, B. (2012). Islamophobia: A concept comes of age. *Ethnicities, 12*(5), 665-681.

Kumar, D. (2012). *Islamophobia and the Politics of Empire*. Haymarket Books.

Marranci, G. (2004). Multiculturalism, Islam and the clash of civilisations theory: rethinking Islamophobia. *Culture and Religion, 5*(1), 105-117.

Mavelli, L. (2013). *Europe's encounter with Islam: the secular and the postsecular*. Routledge.

Morgan, G. (2016). *Global Islamophobia: Muslims and moral panic in the West*. Routledge.

Morsi, Y. (2017). *Radical skin, moderate masks: De-radicalising the Muslim and racism in post-racial societies*. Rowman & Littlefield.

Poynting, S., & Mason, V. (2007). The resistible rise of Islamophobia: Anti-Muslim racism in the UK and Australia before 11 September 2001. *Journal of sociology, 43*(1), 61-86.

Ragazzi, F. (2017). Countering terrorism and radicalisation: Securitising social policy? *Critical Social Policy, 37*(2), 163-179.

Saeed, A. (2007). Media, racism and Islamophobia: The representation of Islam and Muslims in the media. *Sociology Compass, 1*(2), 443-462.

Sayyid, S., & Vakil, A. (2010). *Thinking through Islamophobia: global perspectives*. Hurst.

Chapter 16

Abranches, M., Theuerkauf, U. G., Scott, C., & White, C. S. (2021). Cultural violence in the aftermath of the Brexit Referendum: manifestations of post-racial xeno-racism. *Ethnic and Racial Studies, 44*(15), 2876-2894.

Bogdanor, V. (2019). *Beyond Brexit: Towards a British Constitution*. Bloomsbury Publishing.

Calhoun, C. (2017). Populism, nationalism and Brexit. *Brexit: Sociological Responses*, 57-76.

Clarke, H. D., Goodwin, M., Goodwin, M. J., & Whiteley, P. (2017). *Brexit*. Cambridge University Press.

Dorling, D. (2019). *Rule Britannia: Brexit and the end of empire*. Biteback Publishing.

Evans, G., & Menon, A. (2017). *Brexit and British politics*. John Wiley & Sons.

Ford, R., & Goodwin, M. (2017). Britain after Brexit: A nation divided. *Journal of Democracy*, *28*(1), 17-30.

Freeden, M. (2017). After the Brexit referendum: revisiting populism as an ideology. *Journal of Political Ideologies*, *22*(1), 1-11.

Gusterson, H. (2017). From Brexit to Trump: Anthropology and the rise of nationalist populism. *American ethnologist*, *44*(2), 209-214.

Hopkin, J. (2017). When Polanyi met Farage: Market fundamentalism, economic nationalism, and Britain's exit from the European Union. *The British Journal of Politics and International Relations*, *19*(3), 465-478.

Kromczyk, M., Khattab, N., & Abbas, T. (2021). The limits of tolerance: before and after Brexit and the German Refugee Crisis. *Ethnic and Racial Studies*, *44*(16), 170-193.

Marsh, D. (2018). Brexit and the Politics of Truth. *British Politics*, *13*(1), 79-89.

Menon, A., & Fowler, B. (2016). Hard or soft? The politics of Brexit. *National Institute Economic Review*, *238*(1), R4-R12.

Norris, P., & Inglehart, R. (2016). *Trump, Brexit, and the rise of populism: Economic have-nots and cultural backlash*. Harvard JFK School of Government Faculty Working Papers Series, 1-52.

Patel, T. G., & Connelly, L. (2019). 'Post-race' racisms in the narratives of 'Brexit' voters. *The Sociological Review*, *67*(5), 968-984.

Rzepnikowska, A. (2019). Racism and xenophobia experienced by Polish migrants in the UK before and after Brexit vote. *Journal of Ethnic and Migration Studies*, *45*(1), 61-77.

Virdee, S., & McGeever, B. (2018). Racism, crisis, Brexit. *Ethnic and racial studies*, *41*(10), 1802-1819.

Wilson, H. F. (2016). Brexit: On the rise of '(in) tolerance'. *Environment and Planning D: Society and Space*.

Chapter 17

Bonilla-Silva, E. (2019). "Racists," "Class Anxieties," Hegemonic Racism, and Democracy in Trump's America. *Social Currents*, *6*(1), 14-31.

Christian, M., Seamster, L., & Ray, V. (2019). New directions in critical race theory and sociology: Racism, white supremacy, and resistance. *American behavioral scientist*, *63*(13), 1731-1740.

Fleming, C. M. (2018). *How to be less stupid about race: On racism, white supremacy, and the racial divide*. Beacon Press.

Giroux, H. A. (2020). Weaponizing racism in the age of Trump. In *Eudaimonia* (pp. 60-70). Routledge.

Harris, T. M., & Steiner, R. J. (2018). Beyond the Veil: A Critique of White Christian Rhetoric and Racism in the Age of Trump. *Journal of Communication & Religion*, *41*(1).

Inwood, J. (2019). White supremacy, white counter-revolutionary politics, and the rise of Donald Trump. *Environment and Planning C: Politics and Space*, *37*(4), 579-596.

Kelly, C. R. (2020). Donald J. Trump and the rhetoric of white ambivalence. *Rhetoric and Public Affairs*, *23*(2), 195-223.

Macklin, G. (2019). The Christchurch attacks: Livestream terror in the viral video age. *CTC Sentinel*, *12*(6), 18-29.

Mondon, A., & Winter, A. (2020). *Reactionary democracy: How racism and the populist far right became mainstream*. Verso Books.

Mudde, C. (2019). *The far right today*. John Wiley & Sons.

Pitcher, B. (2019). Racism and Brexit: Notes towards an antiracist populism. *Ethnic and Racial Studies*, *42*(14), 2490-2509.

Poynting, S., & Briskman, L. (2018). Islamophobia in Australia: From far-right deplorables to respectable liberals. *Social Sciences*, *7*(11), 213.

Quek, N. (2019). Bloodbath in Christchurch: The rise of far-right terrorism. *RSIS Commentaries*, (047).

Saull, R. (2018). Racism and far right imaginaries within neo-liberal political economy. *New Political Economy*, *23*(5), 588-608.

Solomos, J., Virdee, S., & Winter, A. (2020). *Global white nationalism: From apartheid to Trump*. Manchester University Press.

become quiet they are grouped in various ways. You perhaps know of patterns that can be formed by causing particles of sand to vibrate on a glass plate. The thought patterns are not so unlike these as one might imagine. You will have to be satisfied by our saying that they form a series of impressions running one into the other in an extended formation. But this ribbon or stream can be broken at almost any point when a thought recalls any portion from the memory.

"This is the best we have been able to do in trying to describe the processes of thought and memory in earthly language."

THE SUBCONSCIOUS MIND

Psychologists have often spoken of the subconscious mind as a vast reservoir in which all sorts of information is stored, and have said that a stream drawn from this reservoir may consist of almost any sort of mixture. In this way they try to account for all that is given through automatic writing. But when such writing or such stream contains ingredients for which there is no evidence that they could ever have been deposited in the reservoir, the analogy fails, and other theories are resorted to or added. These theories are principally two. The first, that this addition was somehow placed there without the knowledge of the conscious mind; the second, that the mind has unknown powers of seeking this extra information. The first explanation is true if a spiritistic or psychometric influence is admitted; otherwise it is simply an assertion made to avoid this admission. The second explanation is also only an evasion of the spiritistic theory, as there is no evidence to support it.

Grant the statements that the knowledge already stored can be recombined, and that spirits can also send information through the same channel, and practically every word of automatic writing can be explained. Some few incidents that are at present classed as psychometry are still a little strange. But spirit influence is not disproven even then. And even if a discarnate intelligence has no part in the proceeding, it is just as simple and just as logical to guess that the psychometrized article itself can influence the mind directly as it is to guess that the subconscious mind can go out and hunt up the information.

After the matter given in the previous chapter was all recorded, this teacher took up the subject of the subconscious mind to the extent of giving quite full directions for judging the origin of messages received through automatic writing. He said:—

"The subconscious mind is an important part of your mortal makeup. We here do not have to reckon with it, as it is always available to us at will. But with you it is usually beyond the control of the will.

"Any disturbance of your physical body is sufficient to influence the thought stored away in your subconscious mind. And when once stirred up these thoughts can recombine with results that are sometimes startling. You of course know a little of this from your dreams. But with some people there is a power of connected action far beyond even that ordinarily found in their dreams. Your psychologists have many records of wonderful performances of the subconscious mind, and many of them are rightly ascribed to that action. But there are also some that are influenced from this side, and you will always have some difficulty in determining to which class they belong.

"But we can state one fact: No action of the subconscious mind uses any information except what has been previously stored there. If anything else appears it has been deliberately placed there at the time by some outside agency. We know this to be true from watching actual operations. We have made many such observations on mortal brains.

"You hear it said that the mind has the power to go out and select this information. But no one tells you how this can be done. You hear that the soul can leave the body. We know that this can be done. But the two statements are not identical. If the mind went out to seek these facts there would ensue a condition of trance, which in most automatic writing never occurs.

"You will hear some spiritualists claim that all unusual subconscious action is caused by spirit influence. This we know to be far from the truth. Spirit influence working through the subconscious mind can sometimes achieve wonderful results. But any spirit influence necessitates a psychic nature on the part of the medium, or the one who is writing. If this is lacking the messages can be quite truthfully claimed to be of subconscious origin, and they will therefore contain no new material, although they may possibly be presented in striking phrases. No medium, however, can write on any subject as quickly or surely when not in a psychic condition, and you will also find that the power of logical combination of facts is rarely more marked in subconscious actions than is possible in normal or conscious thoughts of the same individual.

"Again, there is in all persons a tendency to exaggerate. This seems to be a universal human trait. You will find that productions from spirit influence are free from such exaggeration. You wonder if spirit cannot be guilty of this. Possibly, occasionally. But spirit soon learns here that such a fault should be cast aside.

"Also, spirit influence usually introduces the sentences to the pencil almost a word at a time as it is written. True subconscious action is likely to manifest in the conscious mind much more in advance.

"The product of the subconscious mind is apt to be marked by idioms that are characteristic of the conscious expression. Any tendencies to use new idioms, a higher literary expression than is customary, the use of new words, different grammar, unaccustomed trends in argument: all these argue for the side of outward influence. Sometimes there are plainly apparent distinguishing characteristics that are known to belong to one who is in the spirit world. These can be copied by the conscious mind, but can the subconscious do this?

"One should also notice the fact that much of the automatic writing that is genuinely influenced from the spirit world is concerned with statements that would not ordinarily be in the person's mind—statements of life in the spirit world under conditions that no medium could know or would naturally imagine.

"We know that there are many statements concerning spirit life that are sent through several separate mediums in almost identical language. It is not always easy to get these statements together, but you have probably found many familiar descriptions in your reading.

"These are all rather delicate shadings to observe. But the careful use of them will show results that an unprejudiced mind cannot question. The various writings will quite decidedly fall into two classes."

The following was also received through the pencil, dealing with the subconscious mind and memory.

"Many of your psychologists believe that all actions of the mind are simply functions of the material brain. We know that they are more especially connected with the spirit brain, and only use the material brain as a vehicle of expression. You have been told the process that takes place when a thought enters a spirit brain and is recorded in memory. Now here is where your psychologists fail to understand. We know that all thoughts and impressions that have been received are recorded in the memory, and under certain circumstances almost any of these can be recalled. It is when some statement of fact is given out that could by no normal means have entered the memory that the psychologists fail to explain the process. We know that it is many times difficult to prove that the incident was never recorded at some time during the person's life. But there are hundreds of cases where this has positively been proven. Now we think no investigator there has ever evolved a satisfactory theory as to how this fact was ascertained. You may know that the mind does apparently obtain facts during hypnosis; but even this has never been explained. If you can accept my statements, possibly you may be able to formulate a theory that will lead to the acceptance of the spiritualistic origin.

"When the facts are obtained in hypnosis, I have observed that there was always some spirit near who was interested in seeing that the experiment succeeded; and if it were possible, the facts were supplied in this way. I have never observed a successful hypnotic experiment which was not aided in this way. In psychometry we must admit that the article itself does stimulate thought and ideas by vibrations which it sends out. But in elaborate descriptions I have also observed spirit assistance. And usually, being more impressionable than the medium, this spirit quickly grasps the more important features of the case and at once proceeds to obtain further information and supply it to the medium.

"It must always be remembered that every living being has one or more guides or spirits who are interested in that particular person. Sometimes in the case of a medium, an entire circle of spirits is at a moment's call, and it is always the delight of some of them to be able to supply the information desired, if it is at all obtainable.

"When it comes to predictions, we are still at a loss to give a complete explanation. We know that higher planes understand, but we have never solved the problem. If we ever get any light on it, it will probably be found that it is mostly beyond our control, even if we could understand it.

"The subconscious mind is always a mystery, seemingly, to investigators on earth. To us it is only the memory part of our intellectual development or equipment. When earth people are willing to concede that there is a soul or mind that uses the brain, perhaps they will understand a little better what the memory is. When they try to place everything in the material brain, they are at a loss to know how to account for the subconscious mind. But if they will only concede a spirit brain that controls the material brain, then it is easier to understand the relation of memory to the mental equipment. We think with mental machinery that is separate from the material brain. So we store the thoughts in ways that do not need the physical brain.

"But in mortal life all conscious thought may influence, and usually does influence, the physical brain; so, in the same way, the store of memory records may, and oftentimes does, influence the physical brain. But as this storehouse is not in the physical brain itself, it is not so easily investigated. Hence the mystery concerning it.

"I think the subconscious mind has been burdened long enough. I would like to try to lift the load. We here know so well its limitations. But it is difficult to arrange any argument that will be convincing to critics there. When the subconscious mind is blamed for all the *foolish* things that purport to come from here, we feel that it is just as well to say nothing. But when our best efforts and finest teachings are laid to the same source, we feel that we must make some effort to have the critics understand.

"The principal trouble is, of course, the failure to understand that the real mind and memory are not dependent upon the physical brain. And when the existence of a soul is denied, the case is almost hopeless. But when some are willing and even anxious to believe in a future existence for the soul, we cannot understand the obstinacy with which its real existence is denied.

"We know that the subconscious mind, through various methods of being stimulated, can send forth some interesting things—interesting because unexpected. Yet we are not aware that any proof has ever been offered that unknown facts come from that source. In some cases it is suspected that the facts may have been somehow unconsciously acquired. Let those cases rest. But there are many where the facts absolutely could not have been normally acquired, and here there is no theory at all that will stand for a moment.

"We wish the critics who are willing to admit the existence of a soul as an animating force instead of a function would take this as the foundation of a theory. They could then reach satisfying conclusions on many of these points. But they do not seem to want to do that."

STUDY AND EDUCATION

"Knowledge is always the goal here for those who have come to know what spirit life really means. But knowledge has to be sought; it is not to be picked up like wild fruit in the forest. It is here in abundance, but we do not always know where to find it. We each have our own desires. Some incline to one study, some to another. If a student makes some discovery, it is heralded abroad so that others can get the benefit. But before such discovery can be made, there is much preparation in the way of reading, attending lectures, and in conversation with other students.

"If a class wishes to follow an entirely new line of study or thought, they usually induce some advanced spirit to outline a course of study for them. In following this it is surprising to see the different methods that the members of the class will adopt. Some are for reading all that has ever been written on each small phase of the subject. Some try to post themselves on just the main features. Others decide to only glance at it and run to something more to their liking. All are free to do as they please. There are no class rules laid down by some authority. As a consequence the class, which may have been quite uniform at the beginning, will before long be in all stages of advancement on the subject.

"You can see from this that we are constantly changing, constantly meeting other students, constantly finding new angles to the study. We do not study all the time though. You must not think of our world as a university where each is striving to outdo the others and gain honors in some scholarship. Life is far different from that. I am only describing the study part. We all have our lighter moments, some more than others, to be sure, but no one studies every moment of the time.

"I am sure you will find the life delightful. I have yet to meet one who does not, after he has arrived at a certain stage of his education. We do see, however, that in the early stages, there are many who find life here somewhat disappointing. One who can only think of existence as a means to outdo someone else in money-getting is not attracted to study, is not happy in company with students, and in some ways finds life a burden. If he has really learned how to use his spirit powers, he can find pleasure in the musical performances and in some other ways of entertainment. But as time passes, he usually begins to learn and to experience the pleasure of doing things himself; and then his true happiness comes. If life on earth could be viewed as one of actively acquiring happiness, instead of passively allowing happiness to be brought to them, the earth would become a far more enjoyable place, and the entrance into this life would be a matter of joy instead of one of penance, which it often is."

COMMUNICATION BETWEEN SPIRITS

"We have little use for vocal communication. Not that we do not often use it, but we more frequently receive the thought by direct impression. And in any communication of some extent, this is always the method, except when there is need for accurate statements that are not so easily presented by the action of thought. We often listen to lecturers in both ways; for a lecture is given vocally. But we can follow the thought at the same time. We do not always get a double impression in this way, for we can in a measure turn our attention to either method, just as you may listen to one person speaking when others are also talking near you. We think over these lectures when alone and fix them in our memory. In doing this we do not send out any thought that anyone else could get. We also have here a sort of selective process. Our own thoughts are private unless we will that they go out.

"When several are together and thinking on one subject, there is a wave of harmony that is often felt or sensed that is sometimes an aid in fixing the thoughts in memory. So it is not unusual for a class to remain together while studying the information given by a teacher or spoken by a lecturer. You will thus see that the custom on earth of having pupils together probably has merit. You may not now be able to perceive any such influence, but the time will come when it will be recognized.

"We also find that different persons have different ability in sending out thoughts. There is as much difference in personality in this respect as you there find in the quality of the voice. We learn to recognize thoughts in the same way. You speak of hearing a familiar voice. We comment on recognizing a familiar thought or way of thinking, and our language has a word that expresses this, which you do not have.

"If we desire to impress several friends with a thought, we have to express it, or give it out, with a little more emphasis than if given to one person—not so much to make it stronger, as to be sure that the varying receptive powers fully grasp all its intricate waves. For some persons detect one's thoughts easier than others.

"We are all accustomed to talk vocally when speaking to a stranger. We seldom succeed in clearly impressing a thought on a stranger until we each learn the other's peculiarities of thinking and receiving. In speaking to a stranger we have a rather formal mode of speech. It is used because it is found best to adhere to one particular style so that all may be sure to understand. In our own circle we lapse into familiar expressions, and some circles who have been together for a long time have acquired what might almost be termed a different dialect. But at large, one language is used for all, and our pet expressions are carefully avoided.

"You will be surprised when you come to see how we can chatter when we have a particularly congenial number together. We are far more free and familiar than you might expect. We have some wonderfully good times, but they are just a little difficult to explain to earth people, for we grow into different customs and adopt different methods of thought and conversation. No one need fear, though, that enjoyment is lessened. We think it is greater in every way, for we have so little to detract from it, and so many things to enhance it."

EVOLUTION

"We have some different viewpoints here from those we held on earth. It is not so serious an outlook to consider the waste of effort, the waste of life, that one meets there on all sides. Here we know better the meaning that lies behind it all, and realize that it is a small matter as compared with the wonderful scheme that lies behind all effort, all evolution. We know that no matter what ills life there may have to undergo, it is but a 'growing pain' in the complete history of that life. When all is known it will be seen that the evils of the earth life are for one purpose only—to train humans in the way to understand right from wrong, and to educate them to choose the right. In the process of evolution many fall by the wayside, many strive and fail, many endeavors are frustrated. But the lesson remains, and the individual has grown to a slight extent. Life may be lost, time may be wasted, apparently, but the end has been achieved in some fashion.

"I am speaking of the effort as a whole. There are cases where evolution has failed in some individuals, and the result is downward instead, because of some perverse trait that turned the effort in the wrong direction. But this is far less than is generally believed. All failures, so-called, are not failures. Many prove to be the greatest successes; for an impress has been made on the soul that will last through eternity. Sorrow is there, to be sure, but sorrow is often a blessing in disguise. When man can learn that it is the effort that counts most, he will think less of the failures and more of the personal benefit that has been achieved. For everyone who fails to gain this education there are thousands who find that their character has been strengthened, their lives made to have more meaning, their happiness—their final happiness—much enhanced. We know that the man who goes through life without effort, who has every want supplied, is apt to be the greatest loser. He has obtained no wealth that he can bring with him to this world.

"If all could realize that *effort* is the building material out of which character is constructed, there would be more personalities who would stand out as conspicuous examples of attainment. In the past generation you placed all emphasis on the so-called successes; the failures were not considered. How could you have overlooked this important part? For, if anything, failure makes a greater impression on the character than any success. When man learns the full truth of this there will be less disappointment over the ones who fall short of their ambitions.

"It might seem that such a view takes away all incentive to succeed; but while material success counts for so much in that life, there is little danger of that. And if the time comes when material achievement has less value, there will have come also the knowledge that success should be the goal for honor's sake, if nothing more.

"This thought should help the down-hearted; it should spur the successful one still more. There is so much sadness there over things that to us seem unimportant. Happiness could be the lot of many who are now feeling the loss of some venture, some labor, some great effort. It is all education, and 'education maketh the full man.'"

THE CHINESE PHILOSOPHER

"We have a visitor from a foreign circle who has been with us some time. He formerly lived in China, and was a thinker when on earth. He has continued his thinking here, and as thought has a universal language, he is at home in all circles, although he knows enough English to converse in that tongue. He says:—

"We strive to send the truth through all channels that offer, but it is only in a few instances that we find that it gets through as we wish.

I am hoping I can add a little to your records as opportunity offers.

"It has seemed to me that the earth people need nothing more than they need an understanding of what is meant by the brotherhood of man, and it seems to me the time is opportune for something to be said from here that will aid in bringing enlightenment. So if I can have your time and pencil when you feel that you can write, I shall be pleased to try to give you my ideas on this subject. I will likely be with this circle for some time, so you need not feel hurried."

Then someone in the circle added:—

"You will enjoy his talks, we know. He has been here many years, but has never lost his interest in earth affairs. He is Chinese, and was a man of note among his people, but probably not one whom you could identify."

To this, at another time, they added:—

"We have learned much from this Chinese philosopher who will write for you. He is a wonderful spirit, and has been a great addition to our circle. He tells us of the old ideas of the oriental races, and later we hope he will tell you his ideas of the religions of Asia as they have developed through the centuries. He was a great student and thinker when on earth, and had access to many old books that are not generally known. When he came here he at once plunged into the same studies with the aid of the libraries here."

Later, he began the writing:—

"I have been in the circle where your language is understood for a long time. We do not use it but I have become somewhat familiar with it, and with your assistance I think I can express my thoughts in it.

"We will begin by saying that the ideas I have wanted to express are religious for the most part, but to a certain extent they have with me been linked up with history. I am therefore inclined to refer to historical events at times in order to give authority to my statements.

"When the Chinese nation was first organized it was scarcely more than a loose union of various tribes. But in a few centuries it became much more unified. And when the early writers put forth their books on ethics, there was a large nation ready to receive and adopt the precepts taught them. So the teachings of Confucius and Lao Tze soon became the common property of all who could understand them.

"When Buddha was born in India, China was not quite ready for a common religion or standard of ethical thought and conduct. And it was therefore much later that the Buddhistic doctrines were circulated in China. When the early teachings of Chinese philosophy were brought into contact with Buddhism, they suffered thereby, and for many centuries Buddhism held full sway. But as the priesthood connected with this religion became more powerful, the value of the religion as a guide for the people waned in direct proportion. Then the old precepts of Confucius and Lao Tze were resurrected and added to the remnants of Buddhism that still existed; and for the most part, that is the condition of religion and ethical thought in China today.

"But here and there among the more studious and thoughtful of the Chinese people there have appeared certain thinkers and writers who have had the courage to go deeper than most into the meanings of religious teaching, and through these there has been kept alive a philosophy that is well worth studying by any people of the world. We have always been a thoughtful people on the whole, and we have taken time to think. We are conscious that we have evolved in this direction far more than any other nation. This is not said in a spirit of boastfulness, but as a statement of fact.

"India has had thinkers also. But Buddhism there has given way to the earlier forms of religion again, and the diversity and multiplicity of gods has led to a thinking that is not as solid and unified as has been attained among the Chinese.

"When the Chinese have had cause to wage war with another people, they have always done so as a matter of self-defense. We have never been an aggressive people. We have encouraged peace, we have thought only of peace, and this spirit has impressed itself in many ways. It has made it much easier to avoid quarrels and disputes, and so has always had a tendency to induce a true brotherly spirit.

"When we have studied the early religions we find that the principal features of them are the thought of a continuance of life after death, and of the effect that right living on earth would have on that life. Your Christian religion is the same at heart. So we can safely conclude that there must be some reason for such unanimity of plan. We have only one solution, and that is that there has always been influence from those who have gone before, and who have learned the things which are essential.

"It is in the application that the various races have made of these impressions, and the additions that have been made in their use, that the religions differ materially. In any case the foundations are sufficient for right living if faithfully followed, and with understanding.

"In the course of the centuries the Chinese race has evolved further ideas, or has possibly received further impressions, which we think are aids in the effort at right living. Many of these have found their way into general literature on the subject. Some are still unknown to the world at large. It is my pleasure to try to give you a few of these ideas—these precepts. It has always been the custom of our writers and thinkers to express themselves in what you might call aphorisms. It is in this manner that I have arranged what I wish to say. We have always felt that an idea should not be buried too deeply in wordy explanation. If possible, it should be put in a form where the idea seems to be expressed by the sentence, rather than by the words that form the sentence.

"You may remember that Confucius says, 'No man should carry more than one dish at a time.' I should like to change this to read,

'No man should carry a dish until he understands its fragile nature.' I mean by this, that we should not attempt to teach ideas which we cannot perfectly express.

"You may not get my exact words, and possibly that may be just as well; for my exact words might not be the best ones. You must remember that your language was unknown to me when on earth, and it is not easy to acquire here where all language is new and so different.

"I would like to give you a few of our old 'sayings' that tend to show or explain our idea of the Great Creator. When I look back to my life there, I am conscious that we did not think as much of our origin as we did of our progress. We paid little attention to the Power that caused our existence. But there were rare times when our thoughts *did* turn in this direction, and I find in my memory some of the records of these thoughts—some of them my own, some from greater minds than mine:—

"When God rules why should we try to usurp His power?

"In strength of character there is the reflection of the mind of God.

"It is always best to turn to the Almighty Power when our own power fails.

"Many times when we grow faint-hearted, it is only that we lose the tie which binds us to Him who supplies all power.

"Some lives are failures because the individual fails to understand that he is only a tool in the hands of the Great Skilled Worker.

"When we doubt the value of life we doubt the existence of the Creator.

"In searching for happiness remember what causes happiness.

"We are apt to forget our blessings when the storms prevent our journey.

"If one can remember why he was happy yesterday he may be happy tomorrow.

"It is always best to burn the weeds lest the seeds spring up anew.

"When we are ready to live it is usually time to die.

"If men love beauty they become beautiful.

"If hope hangs herself love is strangled also.

"Many can learn if the few are taught.

"When love forsakes, life is gone.

"If love is worthy it lives forever.

"When love survives, nothing else matters.

"If death is sure, life is certain.

"When old men laugh, young men should take heart.

"If your conscience bids you stop, heed it. If a man bids you cease, question him.

"When the earth dissolves in smoke, man will still be pursuing his onward path.

"It is the soul that lives; the mind is only its guide.

"It is the egotism of a man that causes him to sneer at immortality."

THE GEOGRAPHY OF THE HEAVENLY SPHERES

"You no doubt have often wondered just where heaven is located. So far as I know, there has been little attempt to indicate from here the position of the various planes. I am not thoroughly posted myself, but I have given it some attention, and I believe I can explain it in a manner.

"In the first place, the statement that 'heaven is all about you' is correct to a certain extent, for spirits of all the lower circles come and go freely through the earth's atmosphere. But it is not the real abiding place of any spirit who realizes where he is. It is in the farthest limits of the atmosphere that the heavenly lands begin.

"We always speak of it as a sphere, and this is a proper designation, in a way, in that it surrounds the earth at a fairly uniform distance. But in another sense this does not fully express the conditions. We will have some difficulty here in making you understand just how this spirit land is placed. It is not the inside of a hollow shell, nor is it the outside of a sphere. It is more nearly described as consisting of various regions—you might almost call them countries. Their extent is impossible to convey to you, because distance is such a relative term. We will have to make a general statement and say that these regions are thousands of miles in extent. They are not like islands in the sky, and yet how else can I describe them? I know I am indefinite, but I am doing the best I can.

"It is in these regions or countries that spirits of the lower plane have their homes. They are not replicas of any portion of the earth, for we have no cities. Sometimes the homes are not far apart, but there are no congested sections. There is room and to spare for everyone, and always will be.

"If you were to attempt to explore these countries by any means at your command, you would sail about in many directions to find the various places. And if you desired to stop and investigate anyone of them, you would find each one very extensive. But you must keep in mind that distance means nothing to us. It is possible to encircle the entire lower planes in a few seconds of earth time; although it is customary to use a rather slower speed than that.

"We do not think of these various places as being separated, for we make no attempt to move any distance except through space. We have clairvoyant vision of nearly everything, but it is all under our control. We see comparatively little of our surroundings except as we experience a desire to view them.

"If we wish to go to any place, it is only a question of desire and will power, and we are almost immediately at the place we had in mind.

"It is a vague picture I am drawing, no doubt. It is not a vague country, I assure you. It is more real to us than even the earth with its mountains and oceans.

"There are other spheres beyond these lower regions. Few of us have actual knowledge of them, except by descriptions given by the few visitors from them, and from messengers who are trained to go to and fro. It is said that they grow more and more ethereal, and soon are beyond the ken of any with whom we communicate.

"In making journeys to other planets, we no doubt go by them, but we cannot see them anymore than you can see our sphere. It is all a question of advancement, an acquirement of higher senses, a knowledge of the more ethereal conditions.

"We are told that some communicators mention the spheres by numbers. It is true that there are circles of advancement here on this lower plane, but it is difficult to understand why they are numbered when communicating. It may show a little the extent of the advancement, but I assure you we do not have them ticketed. It is easy to fall into the suggestions given by earthly inquirers, and many seem to have done so."

THE END

Veilleux-Lepage, Y., Daymon, C., & Amarasingam, A. (2020). *The Christchurch Attack Report: Key Takeaways on Tarrant's Radicalization and Attack Planning.* Technical Report. ICCT.

Wodak, R. (2020). *The politics of fear: The shameless normalization of far-right discourse.* Sage.

Chapter 18

Ayoub, M. (1991). Islam and Christianity between tolerance and acceptance. *Islam and Christian-Muslim Relations, 2*(2), 171-181.

Bhattacharyya, G. (2008). Globalizing racism and myths of the other in the "war on terror.". *Thinking Palestine*, 46-61.

Fetzer, J. S., & Soper, J. C. (2005). *Muslims and the state in Britain, France, and Germany.* Cambridge University Press.

Friedmann, Y. (2003). *Tolerance and coercion in Islam: interfaith relations in the Muslim tradition.* Cambridge University Press.

Lewis, B. (2014). *The Jews of Islam.* Princeton University Press.

Meer, N., & Noorani, T. (2008). A sociological comparison of anti-Semitism and anti-Muslim sentiment in Britain. *The sociological review, 56*(2), 195-219.

Modood, T. (1990). Muslims, race and equality in Britain: Some post-Rushdie affair reflections. *Third Text, 4*(11), 127-134.

Özyürek, E. (2005). The politics of cultural unification, secularism, and the place of Islam in the new Europe. *American Ethnologist*, 509-512.

Romeyn, E. (2014). Anti-semitism and Islamophobia: spectropolitics and immigration. *Theory, Culture & Society, 31*(6), 77-101.

Smooha, S. (2004). Jewish ethnicity in Israel: Symbolic or real?. *Jews in Israel: Contemporary social and cultural patterns*, 47-80.

Torstrick, R. (1995). "Educating for democracy" in Israel: Combating or perpetuating racism? *Identities Global Studies in Culture and Power, 1*(4), 367-390.

Werbner, P. (2000). Divided loyalties, empowered citizenship? Muslims in Britain. *Citizenship Studies, 4*(3), 307-324.

Werbner, P. (2011). Revisiting the UK Muslim diasporic public sphere at a time of terror: from local (benign) invisible spaces to seditious conspiratorial spaces and the "failure of multiculturalism" discourse. In *Pakistan and Its Diaspora* (pp. 43-79). Palgrave Macmillan, New York.

Chapter 19

Becker, H. S. (1966). Whose side are we on. *Social Problems*, 14, 239-47.

Ebaugh, H. R. (2009). *The Gülen movement: A sociological analysis of a civic movement rooted in moderate Islam*. Springer Science & Business Media.

Esposito, J. L. (2010). *The future of Islam*. Oxford University Press.

Layton-Henry, Z. (1992). *The politics of immigration: immigration, 'race' and 'race' relations in post-war Britain*. Wiley-Blackwell.

McGhee, D. (2008). *The End of Multiculturalism? Terrorism, Integration and Human Rights: Terrorism, Integration and Human Rights*. McGraw-Hill Education (UK).

Safi, O. (2003). *Progressive Muslims: on justice, gender and pluralism*. Simon and Schuster.

Said, E. W. (2001). *The Edward Said Reader*. Granta Books.

Chapter 20

Dreyfuss, R. (2006). *Devil's game: How the United States helped unleash fundamentalist Islam*. Macmillan.

Jenkins, P. (2007). *God's continent: Christianity, Islam, and Europe's religious crisis*. Oxford University Press.

Bowen, J. R. (2010). *Why the French don't like headscarves*. Princeton University Press.

Khaldun, I. (2015). *The muqaddimah: an introduction to history-abridged Edition*. Princeton University Press.

Index

www.ingramcontent.com/pod-product-compliance
Lightning Source LLC
Chambersburg PA
CBHW032222080426
42735CB00008B/679